Richard Francis Burton

Unexplored Syria

Visits to the Libanus, the Tulúl el Safá, the Anti-Libanus, the northern Libanus, and

the Aláh. Vol. 1

Richard Francis Burton

Unexplored Syria
Visits to the Libanus, the Tulúl el Safá, the Anti-Libanus, the northern Libanus, and the Aláh.
Vol. 1

ISBN/EAN: 9783337245108

Printed in Europe, USA, Canada, Australia, Japan

Cover: Foto ©Andreas Hilbeck / pixelio.de

More available books at **www.hansebooks.com**

UNEXPLORED SYRIA

VISITS TO

THE LIBANUS, THE TULÚL EL SAFÁ,

THE ANTI-LIBANUS, THE NORTHERN LIBANUS,

AND THE 'ALÁH.

BY

RICHARD F. BURTON

AND

CHARLES F. TYRWHITT DRAKE.

IN TWO VOLUMES.

VOL. I.

LONDON:

TINSLEY BROTHERS, 18 CATHERINE ST. STRAND.

1872.

TO

MY FATHER,

HENRY RAYMOND ARUNDELL,

THESE PAGES

ARE AFFECTIONATELY INSCRIBED.

الملك يبقى بالكفر ولا يبقى بالظلم

Kingdom endureth without the True Faith (*i.e.* El Islam); but it endureth not with tyranny. (*Hadis, or Saying of the Prophet.*)

We live in an age of free-thinking and plain-speaking, ' rarâ temporum felicitate, ubi sentire quæ velis, et quæ sentias docere licet.' (*Christian Theology and Modern Scepticism*, by the Duke of Somerset, K.G.: London, 1872.)

PREFACE.

I HASTEN to own, before reviewers tell me so, that this production is what my great namesake, Robert Burton of melancholy and merry, of facete and juvenile memory, honestly termed a 'Cento:' it is a *pot-pourri*, a gathering of somewhat heterogeneous materials—all, however, bearing more or less upon the subject of Unexplored Syria.

For instance, with reference to the contents of Volume I., the general remarks are mine. The first chapter is by Mrs. Burton, with my annotations. Chapter ii. is, again, my property. Appendix No. 1 contains observations for altitude, taken by Mr. C. F. Tyrwhitt Drake and myself, and computed by Captain George, R.N. Appendix No. 2 offers a short specimen of neo-Syrian Proverbs: it forms part of a much larger collection, which I have not had time to prepare for the press; and it may curiously be compared with the ancient proverbial philosophy of the Holy Land. In Appendix No. 3 my friend and fellow-traveller contributes an essay upon 'Writing a Roll of the Law, according to the rules laid down by Maimonides and other Hebrew authorities.' Appendix No. 4 contains a paper by myself upon the 'Hamah

Stones;' followed by the interesting remarks of Mr. Hyde Clarke, and accompanied by transcripts reduced to quarter-size. I need hardly draw attention to these 'Memorials,' which, first cursorily mentioned by Burckhardt in A.D. 1810, now appear in lithograph for the first time.

As to Volume II.: in chapter i. I tell the tale of travel; whilst chapters ii. and iii. are the handiwork of Mr. Tyrwhitt Drake. The *catalogue raisonné* of my collections in Syria and Palestine is by myself, with the able assistance of Dr. C. Carter Blake, Professor Busk, Messrs. A. W. Franks and John Evans, and Dr. Barnard Davis. In Appendix No. 2 my old and valued friend, W. S. W. Vaux, has taken the trouble to decipher, as far as was feasible, the eighty-one original Greek inscriptions collected in the Haurán Mountain (Jebel Durúz Haurán) and in the 'Aláh by Mr. Tyrwhitt Drake. Messrs. William Carruthers and James Britten have been good enough to catalogue for Appendix No. 3 the small collection of Alpine plants which we brought from the apex of the Libanus. Mr. Gwyn Jeffreys kindly catalogued the shells brought home by me; and Dr. Percy and Mr. Reeks named the geological specimens.

The original plans and sketches are all the work of my *compagnon de voyage*. The map, which alters the aspect of Northern Syria, has been drawn by Mr. Keith Johnston from the materials thus supplied to him, and supplemented by the sketches of Count Léon de Perthuis and M. F. Bambino, Vice-consul for France at Hums and Hamah. To these I also have added a few observations.[1] The frontispiece of the first volume is the artistic production of Mr. Richard Knight;

---

[1] Some of the bearings, especially those from Jebel Sannín, proved, when protracted, so erroneous, that future travellers are advised to ascertain if there are any peculiar elements of disturbance upon this wind-lashed crest.

whilst that of the second is a photograph put on stone by those able lithographers Messrs. Kell Brothers for the Anthropological Institute of Great Britain and Ireland. The second volume concludes with an Index; and I here take the earliest opportunity of apologising to the public for the absence of so necessary an adjunct from my last two volumes, *Zanzibar,—City, Island, and Coast* (Tinsleys, 1872). Finally, my thanks are due to Messrs. Robson and Sons, my printers, for the prodigious trouble caused to them by the state of a manuscript written on board ship, and subjected to various corrections.

It need hardly be remarked, that while we (the writers) all hold ourselves responsible to readers for our own sentiments, opinions, and statements, we disclaim being called to account for those of one another. This principle of limited liability we would extend, like those who give evidence before 'Select Parliamentary Committees,' even to such small matters as Arabic orthography.

The discoveries contained in these volumes originated from the Palestine Exploration Fund. The distinguished Committee of that Society declined, somewhat imprudently, I thought, to secure the services of Mr. Tyrwhitt Drake, who understood that he had returned to Syria as its representative. Thereupon I proposed to him that we should proceed, when leisure offered, to the field of action, and leave nothing save details for the Exploration Fund to explore. We succeeded, despite many risks and chances. We carried off the cream of discovery; but during the process, and in the moment of victory, we discovered how much more than we expected still remains to be discovered.

Unfortunately the *Œil-de-bœuf* still reigns to a considerable degree over the learned societies of the day, from those 'Fifty Immortals,' the French Academy, downwards. A spirit of clique too often succeeds in ignoring the real explorer, the true inventor, the most learned writer, and the best artist; in fact, the *fauteuil* is denied to the right man; the pin-cushion stuck full of pins is still the fittest legacy. Party is not rarely successful against Principle. The Pharisee—with his aggressive and vigorous but narrow-minded nature; with his hard thin character, all angles and stings; with his starch and inflexible opinions upon religion and politics, science, lite-rature, and art; and with his broad assurance that his ways are the only right ways—forms not unfrequently a minority that rules with a rod of iron the herd headed by Messrs. Feeble-mind and Ready-to-halt. And this we find notably the case in the present phase of our national life, when the Battle of the Creeds, or rather of 'Non-Credo' *versus* 'Credo,' has been offered and accepted; when every railway-station is hung with texts and strewed with tracts for the benefit of that working-class which now monopolises public interest; when the South Kensington Museum offers professional instruction in science and art for women—that is to say, for the girl be-fore she becomes a mother—suggesting that creation by law may be as reasonable as creation by miracle; when Secular-ism draws the sword against Denominationalism; and, briefly, when those who 'believe' and those who do not can hardly, as the saying is, 'keep hands off one another' in a *mêlée* which suggests a foretaste of the mystical Armageddon.

The following note, an *abrégé* of a paper addressed by me to the leading journals in the capital, may here be reprinted as a proof that I wish the Palestine Exploration Fund all success, despite these remarks, by which the Society, it is hoped, will not feel aggrieved. The Fund has undertaken the goodly labour of subjecting the Holy Land to an Ord-nance Survey, and we all look forward to its result. But the present staff will take, at the present rate, treble the time proposed for finishing the work; the three years will grow to nine before they can show final results. At least three hill-sketchers and four assistant-surveyors and astronomical observers are peremptorily required, but this pauper country cannot afford the miserable pittance of 1500l. per annum. To my mind there are few things less intelligible than the scanty interest which the Jewish as well as the Christian world takes in the Holy Land. I am especially astonished that the various Protestant communities should feel so coldly about a work which a French writer has declared, somewhat *à la française,* to have the force of a fifth Gospel, because it completes and harmonises—I may add, that it makes intelligible—the other four.

'The return of Mr. C. F. Tyrwhitt Drake to Damascus on November 5, after his dangerous *reconnaissance* of the 'Aláh or uplands lying between El Hamah (the Hamath of the Old Testament?) and Aleppo, enables me to say a word for the cause lately advocated by the "Hon. Sec. Palestine Exploration Fund." My friend and fellow-traveller, during a journey of thirty-five days, averaging seven hours of riding per diem, sketched and fixed the positions of some fifty ruins, which, in presence of the Circassian immigration, now a *fait accompli,* are fated soon to disappear from the face of earth; he is also sending home twenty to twenty-five Greek inscriptions, of which six or seven have dates; and before joining Captain Stewart, R.E., he will explore the Harrah or 'Hot Country,' a pure white blank in the best maps, which, however, have not yet had the opportunity of being good. All except the hydrographic charts have been hurriedly executed; the bearings are mostly in confusion, and the proper names of places are hideously distorted. Let me offer, as a proof, the positions for Palmyra supplied to me by Mr. Stanford, of Charing-cross, who assures me that the position of the old Phœnician city is not given in Ritter's *Erdkunde:*

	Lat.	Deg.	Min.	Sec.	Long.	Deg.	Min.	Sec.
1. Duc de Luynes's map; Lt. Vignes' position	N.	34	32	30	E.	38	14	39
2. Lt.-col. Chesney's map, published by Walker	N.	34	15	00	E.	38	35	00
3. Carl Ritter's map . .	N.	34	17	30	E.	38	32	30
4. Major Rennell's map .	N.	34	24	00	E.	38	20	00
5. Murray's Handbook for Syria has adopted from Rennell and Vignes'	N.	34	35	00	E.	38	14	39

'Here, then, the extremes of difference in latitude amount to seventeen miles, and in longitude to twenty miles, or a total of thirty-seven miles, in fact nearly thirty-eight; and it must be remembered that Palmyra lies within an easy four days' ride of Damascus.

'Newly transferred to Syria and Palestine, I imagined—and many would do the same—my occupation as an explorer clean gone. The first few months, however, proved to me that although certain lines of transit have been well trodden, yet few travellers and tourists have ever ridden ten miles away from the high-roads. No one, for instance, would suspect that so many patches of unvisited, and possibly at the time unvisitable, country lie within a day or two's ride of great cities and towns, such as Aleppo and Damascus, Hums and Hamah. When the maps show a virgin-white patch in the heart of Jaydur, the classical Ituræa, students naturally conclude that the land has been examined and has been found to contain nothing of interest—the reverse being absolutely the case. Finally, as will presently appear, there are valid reasons why these places have escaped European inspection; the traveller at once knows that an unexplored spot means one either too difficult or too dangerous for the multitude to undertake.

'A correspondent has effectively pointed out the nature of the work required by the Bible lands proper, "from Dan to Beersheba," where there is nothing barren of interest. It is to be hoped, however, that the funds will soon permit an archæologist to follow the surveyor. Although the East moves slowly, still she moves; but her present movement is all towards the change of ancient and Oriental to modern and European art, and in many places to the destruction of the most valuable remains of antiquity. The ruins of the 'Aláh are being pulled to pieces in order to build houses for Hamah. The classical buildings of Saccæa are torn down and set up into rude hovels for the mountaineers who have fled from the Anti-Libanus and the Hermon. Patterns which possibly antedate the Pyramids are making way for cheap English calico prints. The porcelain sent from China is sold or stowed away, and the table is decked with tawdry bits of French stuff, all white and gold, and worth, perhaps, a franc apiece.

'Allow me to conclude with again attempting to impress upon subscribers to the Palestine Exploration Fund that Syria, north of Palestine proper, is an old country, in more than one aspect — geographical and technological, for instance—virtually new. A Land of the Past, it has a Future as promising as that of Mexico or of the Argentine Republic. The first railway that spans it will restore to rich and vigorous life the poor old lethargic region: *Lazare, veni foras !*—it will raise this Lazarus of eastern provinces, this Niobe of the nations, from a neglected grave. There is literally no limit that can be laid down to the mother-wit, to the ambition, and to the intellectual capabilities of its sons; they are the most gifted race that I have, as yet, ever seen. And when the Curse shall have left the country—not the ban of superstition, but the bane and plague-spot of bad rule—it will again rise to a position not unworthy of the days when it gave to the world a poetry and a system of religion still unforgotten by our highest civilisation.

'Your obedient servant,
'RICHARD F. BURTON.

'Garswood, Dec. 31, 1871.'

My twenty-three months at Damascus (October 2d, 1869, to August 18th, 1871) were, I may here remark, rendered bitter by contact with a tyranny and an oppression which even that land of doleful antecedents cannot remember. The head and front of offence was one Mohammed Ráshid—not to be pronounced or confounded with Rashíd the 'upright,' the 'treader in the right path'—who held the responsible office of Wali or Governor-general. The politics of this unworthy man were alternately French and Russian, whilst, like the Oriental educated in Europe, he hated all Europeans. Similarly, a certain Tahir Pasha, who took such strong part in the massacres of 1860, had studied six years at the Woolwich Artillery College. Brought into collision with him by his utterly ignoring the just claims and even the rights of British subjects and protégés—a proceeding in which he was supported by those whose duty was to do otherwise—I had to battle with hands bound. But at last the truth prevailed. Not even the attention of an acknowledgment was paid to the telegrams and the solicitations of certain Consuls-general resident at Bayrut; their protégé, the infamous Wali, was recalled in disgrace and degradation, whilst the Mushir, or commander-in-chief, was ordered by telegraph to send him, in case of resistance, ironed and fettered to Constantinople. My *Personal Adventures in Syria and Palestine* will, I hope, place the whole subject in the clearest light, and Messrs. Tinsley have kindly undertaken to father the work.

Sweeping changes throughout the province followed the removal of Mohammed Ráshid in September 1871; and every measure which, since October 1869, I had ventured to recommend in the interest of our Ottoman allies was at once carried out. The reform was so thorough and so complete, that presently her Majesty's ambassador at Constantinople was directed officially to compliment the Porte upon its newly-initiated line of progress.

Wonderful is the irony of events. Meanwhile (August 18th) I had left Damascus under a recall. Being the civil, military, and ecclesiastical capital of the country, the head-quarters of the Government and the High Courts of Appeal, and the residence of the chief dignitaries, it was reduced to a Vice-consulate. We now rank there, greatly to the detriment of British interests, and to the injury of English residents, and missionaries, and school-teachers, with, but after, Spain, Portugal, and Greece, because the representatives of those powers, often Rayyáhs or subjects of the Porte, are senior to the British Vice-consul. Persia, with her usual diplomatic sagacity, has long ago directed a Consul-general to reside at Damascus. Russia and Prussia, France and Italy, have not yet been driven by economy, and the hard necessity of saving 300*l.* per annum, to speak through Vice-consuls.

Yet the English public is surprised to hear from the British Vice-consul in Damascus that certain English travellers have been made prisoners at Kerak.

To conclude: Critics and reviewers, who honoured with their notices my last volumes upon Zanzibar, appear in some cases to have acted upon the now recognised principle, 'Abuse the plaintiff's attorney.' Instead of reviewing the books, they have here and there reviewed the author. However amusing may be such a process to the writer, and exciting to the reader, I would protest against it in my own interest. Few lessons indeed, morally as well as in a literary sense, are more useful and beneficial than an able and temperate review. Let me name the *Observer* of February 4th, 1872. One of its remarks particularly attracted my attention : 'Many considerations, we are told, argue this (Wanyika) race to be a degeneracy from civilised man, rather than a people advancing towards civilisation. It is to be wished that Captain Burton had told us what some of the considerations are.' The fact is, that I had left the words as they were written in 1857, when I believed in the old Arab and Persian civilisation of the Coast, and in the great 'Monomoesi Empire' (Unyam wezi) of now obsolete geographers. I had neglected to append a note showing that my opinions about the settled abodes of the maritime classes had been greatly modified. On the other hand, nothing can be less profitable to an author or reader than a long tirade of personal comment and of unanswerable sneer, peevish and petulant withal, like that of the once-respected *Examiner* (February 3d, 1872). What could the most docile of men make of a literary verdict like this? 'We are afraid that these two rambling, egotistical, and excessively bulky volumes will prove tiresome reading even to the most arduous student of African travel.' The worst and the most irritating part of such *critiques manqués* is that, to quote what was said by a reviewer of a very different stamp, ' they declared their misjudgments with that air of supercilious authoritativeness, which, whilst it sometimes disfigures the style of an able critic, is always observable in the utterances of a pretender in critical art.'

RICHARD F. BURTON.

Athenæum Club, May 15, 1872.

CONTENTS OF VOLUME I.

c

APPENDIX.

I.

II.

III.

IV.

ILLUSTRATIONS.

The three steps referred to in page 110, beginning from the seaboard, may thus be supplemented :

1. Sáhil; Shore (עמק) ;

2. Wusút; Hill (שפלה)—Volney (i. 190) mentions only Nos. 1 and 3, ignoring the Wusút; and

3. Jurd; Mountain (הר).

The Sáhil, shore or coast,[1] opposed to Aram, the upland plateau which may be said to form Syria and Palestine, is a strip of ground, here flat, there broken, at this part barely exceeding two miles in breadth, and extending from the lower slopes of the Libanus to the sea.

[1] It is the ancient Kana'an (Canaan, the lowland), and the Palesheth (Philistia), the Greek Paralía (παραλία), and especially the Macras and the Macra-pedium of Strabo, opposed to Shephelah (שפלה, Josh. xi. 16) of the Hebrews, whence the Arabic Sofalah. 'Aram,' in its widest sense, includes all the uplands lying between the Mediterranean and the middle course of the Euphrates, from Phœnicia and Palestine to Mesopotamia, Chaldæa, and even Assyria. Upon the disputed point of 'Shephelah,' the following note by Mr. C. F. Tyrwhitt Drake (Report of Palestine Exploration Fund, Quarterly Statement, April 1872) will be found valuable :

'"Shephelah" has been wrongly rendered "plain" and "valley" in the A.V. (*e.g.* Zech. vii. 7 and Josh. xv. 33). Eusebius says that the country about Eleutheropolis was still called Shephelah in his time. It is in fact the district of rolling hills situated as above mentioned, and forms a most marked feature in the physical geography of the country. It is not, however, so far as I am aware, shown on any map otherwise than as a series of spurs or shoulders running down from the main range, which in reality it is not.

'It is very important that these natural features should be well understood and carefully borne in mind, as most important in helping to clear up the obscurity in which the geography of the Old Testament is now enveloped. These distinctions of mountain, hill, and plain are more than once mentioned in the Talmud (cf. tract Shevith, &c.). Rabbi Jochanan says that from Beth-horon to Emmaus is mountain (הר); from Emmaus to Lydda, hill (שפלה), and from Lydda to the sea, plain (עמק); which is perfectly correct, as Amwas is situated at the base of a spur from the mountains, and the hills extend to within a very short distance of Lidd, beyond which is the plain.'

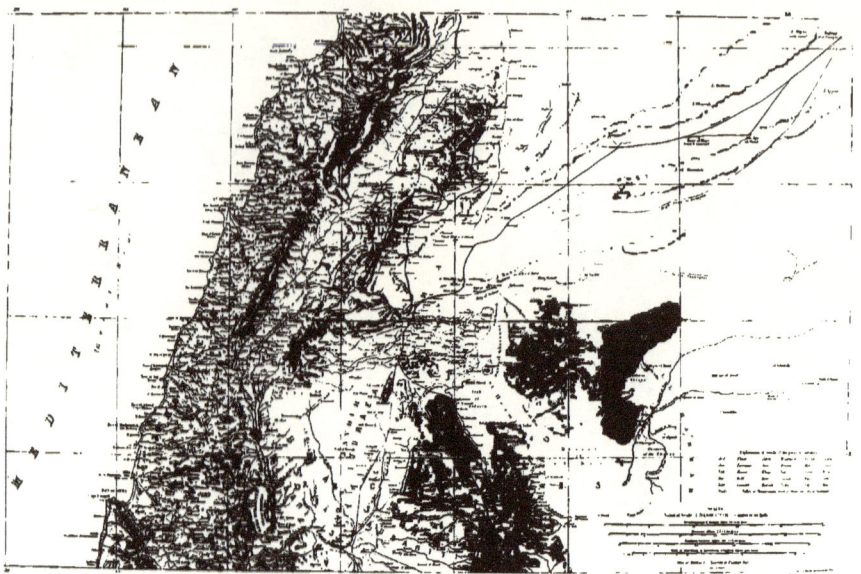

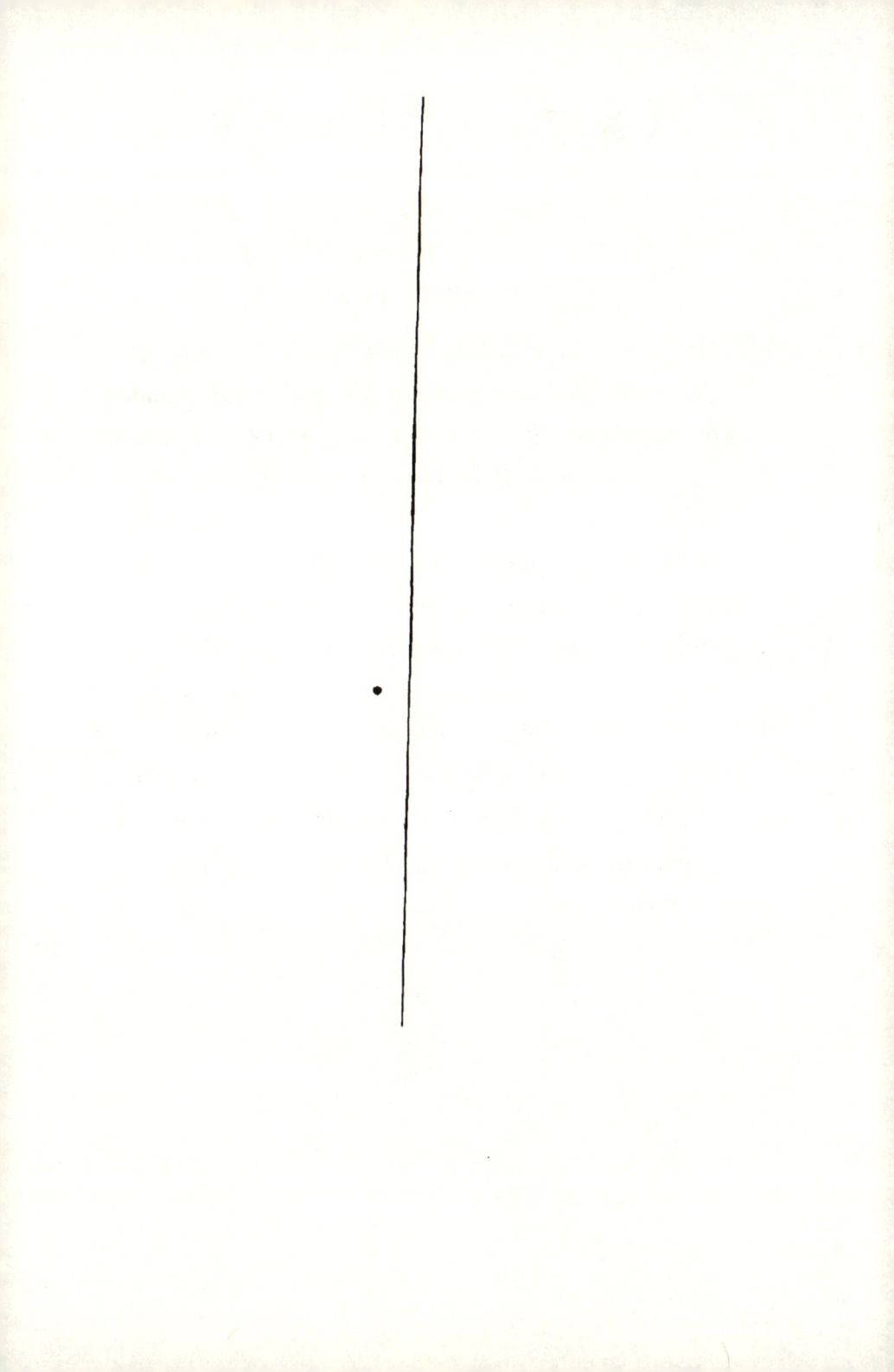

UNEXPLORED SYRIA.

GENERAL REMARKS.

My eyes were still full of the might and majesty of the Chilian Andes, and of the grace and grandeur of Magellan's Straits—memories which fashionable Vichy and foul Brindisi had strengthened, not effaced—as I landed upon the Syrian shore on Friday, October 1, 1869.[1] The points of resemblance and of difference between the South Pacific coast and Mediterranean Palestine at once struck my glance. Both are disposed nearly upon a meridian; mere strips of flat seaboard, mostly narrow, rarely widening, bounded by two parallel Cordilleras, flanking waterless deserts on the far eastern lee-land: the

---

[1] My last appointment had been at Santos, São Paulo, the Brazil.

northernmost are notably the highest blocks of mountain; and the low-lying southern extremities, in Asia
as in America, are ever rising by secular up-growth;
whilst either shores, Pacific and Mediterranean, are
subject to remarkable oscillations of level, chiefly the
result of Plutonic agencies. Both coasts are subtended by currents with northerly sets; both lands
depend greatly upon snow for their water-supply;
both show the extremest contrasts of siccity and humidity, of luxuriance and barrenness; and both abut
upon a 'desert,' an extensive tract of extreme aridity.
In both, as was said by a lover of Spain, God has
still much land in His own holding. Syria and
Palestine are, indeed, an Eastern Chili dwarfed and
grown old—whose wadys (*Fiumaras*) are measured
by yards, not furlongs; whose precipices answer to
feet, instead of metres; whose travelling distances
are registered in hours, not in days and nights. The
former boasts of its Hermon, its Libanus, and its Anti-
Libanus; the latter caps them with her Maypú,
her Tupungáto, and her Aconcágua—names which,
by the bye, drew groans as I pronounced them at the
last anniversary dinner of the Alpine Club—while
lakes and rivers, plains and valleys, cities and settlements, storms and earthquakes; in fact, all the geo-

graphical, the physical, and the meteorological, as well as the social features of the two regions, show a remarkable general likeness, but every thing upon a similar scale of proportion.

On the other hand, the difference in all that may most interest the. imagination, fire the fancy, and upheave the heart is yet more pronounced than the resemblance. The New World, which had been my latest scene of action, wearies with its want of history, of association, and consequently of romance; it was born to the annals of humanity within the space of four centuries; its aborigines, so to speak, were savages that can interest only in Fenimore Cooper; its legends are raw and grotesque, wholly wanting the poetical charms, tender and delicate, of South-European paganism; whilst art and science were, till the other day, words unknown to it. It is the prose of prose, the veriest reality. Its past is insignificant; its present is the baldest and tamest of the kind; and the whole of its life of lives dwells in the future—a glorious and gorgeous realm, ever dazzling the eyes, and serving chiefly to cast a grayer, sadder tone over the things that are.

The Old world of Palestine, again, is oppressively old, as the New is uncomfortably new: it is over-

ripe, while its rival is yet raw; it makes the dis-
satisfied poet cry,

' The world is weary of the past.'

In these regions we find hardly a mile without a
ruin, hardly a ruin that would not be held deeply
interesting between Hudson's Bay and the Tierra del
Fuego; and, in places, mile after mile and square
mile upon square mile of ruin. It is a luxuriance
of ruin; and there is not a large ruin in the country
which does not prove upon examination to be the
composition of ruins more ancient still. The whole
becomes somewhat depressing, even to the most ar-
dent worker; whilst everywhere the certainty that
the mere surface of the antiquarian mine has been
only scratched, and that years and long years must
roll by before the country can be considered explored
—before even Jerusalem can be called ' recovered'—
suggests that the task must be undertaken by Societies, not by the individual.

Of history, again, of picturesque legend, of theology and mythology, of art and literature, as of
archæology, of palæography, of palæogeography, of
numismatology, and a dozen other -ologies and -ogra-
phies, there is absolutely no visible end. And if the
present of the New World be bald and tame, that of

the Syrian Old World is, to those who know it well, perhaps a little too fiery and exciting, paling with its fierce tints and angry flush the fair vision which a country has a right to contemplate in the days to be.

The reader will understand this mingled feeling— a feeling never absent except in books—with which this pilgrim cast his first look upon the 'holy, beautiful Hermon;' a commonplace hogsback (χοιρἁς), where he had been led to expect a mighty and majestic Mont Blanc; upon the short barren buttress of Carmel by the Sea (*la Vigne du Seigneur*), type of graceful beauty to the Hebrew, and now crowned with a convent not quite useless, and with a French lighthouse decidedly useful, though uncommonly expensive;[2] upon the insignificant lines, the dull tintage, and the sterile surface of the Libanus—that Lebanon which served the Israelites as a *beau idéal* of glory and majesty; upon the memorial Ladder of Tyre,

---

[2] The French company (L'Administration des Phares) of Constantinople must administer to advantage, must make money, even at Carmel. Whilst a ship, say of 740 tons, pays 8*l*. for lightage-fees up the English Channel to Liverpool, the same vessel going the usual Mediterranean round of Papayanni & Co.'s steamers expends 30*l*., or 3*l*. 10*s*. at each port. For Gibraltar light a vessel contributes 2*s*.; at Bayrut she is mulcted 370 piastres, or within a few pence of 3*l*.

much resembling from afar a snowy patch taken from
the Dover cliffs; and upon Bayrut, classic Berytus, a
little city of the true harbour-town species, with
terraced lines and tenements flat-roofed enough to
support a bran-new settlement in Southern Italy.
There was, indeed, to me something almost quaint
in the contrast between the pictures which the fancy
of childhood, aided perhaps by Mr. Bartlett and others
of his craft, had traced and had deepened till the
print might have been indelible, and the realities
which rose somewhat misty and cloud-veiled above the
light-blue Mediterranean wave.   Like almost all realities, the scene declined answering to the anticipation.
The comparison presently suggested the want of a
realistic description, showing sights and things as
they are; not as they are wished to be, nor as they
ought to be — realistic chiefly as to the outer and
visible part of such things and their bearings; thus
serving to set off the other, and to many the more
interesting, phase of the subject, 'la merveilleuse
harmonie,' as M. E. Renan expresses it, 'de l'idéal
évangélique avec le paysage qui lui sert de cadre.'

I doubt whether this explanation will satisfy the
man of artistic tastes, who writes to me, 'Surely you
will not "unweave *all* our rainbows"? Who will be

the gainer by reading your comparison of the plain of Sharon with the Bedfordshire fields? I, for one, am certain that many take a delight in believing the contrary.' But surely this belief, which thus depends upon 'delight,' may be attacked to advantage, not only because it makes physical size and topical beauty the chiefest charm of the Holy Land, but also because it dwarfs the true importance and grandeur of its effects upon humanity, by setting its events in a frame far too large and fair. A great action appears the greater by being placed upon a small theatre. Pombal was a giant in Portugal; and though we still do right to measure—despite the Dean of Westminster—the power of a country by its size, yet we ever take the highest interest in those bygone days when the smallest of nations, Egypt and Greece, were perhaps the greatest. Why, then, make 'the mighty wall of Lebanon rise in indescribable majesty:' had Dr. Robinson never sighted the Alps, or the White Mountains of his native land? What means the 'eternal snows of the royal Hermon:' did Dr. Tristram ever see his favourite mountain all berry-brown in September and October? Why quote of a poor bell-shaped, onion-topped mound,

'What hill is like to Tabor's hill in beauty and in fame?'

Had M. Chasseaud never glanced at Patras or Reggio,
to quote no others, when he asserts : ' It would be
superfluous to say that the immediate neighbourhood of the hills defining the landscape about Beyrout is, without one solitary exception, the finest and
the most fertile in the known earth'?[3]

The fact is, we find here, and not elsewhere, a
complaint which may be called 'Holy Land on the
Brain.' It is no obscure cerebral disorder, like the
morbid delusions of the poisoner : it rather delights
to announce its presence, to flaunt itself in the face
of fact. This perversion of allowable sentiment is
the calenture which makes patients babble of hanging gardens and parterres of flowers, when all they
beheld was sere and barren. The green sickness
mostly attacks the new and unseasoned visitor from
Europe and North America, especially from regions where he has rarely seen a sun. It is a
'strange delusion that the man should believe,'
Carlyle says, 'the thing to be which *is* not.' As
might be expected, it visits the Protestant with
greater violence than the Catholic, whose fit assumes
a more excited and emotional, a spasmodic and hys-

---

[3] *The Druzes and the Lebanon*, by George Washington Chasseaud.
London, Bentley, 1855.

terical, form, ending, if the patient be a man and a poet, in a long rhapsody about himself, possibly about his childhood and his mother. It spares the Levantine, as yellow Jack does the negro: his brain is too well packed with the wretched intrigues and the petty interests of a most material life to have room for excitement at the 'first glimpse of Emmanuel's Land.' A long attack of the disorder—which is, however, rare—leads from functional to organic lesion. Under such circumstances, the sufferer will, to adduce only one instance, hire a house at Siloam, and, like the peasant of yore, pass his evening hours in howling from the roof at the torpid little town of Jebus, 'Woe, woe to thee, Jerusalem!' The characteristic and essence of the complaint are not only to see matters as they are not, but to force this view upon others; not only to close the eyes of body and mind to reality, but also firmly to hold that they are open, and to resent their being opened by any hand, however gentle. A few limestone blocks stained with iron rust become 'beautiful blush marble,' because they are the remains of a synagogue at Tell Hum—which, by the bye, is *not* Capernaum. Men fall to shaking hands with one another, and exchange congratulations, for the all-sufficient reason that the view before them embraces the plain of Esdraelon. The melon-shaped article which roofs the greater Rock in the Noble Sanctuary becomes an 'exquisite dome;' and so forth unto nausea. In art, poetry, and literature generally, 'Holy Land on the Brain' displays itself by an exaggeration of description which distorts the original; by sentimental reminiscence; by trite quotation, more or less apposite; and sometimes by a trifle of pious fraud. Its peculiarity in the Englishman and the Anglo-American is the rapture with which it hails the discovery in some ruinous heap of some obscure Scriptural name, belonging to some site still more obscure. As it especially afflicts writers of travels and guide-books, the sober and sensible tourist in Syria and Palestine must be prepared for not a little disappointment. Finally, it is in some few patients incurable: I have known cases to which earthly happiness and residence in the Holy Land were convertible terms. It endures time and absence, affecting the afflicted one with something of that desiderium, that 'sad and tender passion which a father nurses for the child whom he has loved and lost.'

Another advantage of the realistic treatment in

the perfect cure for all such complaints is its power
of turning the thoughts from the interminable vista
of bygone days, and of fixing them upon the times
that are, and the times to come—a process which
in Syria and Palestine has been grossly neglected.
Syria indeed, north of Palestine Proper, is, I have
said, and I repeat it, an old country in more than
one aspect virtually new. A long and a happy life
is still before it, the life which shall be called into
being by the appliances of a later civilisation. The
ruined heaps strewed over its surface show what it
has been, and enable us to look forward to what it
shall be. The 'Holy Land,' when provided with
railways and tramways, will offer the happiest blend-
ing of the ancient and the modern worlds; it will
become another Egypt, with the distinct advantages
of a superior climate, and far nobler races of men.

I visited the Libanus, with the half-formed fan-
cies of finding in it a *pied à terre*, where reminiscence
and romance, tempered by reality and retirement,
might suggest *inveni portum;* where the side, aweary
with warfare and wander, could repose in peace and
comfortable ease. The idea of pitching tent for life on
'Mount Lebanon'—whose Raki and tobacco are of
the best; whose Vino d'oro has been compared with

the best; whose winter climate is likened to the charms of early English summer, and whose views are pronounced to be lovely; in a place at once near to and far from society—I must cut short the long string of imaginary excellences — was riant in the extreme. Pleasant illusions dispelled in a week! As the physical mountain has no shade, so has the moral mountain no privacy: the *tracasserie* of its town and village life is dreary and monotonous as its physical aspect; broken only by a storm or an earthquake; when a murder takes place, or when a massacre is expected; when the Mount of Milk threatens to blush with blood; when its population, which, at the call of patriotism, would hide their guns and swords, are ready and willing, under the influence of party feeling, to deal death like Cyrillus, or to meet it like Hypatia. And I hasten to say that Europeans as a rule, with a few notable exceptions, set in these matters the very worst example. For the reasonable enjoyment of life, place me on Highgate's grassy steep rather than upon Lebanon. Having learned what it is, I should far prefer the comfort of Spitalfields, the case of the Seven Dials, and the society of Southwark.

Such was Syria under the rule of Rashid Pasha,

the late Wali, or Governor-general. And as my four years in the Brazil were saddened by the presence of the fatal though glorious five years' war with Paraguay, so my residence of nearly two years in the Holy Land, from October 1, 1869, to August 20, 1871, was at a peculiarly unfortunate time, when drought and famine combined with despotism and misrule to madden its unfortunate inhabitants.

The following pages by no means exhaust the information which I collected in Syria and Palestine. The book is an instalment respectfully offered to the public rather as a specimen of what remains to be done, than as a proof of what has been done by myself with others. Though the explorations are upon a small scale, they have all the value of novelty; and by pointing out the direction and the proper measures, they may stimulate and encourage future travellers to enlarge the field of correct topography.

An abstract of these volumes has been offered for the benefit of those who have no time for perusing anything beyond its preface. The first chapter, I repeat, in which we determined the forms and bearings of the Cedar Block, the true apex of the Libanus, was written by my wife: I have added to it a few philological notes and explanations. The second chapter contains a visit made by my friend Mr. Charles F. Tyrwhitt-Drake, and by myself, to the unknown and dangerous region called the Tulúl el Safá—Hillocks of the Safá district—a mass of volcanic cones lying east of the Damascus swamps called 'Lakes.' I alone am answerable for the text; whilst my fellow-traveller responds for the map of the cones, and for the plan of the far-famed cave 'Umm Nírán.' The third chapter (first in Vol. II.), written and illustrated under precisely the same conditions, is an exploration of the northern Anti-Libanus, a region which seems hitherto to have escaped the tourist and the traveller, and which still appears a blank of mountains upon the best of maps. The appendices which contribute so much to swell the bulk of these volumes are simply necessary: an endless succession of labour left me no time for working the matter into the text, nor perhaps would it have been advisable so to do. As the book now stands, the heterogeneous matter, much of it being the valuable contribution of friends and well-wishers, is relegated to the end, where it can most easily be found.

A few words concerning Volume II. A sudden and unexpected departure from Damascus prevented my carrying out a variety of exploration-projects, matured during a residence of twenty-three months, by collecting for them much preliminary and hearsay information. It was a great comfort under somewhat trying circumstances for me to know that these novelties would fall to the lot of one fully competent to do them justice. Mr. C. F. Tyrwhitt-Drake, who accompanied us in July 1870 to the Cedar Block, and who in March 1871 returned from England ⋅to Northern Syria, considering himself the representative of the Palestine Exploration Fund, is no common traveller. He has visited and collected in Morocco and other Moslem regions of North-western Africa; he is familiar with Egypt; and his survey of the Tih, or Desert of Wandering, made in conjunction with Mr. (now Professor) E. H. Palmer of Trinity College, Cambridge, a linguist and an Orientalist already of note, has made his name familiar to geographers. He is well acquainted with conversational Arabic; he is versed in the manners and customs of Moslem people, who respect him as a hard rider and a good shot, not to mention other weightier reasons; and he is inured to all the small hardships, the privations, and the fatigues inseparable from explorations and from gipsying over rough countries in the inner and the outer East. He has read at Cambridge, and he is practised in copying inscriptions; whilst his photographs, his drawings, and his coloured sketches speak for themselves. A diligent student of natural history, his specialty should be topographical surveying; he has an unusually keen eye for ground, and a trained judgment in determining distance, which render his compass-sketches as correct as those made by most men with the theodolite. A glance enabled him to set right Captain Wilson's (R.E.) plan of the environs of Jerusalem, where M. C. Clermont-Ganneau, Drogman-Chancelier to the Consulat de France, and I, by chatting with the peasants, had found (April 19) in the Mashárif Hills, immediately on the right of the high road to Nablus, the true site of Scopus, which topographers had placed too far east.

I have thus spoken of Mr. Tyrwhitt-Drake as a fellow-traveller: I will not trust myself to speak of him as a friend. Suffice it to say, that during three tedious months of contending unsupported against all that falsehood and treachery could devise, he was ever ready to lend me the most valuable and energetic assistance. Those only who have been

placed in a similar predicament can appreciate at
its real worth the presence of a true-hearted Englishman, staunch to the backbone, inflexible in the
cause of right, and equally disdainful of threats and
promises. I speak with allowable enthusiasm : in
this asthenic age of England and the English — a
physical as well as mental asthenia, which some
derive from tea taking the place of ale, and which
others date from the first attack of cholera — such
men are rare.

My friend tells his own tale of travel in the
second part of this volume, which he has entitled
' The Northern Slopes of Lebanon,' and the ''Alah,
or Highland of Syria.' The latter is an absolute gain
to geography, as the road lay through a region
hitherto marked on our maps 'Great Syrian Desert.'
The limestone ruins in the Jebel el Zowi were explored and described by the Count de Vogüé ; but
the basaltic remains in the extensive and once populous plain lying to the north-east and the south-east
of Hamah have been visited, sketched, and portrayed,
for the first time, I believe, by my friend.

CHAPTER I.

CARTOGRAPHIC AND OTHER NOTES ON THE WATER-SHED
OF THE BA'ALBAK PLAIN, ON THE 'CEDAR BLOCK,'
AND ON THE NORTHERN LIBANUS.

PART I.

I ARRIVED on December 31, 1869—why will not travellers be less chary of their dates?—at Damascus,
where a bare-walled whitewashed cottage had been
hired, and where the usual troubles of settling ourselves awaited me. Everything was to be done:
the tenement wanted 'cleaning' and repairing; the
stables and outhouses required additions which were
often reconstructions; servants were to be engaged;
horses and asses were to be bought. I found myself
face to face with the difficulties of Arabic; of strange
weights and measures; of new ideas; of outlandish
manners and customs, which took me back half-a-
dozen centuries, and which made me feel six times
farther away from home than when living in Brazil.
The hardest trial of all was to feel that every soul
had a deep design upon my purse, from the little
lad who stole my kitten for a *khamsah* (5 farthings)
to the gray-headed dragoman who wore two medals

presented to him by her Majesty's government, and
who would rather mulct me in a piastre (2½*d.*) than
not mulct me at all. However, there was a certain
amount of so-called 'society;' a few visits were to be
exchanged with the little European colony, almost
all consular, missionary, medical, and educational;
whilst many and long were the visitations from
and to all Haríms — we here drop the 'harem'
—who wished to enjoy an emancipation of a few
hours, and the pleasant ride up to our green
little village. At times also some relative or
friend from the distant fatherland dropped down
upon us like manna from the skies; and the
result was a rapid fleeting of time, with long rides
into the country, minute inspection of the bazaars,
and solemn interviews with white - bearded Abú
Antíká (father of antiquities) and other vendors of
rococo and *bric-à-brac.*

Briefly, these every-day cares tasked me at Damascus for some three months; and it was early
April (5, 1870) before I could find leisure for a holi-
day excursion to Palmyra. We returned after the
seventeenth day, delighted with our 'outing,' despite
all manner of small troubles. I may here quote the
short account of my trial trip, which found its way

into the home papers : such sketches, drawn from Nature upon the spot, often have a freshness of local colouring and a perspective of events which drawings finished in the study notably want.

Damascus, May 7, 1870.

Perhaps the welcome intelligence that the road to Tadmor or Palmyra is now open to European travellers may procure a place for these lines in your columns.

Until the present time, a traveller visiting Syria, perhaps expressly to see Tadmor, after having been kept for months in hopes, had to return as he came. Only the rich could hope at all, as it was necessary to hire a large Bedawin escort; for which even 6000 fr. and more have been demanded. Add to this the difficulties, hardships, and dangers of the journey. I allude to the heat of the arid desert, to chances of attack, to want of water, and to long forced marches by night, and hiding by day, thus seeing literally nothing of the country. Another drawback was the customary halt of two days at a place to see which so much had been sacrificed, and where twelve or fifteen could be well spent. Thus Tadmor, except to a few English travellers, has been totally excluded from the Oriental tour.

For more than a generation the Porte has deliberated about establishing a *cordon militaire*, extending from Damascus, *viâ* Jayrud, Karyatayn, Palmyra, and Sokhnah, to Dayr on the Euphrates. The wells were to be commanded by block houses, and the road to be cleared by movable columns; and thus the plundering Bedawin, who refuse allegiance to the Sultan, would be kept perforce in the Dau or Desert be-

tween the off-sets of Anti-Libanus and the fertile plains of
Nejd. This project—for which M. Denouville hopes and
fears in his charming little work on the Palmyrene—has at
length been rescued from the fate of good intentions. Omar
Bey, a Hungarian officer, with some 1600 men, is now at
Karyatayn, a three days' infantry march from Palmyra, and
waits but carriage and rations to make the next move.

A certain semi-official business compelling Captain Burton to visit Karyatayn, which is within his jurisdiction, I
resolved to accompany him, in the hopes of pushing on to
Palmyra. In this enterprise I was warmly seconded by the
Vicomte de Perrochel, a French traveller and author, who
has twice visited Damascus with the hope of reaching Tadmor, and M. Ionine, the Russian consul for Damascus. We
were mounted upon horses, and were wrongly persuaded not
to take riding-asses—they would have been a pleasant change
on long days. We engaged an excellent dragoman, Melhem
Wardi of Beyrout, six servants, a cook, twenty-eight muleteers, fourteen mules and twenty-eight donkeys to carry bag-
gage, tents, provisions, and barley for horses. These were
escorted by one officer and two privates of irregular cavalry.

On the second day, Da'as Agha, a noted sabre, chief of
Jayrud, and commanding one hundred and fifty lances, joined
us with ten of his men. He still looks forward to military
employment; and it will be surprising if they do not utilise
such a capable man. The Wali or Governor-general Rashid
Pasha, his agent Holo Pasha, the Mushir or Field-marshal
commanding in Syria, and other high officers, lent us their
aid. On our fifth day, when we arrived at Karyatayn, Omar
Bey gave us a cordial welcome, and placed at our disposal

eighty bayonets and twenty-five sabres, commanded by two officers. We arrived at Palmyra only on the eighth day, as we diverged hither and thither to see and examine the country; but we rode back to Damascus at a hand gallop in four.

Nothing can be more simple than the geography of the country traversed. We crossed one small divide between the Marj, or Damascus Plain, and the extensive valley which, under a multitude of names, runs nearly straight up north-eastward to Palmyra. After leaving Karyatayn, however, we went by the Baghdad or eastern road, called Darb el Basir from the Basir well and ruin; and we returned by the Darb el Sultani, the main or direct road, with a slight digression to the Ayn el Wu'ul (Spring of the Ibex Antelopes). At no season is water wanting. The seventeen camels hired by us at Karyatayn were a complete waste of money. This is always supposing that the traveller rides in two days from Karyatayn to Palmyra, and that he camps for the night at the Ayn el Wu'ul, in order to water his animals on arriving and in the morning before starting, there being no other supply between the two villages.

Everything that we saw in the shape of Bedawin ran away from the hundred and five men who formed our escort. A ghazu or war-party of two thousand would not have attacked us; and thirty Englishmen, mounted on good horses and armed with breechloaders and revolvers, could, I believe, sweep the whole desert from end to end.

Murray's Handbook requires much reform. The plan of Palmyra is not only defective, but erroneous: the author visited it perhaps under the old difficult conditions. Travelling by night would have deceived him as to distance—which he makes twenty, instead of fifteen, hours—and a constant feeling of insecurity as to attack would have enhanced many fanciful difficulties. A Bedawi shaykh can guarantee only from his friends; he cannot protect from inimical tribes; whereas we had the advantage of being independent.

If you ask me whether Palmyra be worth the trouble, I will reply Yes and No. No, if you merely go and come, especially after the splendours of Ba'albak; not for the broken Grand Colonnade, nor for the Temple of the Sun (the *fredaine* of a Roman emperor). Yes, if you would examine the site, the neighbourhood, and the old Palmyrene tomb-towers, which here represent the Pyramids. But who can pretend to do this in two days? We could not in five: it requires twelve or thirteen at least. The site is very interesting. Of Palmyra, as of Paestum, we may say:

'She stands between the mountains and the sea'

of desert, whose ships are camels, whose yachts are high-bred mares, and whose cock-boats are mules and asses. She lies on the threshold of the mountains, which the wild cavalry cannot scour as they do the level waste. The water is detestable, the climate unhealthy—all of us suffered more or less—and the people are ugly, dirty, poor, ragged, and ophthalmic. Let those who follow us encamp amongst the trees, a threshing-floor near three palms, close by the fountain; not near to and east of the Grand Colonnade, as did our muleteers, for the benefit of being at the side of a favourite well.

Yet it will not be difficult to revive old Tadmor. When there shall be protection for life and property, a large tract can be placed under cultivation. We found, by excavation, an old rain-cistern. Even the aqueducts may be repaired; and food need not be brought, as now, from Homs and Hamah, a four days' march.

There are three tomb-towers, which still may yield results. The people call them Kasr el Zaynah (Pretty Palace), Kasr el Azbá (Palace of the Maiden), and Kasr el Arús (Palace of the Bride). Explorers, however, must bring ropes and hooks, ladders which will reach 60 to 80 feet, planks to bridge over broken staircases, and a stout crowbar. We had none of these things. I have little doubt that the upper stories still contain mummies, tesseræ, and other curiosities. We made sundry excavations; but we lacked implements, and our stay was not long enough for good results.

The march from Damascus to Palmyra may be done, as we did on return, in four days, by strong people well mounted. The first is from Damascus to Jayrud, or better still, 'Utnah, a village half an hour beyond. The second to Karyatayn is a long day, *i. e.* nine hours of hand gallop, or fourteen of walking. At Karyatayn an escort is necessary, and would always be granted on receipt of an order from head-quarters. Those who have no camels must camp for that night three hours out of the direct road, by Ayn el Wu'ul, the before-mentioned well in the mountains. Those carrying water can proceed by a more direct road, *viâ* a ruin in the desert called Kasr el Hayr, which looks like a chapel, and near the remains of an aqueduct. They must choose between three hours' extra ride and the expense and slowness of camels. These two last days from Karyatayn to Palmyra may be done with twenty-four hours of camel-walking, thirteen of horse-walking, or with twelve of dromedary or hand gallop. However, my experience is, that we usually started at 6.30 or 7 A.M., and encamped after having been out twelve or thirteen hours; but this included breakfast and halts, sometimes to inspect figures, real or imaginary, in the distance; sometimes a 'spurt' after a gazelle or a wild boar. May is the height of the season; and the traveller need not fear to encounter, as we did, ice and snow and alternate siroccos and furious sou'-westers. This year has been a phenomenon. I expect many friends to follow my example; and I am ready to give ampler details to all who ask for them.—I remain, sir, &c. Isabel Burton.

The whole of May and a considerable part of June were spent at Damascus. Although we had a house on the highest ground, in the Sálihiyyah or northern suburb, the heat became intense, stifling. Between the solstice and the autumnal equinox all the English, and most of the Europeans, exchange the fetid City of the Caliphs for a villeggiatura; some contenting themselves with El Hámah, the first station on the French road to Beyrout; others pushing to Rasheyyá, on the western slopes of Hermon, distant two short days. The quarters belonging to Mr. Consul-general Wood, C.B., and kindly lent by him to the English consulate, are at B'lúdán, a little village near Zebedání,[1] about twenty-seven indirect

---

[1] Yakút (*Kitáb mu'jim el Buldan*) writes Zabedani and Ba'alabakk. The people pronounce the names Zebedání and Ba'albak.

miles to the north-west of Damascus: fast riding
will cover the distance in four hours; whereas mules
take ten, and camels rarely arrive there before the
second day.

The duty of a consular officer in Syria is to scour
the country as often as possible, to see men and matters with his own eyes, and personally to investigate
cases which are brought before him at head-quarters
in such disguise that all except the truth appears.
My husband's presence being required at Ba'albak in
July, I gladly embraced the opportunity of visiting the far-famed ruins. We were accompanied by
Messrs. Palmer and Tyrwhitt-Drake — the former
employed by the Ordnance Survey of the peninsula
of Sinai, and subsequently by the Palestine Exploration Fund; and the latter travelling at his own
expense, to investigate the natural history of Palestine, partly aided by the University of Cambridge.
After hard work, and harder living, with not a few
anxieties and risks on Mount Sinai, in the Badiyat
el Tih, or Desert of the Wandering,[2] and at Petra
and its ill-famed vicinity, these gentlemen were rest-

---

[2] May I suggest that this term, universally translated 'Desert of
the Wanderings,' may mean with more probability the 'Desert of the
(general) Wandering,' that is to say, where men wander and may lose
their way?

ing themselves by a run through Northern Syria and Palestine.[3] It was settled amongst us that we should do a little geography, and determine once for all the disputed point—the apex of the Libanus range.

As will presently appear, the best and most modern maps of Syria and Palestine[4] that Europe has produced display unexpected inaccuracies; and even the hydrographic charts, though they give the coast-lines correctly, are by no means equally happy

[3] Here, and in other parts of this volume, the term 'Syria and Palestine' is applied to the whole country extending from El Arish to Aleppo; the warning may prevent confusion with the Syria-Palestina (*e. g.* Philistine-Syria) of the Greeks, in fact the Land of Israel, the To-Netr, or Terra Santa.

[4] The following are chiefly alluded to :

(*a*) Map of Palestine, by the late A. Keith Johnston, F.R.G.S. Stanford, London; no date (a very bad practice, and apparently British).

(*b*) Map of Turkey in Asia. Same author, publisher, and defect.

(*c*) Map of the Holy Land. By C. W. M. Van de Velde. Gotha, Perthes. Second edition, Stanford, 1865.

(*d*) Carte du Liban, d'après les Reconnaissances de la Brigade Topographique en 1860-1861. Donnée au Dépôt de la Guerre, 1862.

Besides the minors, viz. I. Karte von Syrien den Manen Jacotins und Burckhardt's gewidmet. Berghaus, Gotha, Perthes, 1835. II. Carte Générale de l'Empire Ottoman. H. Kiepert, 1867. III. Syria. By W. Hughes, F.R.G.S. Printed for the Society for the Diffusion of Useful Knowledge. IV. Map appended to vol. iii. of Robinson and Smith's *Biblical Researches.* H. Kiepert, 1841. V. New Map of Palestine, &c. (from the Revs. E. Robinson, E. Smith, and J. L. Porter; by

in the parts of the Libanus which they include.
Looking at the position of Palmyra,[5] to give no
other instance, I may fearlessly assert that the present state of Syrian cartography is less satisfactory
than the topography of the Brazilian 'Sertão,' and
that the Anti-Libanus has not yet been so correctly
traced as the Andes. The survey of the Holy Land
lately proposed in the United States, as well as in
England, will find novelties enough, and will smooth
the way for the archæologist, the mineralogist, and
the technologist. At present 'The Mountain,' as men
call it, is scientifically almost unexplored; and to a
careful observer every trip of a few days produces
something new. During his rides my husband has
found in various parts, where they were least expected, deposits of lignite and of true coal, and extensive strata of bituminous schists and limestones,

---

H. Kiepert), for Murray's *Handbook for Syria and Palestine.* VI. Map
of Damascus, Hauran, and the Lebanon Mountains, from personal
Survey. By J. L. Porter. *Five Years in Damascus.* Second edition.
London: Murray, 1870. VII. New Map of Palestine and the adjacent
Countries. By Richard Palmer. VIII. Palästina. Von A. Petermann
(the worst of all), Stieler's *Hand-Atlas.* IX. Keith Johnston's Map
of Palestine, published in 1856. It has gone through five editions, each
time with some corrections, the latest being in 1870.

[5] See Preface for the discrepancies.

leading down to the finest bitumen or asphalt (*hum-mar*), the 'slime' of Holy Writ, quaintly called by our ancestors 'Jew's pitch.' So far from being confined, as has been popularly stated, to the valley of the Upper Jordan, this semi-mineral exists almost everywhere in the Howára or chalk formation, alternating with the Jurassic limestone: hence its origin in the Lacus Asphaltites, where it is degraded from the cretaceous matrix, and not, as the ancients declared, found floating upon the waters.[6] Mineral springs, especially sulphureous, chalybeate, and aluminous, are common; magnetic, specular, and pyritic ores, with hydrates of iron, abound, and copper is found in its native state. The coarse sandstone formations which crop out of the barren gray fields of secondary limestone[7] often contain, as the landslips (خسفات) near Kufayr and Jezzin show, remains of

---

[6] It need hardly be remarked that the Rev. Mr. Porter's theory (*Giant Cities of Bashan*, p. 264; London: Nelson, 1869) about asphalt being thrown up from the bed of the Jordan valley, and that the 'travellers' tales' concerning the generation of bitumen in the so-called Dead Sea, recorded by Tacitus and others, are simply fabulous. The bitumen and bituminous schist are washed out of the chalk formation, especially after earthquakes.

[7] I find in the *Recovery of Jerusalem* (p. 8), that 'the limestones about the "Holy City" are of the tertiary formation,' when they are distinctly secondary.

stone pine-forests (*P. Pinea* and *Halepensis*), rich in semi-mineralised Dammar, locally called Sandarús and Alfúnah; in alum and in sulphur, with other pyrites. The Hermon Mountain and the Anti-Libanus range produce two plants, both called Zalluá (زلوع). They are famed for tonics like the once well-known and now neglected *Chob Chini*, or Chinese Orris. The hills behind B'lúdán are grown after snow time with a kind of rhubarb;[8] the root is used medicinally by the peasantry, and the stalks which appear in spring are made, especially at Ba'albak, into sherbet; they are also seasoned with salt, like salad, or boiled and eaten with sugar as amongst ourselves. Rhubarb, it will be remembered, became an edible throughout England only in the latter part of the last century, and, like tea, it found at first but little favour.

The route from B'lúdán to Ba'albak lies up the Zebedání Valley to the Jisr el Rummánah — 'of the Pomegranate'—a common one-arched Saracenic affair, of which Mr. Porter (Murray's Handbook, 526) makes a 'Roman bridge, showing that we are in

---

[8] Here known as 'Ribás,' which properly means sorrel (rhapontic), the classical Arabic name being 'Răwand,' probably borrowed from the Persian, and perverted to Rewand, and even to Ráwand.

the line of the old Roman road from Damascus to Ba'albak.'[9] There are in this neighbourhood the ruins of two temples or Nymphæa, of a necropolis, and of three towns, which point out the line with less uncertainty. We then crossed the Saradah stream, and zigzag'd up the right bank of the Yahfúfah Valley to the village which contains the sepulchre of Nabí Shays[10] (Seth, the son of Adam). It is of the common Moslem pattern, raised upon two steps of masonry. The faithful have located almost all the Adamical and Noachian patriarchs around Damascus, which gave, according to some, the handful of red clay, 'the origin and true earth,' for the material part of our first father. Others prefer the Ager Damascenus, a bow-shot from Hebron, the city 'built seven years before Zoan in Egypt,' and claiming precedence over

[9] Like Madame Ida Pfeiffer's 'bridge of Roman architecture at Lycus' (*Visit to the Holy Land*, p. 205). Both are as recent as the ' Roman bridge' at Preston.

[10] 'Ab Seth,' Father Seth, whose name is composed of the initial and terminal letters of the Hebrew alphabet. According to a writer in the *Astronomical Register* (Dec. 1870), this alphabet is astral. The first twelve letters, from *a* to *l*, forming the popular name of the Deity (Al, Alat, Allah, &c.), are the twelve signs of the zodiac; the rest are—13 Eridanus, 14 Southern Fish, 15 Band of Pisces, 16 Pleiades, 17 Beta Tauri, 18 Orion, 19 Belt of Orion, 20 Delta Canis, 21 Canis Major, 22 Southern Cross.

VOL. I.   D

Damascus, although writers will call the latter the
'most ancient city in the world.' Adam is buried,
some declare, in the Muna Valley near Meccah; others
say that his head is under Calvary, and his feet
under the Hebron mosque;[11] Eve's tomb is undoubtedly at Jeddah, yet the hill-side (Jebel Arba'ín)
where Cain slew Abel lies hard behind our house
in the Sálihíyah suburb. Here an iron-riveted
slope of the hardest limestone looks from afar as if
a torrent of oxidised blood had poured down it to
the foot of the white building known as the Arba'ín
Rijál (the Forty Martyrs).[12] Cain's last home is on
the hideous rim of the Aden crater; Abel's looks
down from its red cliff upon the cool green valley

---

[11] According to SS. Epiphanius and Ambrose the blood of the
Redeemer dripped upon the tomb of the first man in token of salvation.
St. Augustine finds it only reasonable that the Physician should go
where the Patient lies. It is, however, an error to suppose, with Dean
Stanley, that the burial of Adam's head by Noah under Cranion or
Calvary is a Christian legend only, although it may have a Christian
origin. The Moslems place the 'Makam Adam' in the enceinte of
Hebron, and St. Arculfus seems to have remarked it there.

[12] They are evidently borrowed by the Moslems from the Latin and
Greek Churches, which still keep the feast of 'those buried at Sebaste.'
Mostly, however, the utterly ignorant Faithful believe the Forty to have
been Mohammedans who died fighting hard against crusading Christians. It is a favourite invocation: there are no less than three 'Arba'ín'
about Damascus.

of the Damascus river near Súk Wady Barada. Seth enjoys a bird's-eye view of the Cœlesyrian vale; the sepulchre of Ham is a few furlongs to the east; whilst Noah reposes at Karak (the Ruin), near the Mu'allakah or suburb of Zahlah: here also is the tomb of the Sáhib el Zamán, *alias* Hezekiah, who heals the aguish. The stature of these patriarchs prodigiously varied: whilst Seth is a Cyclops 100 feet long, and whilst Nabi Nuh (Noah) measures 104 ft. 10 in. by 8 ft. 8 in. in width, and 3 ft. 3 in. in depth, his son Nabi Ham, a deplorable pigmy— size being here carefully proportioned to religious merit—covers only 9 ft. 6 in. between the head- stone and the footstone, in fact he was only as long as his father was broad.[13] I am sure of these

---

[13] Although this ' grave of Noah' is a palpable absurdity in shape and proportions, curious to say, the author of the *Giant Cities of Bashan* quotes it, with other silly Moslem impostures or ignorances, as ' traditional memorials of primeval giants.' He would see similar enormous tombs even in the Jebel Kalbiyah of the Nusayri race, where no Rephaim are said to have existed. And near Karn Kaytú Messrs. Drake and Palmer found a gondola-shaped monolithic sarcophagus thirty feet in length by seven feet in breadth, in fact a family sepulchre. Barbarians everywhere confound size, the rudest element of grandeur, with grandeur itself: Adam was our first father, consequently his head touched the skies till he was reduced to a handful of miles. Moses was a great man, *ergo* he was sixty feet high; yet his tomb, to the west of the Jordan be it remembered, is not more than fourteen feet in length.

measurements; they were confirmed to me by our friends Mr. and Mrs. Rattray over a cup of tea at Kh'raybah.

Before leaving Damascus, Captain Burton applied to the Govenor-general of Syria for official permission to clear away the hideous Saracenic wall which, pierced for a wicket, masks the smaller temple of Ba'albak, called of Jupiter or of the Sun. This was a step preparatory to levelling the interior, and to under-pinning the falling keystone of the noble portal. I have before related how our good intentions were foiled, and there is no objection to the story being repeated here.

You were so kind as to insert a letter from me last May concerning 'Tadmor in the Wilderness,' and I shall feel glad if you find a pendent letter about Ba'albak, its rival in the traveller's interest, worthy of a similar favour. Many of your readers have visited or intend to visit its magnificent ruins—gigantic remains which Rome herself cannot show—and they will be thankful for the information which my five days under canvas in the midst of its temples enable me to give them.

For some months past my husband has been making interest with Rashid Pasha, the Wali, or Governor-general of Syria, to take certain precautionary steps for the conservation of old Heliopolis. In the early Saracenic times the temple, or rather temples, had been built up into a fort;

whence, as at Palmyra, they are still known to the Arabs
as El Kala'ah (the Castle). Of late years the moat has been
planted with poplars, dry walls have divided it into garden
plots; and thus the visitor can neither walk round the building, nor enjoy the admirable proportions, the vast length of
line, and the massive grandeur of the exterior. Similarly, the
small outlying circular temple called Barbárat el Atíkah (La
Sainte Barbe) has been choked by wretched hovels. The
worst, however, of all the Saracenic additions are—first, a
capping of stone converting into a ' Burj' (tower) the south-
eastern anta or wing of the smaller temple dedicated to the
Sun, and popularly known as that of Jupiter; second, a
large dead wall with a hole for an entrance, through which
travellers must creep, thrown up to mask the vestibule and
the great portal of the same building. Inside it there has
been a vast accumulation of débris and rubbish; a portion
was removed for the visit of H.R.H. the Crown Prince of
Prussia in 1869, but the whole area wants clearing. Finally,
nothing has been done to arrest the fall of the celebrated keystone in the soffit, which began to slip about 1759; which falls
lower with every slight earthquake (we had one at 6.15 P.M.
on June 24, 1870), and which, if left unsupported, will bring
down with it the other five monoliths of the lintel and sides,
thus destroying one of, if not *the* grandest of ancient entrances
the world can show.

On July 21 we left B'lúdán, accompanied by Messrs.
Drake and Palmer, who were finishing with a tour through
Palestine their hard work and harder times in the 'Tíh' and
the mountains of Sinai. We were very happy to have the
society of these gentlemen as far as the cedars of Lebanon,
and we only regretted that the journey was so short. Rashid

Pasha sent from Damascus Mr. Barker, chief civil engineer to the government of Syria, whose duty it was to undertake the actual work.

After examining the Saracenic capping of large stones overlying the south-eastern anta of 'Jupiter,' and which seems to crush down the cornice and to exfoliate the columns at the joints, it was judged inadvisable to remove them. The cornice, broken in two places, inclines slightly outwards, whilst the stones are disposed exactly over the centre of gravity, and serve to diminish the thrust: we therefore left with regret this hideous addition, this *bonnet de nuit*, which must now be regarded as a necessary evil. I may here remark for the benefit of your general readers, that no one can form an idea of the size of the stones used for building Heliopolis unless they have seen them. The three famous ones, measuring 64 ft., 63 ft. 8 in., and 63 ft. long, each 13 ft. in height and breadth, and raised to a height of 20 ft. or more, take away one's breath, and compel one to sit before them, only to be more and more puzzled by thinking how very superior in stone-lifting and transporting the Pagans must have been to us Christians of 1870.

The first work was to demolish the ignoble eastern masking wall. At an interview with the local authorities it was agreed that they should supply labour, on condition of being allowed to carry off the building material. During our stay of five days the upper part of the barbarous screen had been removed, much to the benefit of the temple, and it was a great excitement to the small population of the village of Ba'albak to see the huge masses of stone coming down with a thud.

We intended next to expose, by clearing away the rubbish-heap at the proper entrance, the alt-reliefs extending on both sides of the great portal. Lastly, we had planned to under-pin the falling keystone with a porphyry shaft, of which there are several in the Jami el Kabir, or chief mosque. The prop was to be as thin as possible, so as not to hide the grand old eagle, emblem of Ba'al, the Sun-god, which occupies the lower surface of the middle soffit stone.

Unhappily, Mr. Barker, immediately on beginning work, was summoned to Damascus by Rashid Pasha, who, after having kindly offered to carry out the improvements, changed his mind suddenly, inexplicably, *à la Turque.* He objected to the worthless building material being given away—the why will not interest your readers. The English nation would have spent hundreds of pounds in such a cause, and we could have done it with pence; but you cannot succeed in making an Oriental brain understand that a few piastres in the pocket are not a greater glory than saving these splendid antiquities. The indolent Eastern will only shrug his shoulders and call you a Majnun—a madman—and if he can put a spoke in your wheel, well, it might give him an emotion, and he will not neglect his opportunity. So Mr. Barker was kept doing no-thing at head-quarters, hardly ever admitted to the 'presence,' and after short, rare visits uncourteously dismissed. I am always sorry to see an Englishman in 'native' employment, and if Mr. Barker had not been born at Aleppo, and knew any-thing of England, he would be sorry too. About the end of August he was ordered to lay out a road between Tripoli and Hamah; not a carriage road, but a mere mule path, which half a dozen Fellahs and donkey-boys could have done as well as the best of civil engineers. Thus poor Ba'albak has been again abandoned to the decay and desolation of the last fourteen centuries. We do not despair, however, of carrying out our views, and we can only hope that when his Excellency has finished his goat-track he will lend help to the cause of science. Perhaps he would, if he could understand how much all civilised people will care about this our undertaking, and how abundantly patronising such a cause would redound to the credit of Constantinople.

I hope that my friends who visit Ba'albak will let this letter supplement 'Murray,' and by all means prefer to the latter the plan of the ruins given by Joanne et Isambert, as that in 'Murray' is very poor.

The temples are doubtless the main attraction, but they are not everything, at Heliopolis. A day may well be devoted to the following programme. Walk up the hill to the south-east of the Kala'ah, examining the remains of the western wall, about the gate now called 'Bawwâbat Doris,' or 'El Sirr.' Visit the rock tombs and sepulchral caves, the remains of the small temple and Doric columns, and the Saracen 'Kubbat,' or dome, under which lies Melek el Amjad, of the Seljukian dynasty. From this high point the view of the ruins and of the valley is really charming. Descend to the nearest *Maklah* (quarries), and measure—as every one does, with different results—the *Hajar el Hablah*, or 'pregnant stone,' as the huge unfinished block is called. Our measurement was 70 ft. long, 14 ft. 2 in. high, and 13 ft. 11 in. broad. It was doubtless cut and prepared for building, but not detached from the quarry at one end; and the extraordinary sight makes you exclaim, 'Something must have frightened them away before they had time to carry it off.' Ride to the 'Kubbat Doris,' so named from a neighbouring village; its eight columns of fine granite have doubtless been removed

from the classic building. Thence proceed to the other quarries north of the temples. After some six indirect miles
nearly due west (279° magnetic) of the ruins, you strike the
sources of the Litani, or river of Tyre, and of the Asi
(Orontes), which rise at the eastern foot of the Lebanon outliers, within one short mile of each other. Concerning these
matters, however, Captain Burton will communicate with the
Royal Geographical Society. On the way you can enter the
tents of the Turkomans, who, though wandering about Syria
since the days of the Crusader, have preserved, like their
neighbours the Nuwar (gipsies), their ancestral language and
customs. From the sources turn to the north-east, and see
the 'Kamu'a Iyad,' named from a neighbouring village;
evidently a memorial column like that of Alilamus, still standing at Palmyra. Thence across the north-eastern quarries,
cut in steps like the Egyptian, to the eastern wall of Ba'albak. This must be carefully examined, and its difference
from that of Tadmor, a succession of mausolea, should be
duly noted.

Most travellers will now gladly return to their tents. If
unwilling to spend a second day, they will remount about
2 P.M., and follow up to its source the little mountain torrent
Ayn Lujuj. If the weather be not too cold, they can descend
the Najmah, or shaft, explore the tunnel with magnesium
wire, and extend the subterranean journey as far as the iron
door reported by the natives. We found the prospect peculiarly uninviting. Retracing your steps down the wady, and
visiting the tombs of the feudal house of Harfush, you strike
the valley of the Ba'albak waters at the source known as the
Ra'as el Ayn. This is by far the quietest and the prettiest
spot for pitching tents, but most people prefer, as we did, for

convenience to encamp among the ruins. Examine the two mosques, the larger built by the Melek el As'ad, son of the celebrated Melek el Zahir, and the smaller, 'Jami' el Mela-wiyah,' dating, as the inscription shows, from A.H. 670, and erected by the Melek el Zahir himself. Those who have spare time might try a little digging in the mortuary caverns which riddle the soft chalky cliff on the proper left of the river valley. Even at Ba'albak little has been done in the way of *fouilles.* The general visitor stays one day, and, after looking at the temples, goes on his way rejoicing that he has 'done' his Ba'albak. M. Achille Joyeau, a young French artist, and *grand prix de Rome,* who, employed by his government, spent some months in measuring and modelling the temples, seems to have made a cross-cut on the south of the remaining six columns which mark the great temples of Ba'al. There has, however, been no work on a grand scale, and I am convinced that excavation would produce valuable results. Lastly, as the sun is sinking behind the giant wall in front, you pass down the valley of the Ra'as el Ayn to the tents or house, and you thus end the supplementary ride.

In fine weather nothing can be more delightful than this excursion. The clear, crisp, pure air at an elevation of 3000 feet above sea level; the abundance of water 'more splendid than glass;' the variety, the novelty, and the glorious associations of the view; the sublime aspect of the ruins crowning the fertile valley, and backed by the eternal mountains; the manifold contrasts of stony brown range, barren yellow flat, luxuriant verdure of irrigated field and orchard; and last, not least, the ermined shoulders of Hermon, Sannin, and Arz Libnan (the Cedar Block) thrown out into such relief by the diaphanous blue sky that they seem to be within cannot-shot

—if these things will not satisfy a traveller's taste, I don't know what will.

ISABEL BURTON.

B'lúdán, near Damascus, Sept. 20, 1870.

And the following note addressed by Mr. C. F. Tyr-whitt-Drake to the Editor of the *Times* will prove that during the year which elapsed since our visit the evil has rapidly increased.

Sir,—Allow me through your columns to plead for the ruins of Ba'albak.

After an interval of fourteen months I have revisited them, and was astonished to see how much damage had been done in that time, chiefly by frost and rain, especially to the seven columns of the great temple.

The third pillar from the east is in a very bad state; its base is undermined northwards to a depth of three feet: some five or six feet of the lower stone have flaked away in large pieces, and the stones are generally scaling.

The cornice above No. 3 and No. 4 is cracked midway between the columns, and as the stone is crumbling, it seems in great danger of falling.

A large mass at the north-west corner of the square base supporting the western column has been broken by frost, and the column now overhangs thirteen inches.

All the columns have been more or less undermined by the natives, who thus endanger them for the sake of the metal clamps worth a few piastres; and unless something is done, these fine columns will soon have fallen.

A few iron bands round the columns connected by bars,

and a little careful under-pinning, would doubtless preserve them for many years, and I have no doubt that permission to do this would readily be obtained from the new Wali of Syria, whom all speak of as an honourable and intelligent man.

Could not a subscription be made in England—I believe 40*l.* or 50*l.* would suffice—and would not some architect or civil engineer, intending to visit Palestine during the ensuing tourist season, volunteer to stay a few days and see the thing done? I fear that if it be not set about within a year, it will be too late.

CHAS. F. TYRWHITT-DRAKE.

Damascus, Nov. 20, 1871.

The Governor-general afterwards denied having summoned our friend Mr. Barker, C.E., and then declared that he did not know what his chief engineer was doing. I soon learned the full significancy of this petty trick, worthy of the school which produced the two bans of Turkey, Fuad and Ali Pasha, the late grand vizier. No foreigner, and especially no consul, must leave his mark upon the land unless he pay liberally for permission to benefit it. A similar neglect of the duty of bribery and corruption occurred to a French traveller at Rhodes. The Giaour, furnished with a Firman permitting him to carry off an inscribed stone, calls upon the Pasha, who is all consent, and who sends his aide-de-camp as an escort of honour, and to collect the corvée.

The stone is found freshly broken in two. The
Frenchman storms, but after cooling down proceeds
to carry off the pieces. 'Nenni,' objects the aide-
de-camp; 'the Firman says stone, not stones.' Mon-
sieur complains excitedly to the Pasha, who threatens there and then to cut off the aide-de-camp's
head. The Frenchman, reassured, at once returns to
his stones, but finds that all have been removed during
the audience. Drop-scene: the Pasha threatening
to decapitate the whole population, who smile with
intense appreciation of the joke; whilst the Frenchman, with torn hair and wringing hands, vanishes
into space.

The valley-plain of Ba'albak (Sahlat Ba'albak),
as the people term it, is popularly but erroneously
called by modern travellers El Buká'a,[14] of which
it is the northern prolongation. The Buká'a and
the Sahlat are simply parts of a great depression
between the once single range which at present is
parted into the Libanus and the Anti-Libanus. It
is a fissure formerly deep and gorge-like, as may

---

[14] The Hebrew Bikath (בִּקְעַת), a plain as Shinar (Gen. xi. 2), or a
plain between mountains, is translated by the Greeks πεδίον, and by
the Latins simply *campus*. Some travellers have identified it with the
Bikath Aven of Amos (i. 5), and have gone so far as to explain Aven
by the Coptic On, the sun. Hence Heliopolis—but very doubtful.

still be seen in the lower course of the Litáni. The latter in geological ages was doubtless the main drain of the Buká'a, when the secular uprise of the latter discharged the waters into the sea. Since that epoch the valley-sole has been raised and levelled by successive strata of moraine swept down from the west, especially about the Sahlat, by modern conglomerates, and by humus still forming. It heads the Ghor,[15] the well-known Jordanic line of erosion; and the 'Eyes of the land,' the three main centres of depression shown upon the whole line, are the Waters of Merom, in a country almost purely basaltic; the Lake of Tiberias, about which the igneous alternates with the sedimentary formation, and the Dead Sea, where the trap completely disappears. When Van de Velde asserts (ii. 466) that the Buká'a throughout its entire length exhibits an unbroken chain of volcanic formations, he should have limited his 'bare and simple fact' to the fissure stretching southward from a little north of Rasheyyá, and to the northern section of the Sahlát Ba'albak, lying chiefly upon the left bank of the Orontes River. The eruption is evidently of more ancient date than

[15] The Hebrew Ha Arabah, the steppe, the desert place. Araboth is applied to the plains of Jericho and Moab.

those which formed the Druze Mountain (Jebel Durúz Haurán), with its adjuncts the Lejá, the Safá,
and the northern and southern Tulúl el Safá. The
water which fed the eruptions was contained in
the Cœlesyrian Valley proper, and it lay there till
within the historic age ;[16] the focus of explosion is
the Birkat el Rám, or Tank of the High Place, lying
on the southern slope of Mount Hermon. The Rev.
Mr. Tristram (*The Natural History of the Bible*, p.
22; London, Society for Promoting Christian Knowledge, 1868) describes it as a ' circular fathomless pool.'
Mr. Tyrwhitt-Drake and my husband, on May 18,
1871, made a boat out of a table-leaf and four air-
filled water-skins, and found the maximum of the
centre, beyond the thick line of vegetation (*Astero-
phyllum Spicatum?*) which clothes the shallows, to
be seventeen feet and a half, with a temperature
of 68° F. In the Buká'a proper, at the section
traversed by the modern French carriage road, the
traces of depressions are distinctly visible in the
uptilting of the outlying eastern buttresses, which

---

[16] Antiochus the Great in his war with Ptolemy was stopped by the
water that had collected in the great meridional fissure, flanked by the
two fortresses, Bronchi (Kabb Iliyás) and Gerrha (Majdal Anjar), which
were held by the Governor of Cœlesyria, Theodotus the Ætolian (Polybius, *Gen. History*, lib. ii. chap. 5).

enclose a valley of a higher plane, bounded farther east by the western slopes of the Anti-Libanus. About the village of Kafr Zabad these white-faced heaps of conglomerate are uptilted eastward at an angle of 35° to 45°; whereas the opposite sides of the Anti-Libanus show highly but irregularly contorted strata.

By the moderns the valley is known as El Buká'a el 'Azíz, in order to distinguish it from other Buká'as,[17] especially from El Buká'a near Salt, eastward of the Jordan, whose forty-five miles of the richest meadow land also appear to represent the now dried-up bed of a lake drained by the Zerka or Jabbok to the Jordan. The 'Beloved,' or the 'Precious,' is divided into two districts, both under the government of Damascus. The Buká'a el Sharkí (Oriental Buká'a), which contains three-fourths of the whole, but which is not so well watered as the other quarter, extends from the Kariyah village to Kafr Zabad: it is sometimes called *par excellence* 'El Buká'a.' The Buká'a el Gharbí (Occidental Buká'a) is bounded northwards by Karak and Barr Iliyás, the little Moslem villages

---

[17] The diminutive form El Bukay'ah is also common in Syria and Palestine.

close to and north of the French road; southwards
by Lusáh and Maydún; eastwards by the Litání
River; and westwards by the unhappy village of Ba-
wárísh and by the Khan Murayját. It clings, in
fact, to the eastern flanks of the Central Libanus.
This 'Valley of Lebanon,' as Hebrew writers know
it, must not therefore in modern days be made synonymous with ' Cœlesyria,' the name which Macedonian conquests gave to the 80 miles between N.
lat. 33° 20′ and N. lat. 34° 40′; whilst the Romans
extended it to the Damascene and to the Peræa or
Trans-Jordanic Palestine.

The aspect of the Buká'a proper much resembles
the fair lowlands of southern England, whilst the
finest views of 'the Mountain' suggest those of Spain
and Portugal. It is a Vega green even in mid-
summer, with trees and herbage and queer misshapen fields where water reaches. The redness of
the sides is not from the vineyards, but from the
oxide of iron, the rust of the decomposed Jurassic
lime, dating with the lower secondary, which en-
riches the ground. It is not ' smooth as a lake,'
but undulating in gentle land-waves, whose depressions are formed by the sundry little river valleys.
It abounds in settlements and hamlets, which are said

to number 137; the greater, which are of high antiquity, usually hug the hill folds, where they can
more easily defend themselves against the campaign
and the razzia. The little villages, which here and there
affect the centre, are of mud hovels built upon dwarf
mounds, the débris of ages; whilst the material is a
dark clay brick, contrasting with the limestone material of the hill hamlets : in this point the view suggests Egypt, and a single steam-engine and sundry
haycocks which have lately appeared add to the resemblance. The hill settlements apparently prefer the
neighbourhood of the white chalky Howára, which,
after the basalt, forms the best of vineyards. The
population must have been even thicker in classical
days : on the eastern side we still trace two important
cities, Chalcis ad Libanum (Anjar)[18] and Gerrha
(Mejdel Anjar), within cannon-shot of each other.
The climate, despite an average altitude of 2500
feet, is rich in fevers as the soil is exuberant in
fertility, and no European resident upon the lowlands can hope to escape repeated attacks. What

[18] Anjar is evidently a modern corruption of Ayn el Jurr, the proper
name of a spring. The peasantry have made it the name of an ancient
king. They call the ruins Husn Anjar, or Anjar el Kadím, and relate
how Caliph Ali rode from Meccah and slew its Jewish ruler Malak
Ankabút (the Spider). The tale suggests a Guinea Coast 'Spider story.'

little of beauty it has is essentially that of contrast, a smiling valley red and rich green parting two blocks of mountains barren, brown, and yellow. Here the Libanus is essentially never picturesque except by moonlight, or when its snow-capped summits gleam through storm-cloud rack above and mist-wreath below. There is even less to be admired in the northern projecting tongue of Ba'albak and in the Safet Block, which, dwarfed by distance, bounds the view to the south.

Beyond Ba'albak the Cœlesyrian Vale breaks into rough parallel ridges and becomes comparatively sterile, the result of deficient water, a want extending from that parallel throughout the northern head of the Libanus and the Anti-Libanus. Here also appear scatters of stones, showing subterranean and igneous action. South of Jubb Jenin the fissure is composed of four distinct meridional depressions, beginning from Jebel el Shaykh (Hermon) to the east, and abutting westward upon the Tau'amát Níhá or Mashgharah (the Twins of the Níhá or the Mashgharah village). These are—1st, the Wady el Yábis, the northern extremity of the Wady Taym[19] and

---

[19] Mr. Porter (*Five Years in Damascus,* 2d edition, p. 7) makes the Plain of Marsyas correspond with the Wady Taym, including the Marj

the uppermost water parting of the Jordan, which separates the Hermon from the Jebel el Minshár, or ridge upon which Rasheyyá town lies; 2d, the Wady el Arís and Marjat el Sh'maysah in a lateral range, where basalt outcrops; 3d, the well-known gorge of the Litáni, with its natural bridge and its Khatwah or 'step across,' visited by every traveller; and 4th, the Maydún depression, lying at the eastern foot of the Libanus.

The people of Ba'albak correctly say that their town lies *'Al 'el mízán* (upon the balance); that is to say, it occupies the flattened crest of the versant which discharges to the north and south; thus the plain lying east of Sanúr is declared to 'drink its own water.' The streamlet formed by the Ra'as el Ayn or Ba'albak fountain is absolutely without water-

---

'Uyun (Ijon), south of the Buká'a proper. Strabo (xvi. 2) would have informed him that Chalcis (not the ruin in the Buká'a, but the place formerly known as Old Aleppo) is the 'Acropolis, as it were, of the Marsyas,' and that the southern boundaries were Laodicea ad Libanum (now Tell Nabi Mindoh) and the sources of the Orontes. When Polybius (ii. v.) speaks of the 'close and narrow valley which lies between the Libanus and Anti-Libanus, and which is called the "vale of Marsyas,"' he must be understood to signify that ancient Cœlesyria continues the vale of Marsyas. Pococke (chap. xii.) tells us that the river Marsyas, now called the (northern) Yarmuk, falls into the Orontes near Apamea, and that the plain doubtless took its name from the stream.

shed, though bounded immediately to the right and
to the left—north and south—by the two great river
systems of Cœlesyria.

On July 26th the travellers proceeded to examine
the spot where lie the true sources of the Litání and
the Orontes. And here I may premise, that in Syria
and Palestine generally, great influents have ever
since historic ages been confounded with sources;
whilst the latter are those represented by the most
copious, not by the most distant fountains. Moreover, Wasserschieds, versants and river-valleys were
and are universally neglected, if, as often happens,
the young spring is drawn off for irrigation: this
will especially appear at the head of the Upper Jordan. Hence we have the historical, which is still
the popular, opposed to the geographical or scientific
source. Again, in highly important streams like the
Jordan, the historical may be differently placed by
the Hebrews, the classics, and the Arabs. Finally,
there is often a mythical or fabulous source, like the
cave near Afka, which forms the Orontes; the Jurah
or sink, in the hill-range called Zebadání, which sends
forth the Barada of Damascus; and the Lake Phiala
(Birkat el Rám), which Josephus made the highest
water of the Jordan.

A slow walk of two hours led through some forty to fifty Turkoman tents, where the women, habited in the normal green and red, were making butter, by swinging a skinful of milk supported by a triangle. Part of the way was over ground which carried a good turf. It is called Marjat el Sahn, and it is owned by the little Fellah-village Haush Baradah.[20] After covering some six indirect and five direct geographical miles, Fáris Rufáil, the guide, informed the travellers that they had reached the Tell Barada. This mound, bearing 279° (Mag.) from the north-west angle of the great temple of Ba'al above the Trilithon, is one of the many tumuli, artificial and natural, which are dotted over the plain. They generally affect the vicinity of a source or a pool, and some of them may have upheld forts to protect the precious element. Upon its western flank appears an inscriptionless sarcophagus of white limestone.[21] The surface ma-

---

[20] Captain Warren, R.E. (*Palestine Exploration Fund*, No. V. p. 189; London, Richard Bentley) translates Haush, which is also written Hosh, 'herd-fold,' thus unduly limiting the generic word for courtyard, *patio*, and so forth.

[21] The classical Arabic name of this article is Náús (ناووس), possibly from the Persian Nawús, a Magian cemetery. The vulgar call it Jurn (a place for drying dates), properly a basin, a caldron, a large pot, also popularly applied to the monolithic lid of the Náús. In Northern Syria the favourite term is Rasad, plural Arsád.

terial is invariably an ashen-gray débris, comminuted and often powdery, remarkably contrasting with the red soil about it. It much resembles Mr. White of Selborne's 'black malm,' which he describes to be a 'warm forward crumbling loam, saturated with vegetable and animal matter.' It is essentially 'rotten,' and it runs down in streams like water when pierced with shaft or gallery. The country folk, who use this material for compost to their plots of vegetables and tobacco, all know that it shows signs of ancient building. We found it well defined in the old Sayyaghah (gold and silver smiths' quarter) at Damascus, Palmyra, and Ba'albak. It may be useful in tracing out the limits of immense cities like Tyre and Sidon; but the ground about the ruins of smaller settlements— for instance, Fákah near Rasheyyá, and Sardánah near Banyás—has been ploughed over till no traces of the gray matter remain, and the rains assist to remove it, especially if it lies upon a slope.

A few yards to the north-west of the mound is the true source of the Litání, a muddy unclean pool, without perceptible current during the dries; an oval, whose longer diameter was about 100 feet in July. It is treeless but rush-fringed, like most of these northern waters, and, as usual, it abounds

in small fish and large leeches, which may seriously
injure man and beast.   The low grassy land about
it (Marjat el Baradah) is flooded in winter; during
the summer, a hole sunk three or four feet deep
readily strikes the water, which percolates from the
uplands.   Hence the place is much affected by the
nomad Turkomans, and the cavalry horses are here
sent by the military authorities for spring grazing.
South of the line drawn through 279° (Mag.) the
fountains of the valley plain, such as the Naba' el
Na'na' (mint spring), and sundry minor supplies,
shed southwards, feeding, when they do not sink,
the Litáni river.   At the source the aneroid gave
an altitude of 3595 feet, Ba'albak itself standing at
3847.

Here the upper part of the river of Tyre is called
El Baradah, and must not be confounded with the
Barada or Chrysoröos (Abana?) of Damascus.   Mr.
Hughes's map (No. III.) derives the latter from the
north-west of the Litáni, and boldly leads it up and
down the southern heights of the Anti-Libanus.   This
change of name in the upper course — almost invariably the case with rivers, valleys, and plains in
this country—accounts for the error of Dr. Robinson
(iii. 143), who, when going from Zahlah to Ba'albak,

did not find the Litáni, which he must have crossed,
and who makes its fountain the streamlet of the
Anjar Valley. This Ghuzayyil (غزيل) water is simply a large influent, gushing plentifully from the
limestone rock at the western base of the Anti-Libanus, and flowing through a lateral valley of a higher
plane than the Buká'a, till it forms in the latter
what classical geographers call the river of Chalcis.
The traveller on the French road sees the stream
on his left, immediately before striking the Khán el
Masna' (*Station de la Citerne*), at the western jaw of
the Wady el Harír (the Valley of Silk), an article of
Damascus manufacture here often plundered in days
gone by.

But nothing will excuse a scholarly writer like
Dr. Robinson, in speaking (iii. 344) of the river
Litáni as the ancient Leontes.[22] Of course, guide-
books and tourists cling to their Leontes. Murray

---

[22] Strabo (xvi. 2) writes, 'between these places [Berytus and Sidon]
is the river Tamyras [the modern Dámúr] and the grove of Asclepias
and Leontopolis,' but he does not mention the river. Pliny (v. 17) also
records the ' town Leontos' (of the lion). Ptolemy (v. xv.) places the
λέοντος ποταμοῦ ἐκβολαί in N. lat 33° 5', and E. long. 67° 30', also
between Bayrut and Sidon. This would point to one of the many
Wadys or Fiumaras, especially the Nahr el Yábis, a mountain stream
probably then perennial, as its modern name the ' Dry River' suggests,
and now flowing only after rain.

(375) informs us that 'the name Lantch or Litâny, which Arab geographers have always given to this river, is unquestionably an Arab form of Leontes.' Another error about the stream occurs in the same page, where the lower course is translated 'El Kâsimiyah, the "Divider," because it separates the lands of Sidon and Safet, or from the name of some distinguished chief.' The fact is, that Kásimiyah is a common term in Syria for a village situated near a Maksam (مقسم), or place of parting, where a road forks or a leat is taken from a stream. And this is precisely the case near the bridge which spans the river above its debouchure. The only 'distinguished chief' connected with it is the Shaykh Kásim, a Shiite saint, whose ruinous domed tomb lies near the left bank.

From the Ayn el Baradah the travellers walked a short mile northward, over a shallow and partially cultivated wave of ground separating the Litáni pool-source from the true head of the Orontes. This spring, called Naba' el 'Illá (علة), issues from the foot of a gray Tell, bearing from above the Trilithon 287° 30′ (Mag.). The trickling source, forming a rushy ditch, supplies, they say, excellent water ; and on the left bank are two clumps and small

fields, especially of cucumbers. The many streams
of the valley-plains north of the rhumb before mentioned, such as the Naba' Haush el Zahab, the Naba'
Haush Tell Safiyyah, and the Naba' el Kaddús, the
largest of the springs, feed the Orontes.

The two sources are separated by a mere ground
wave;[23] they lie on the lowest level of the Ba'albak
plane, which falls from east to west with a long gentle
slope; whilst two distinct river-valleys, running north
and south, have been formed by the erosion of the
twin streams. The depression is disposed along the
eastern base of the Libanus, which is here marked
by two buttress-like outliers of ruddy surface : the
Tell Mughur el Saídah (Caves of the Virgin?) bears
north-west (Mag.) and the Tell Jabú'a due west (Mag.)
from the southern or Litání source.

Maps C and D, which, being on a larger scale,
might be expected to show the positions correctly,
have failed the most. C places the Haush Baradah,

[23] A remark which I made many years ago touching the water-
partings of the largest river-systems being seldom what we should
expect to find them, gigantic mountain ranges, has lately been enforced
by the discoveries of Mr. R. B. Shaw (*Proceedings of the Royal Geographical Society*, vol. xv. No. 3, p. 177), who reports that the great
basins of Southern and of Central Asia are separated by ' merely a few
yards of level sand.'

a little village, near the true source of the Baradah,
alias Litání; but it brings the latter from fourteen
direct miles to the north. D prolongs the stream
fifteen miles north, and both throw it across the
watershed of the Orontes. Berghaus (No. I.), whose
Anti-Libanus is a marvel of incorrectness, makes the
'Quell-see des Leontes' a pool, apparently following
Burckhardt; but he places it to the south-west,
whereas it lies west, of Ba'albak. Mr. Hughes (No.
III.) is also correct about the pool-source; but he
has, I have shown, confounded the Baradah and the
Barada of Damascus. Dr. Robinson (No. IV.) ignores
the Haush Baradah and the Naba' el 'Illá. The rest
seem simply to have drawn a frayed ribbon by way
of mountain, and to have derived from the fringings
certain cobweb lines meaning rivers.

The Orontes or Axios[24] has fared no better. C

[24] According to Strabo (xvi. 2, 7) the oldest name of the stream was
Typhon, from the serpent here struck with lightning. It was changed
to Orontes, the name of a man who bridged it; the site is near the
modern Metawili village of Hurmul. The legend of its underground
course doubtless alludes to the deep and shady gorge below Már Márún's summer quarters. The other Greek name "Αξιος is evidently the
Arabic 'Asi' (عاصي), meaning the rebel: Sozomeni *Historia*, vii. 15,
quoted by Pocöcke, chap. xii. Mr. Hyde Clarke (on the pre-Israelite
population of Palestine, &c.) has lately been developing a remarkable
theory (*Palestine Exploration Fund*, No. II. pp. 97-100), namely, that

and D bring it from the north-east of the Yunín
village, and about ten miles east-north-east of its
proper position. Mr. Hughes (No. III.) makes it rise
near the hamlet of Lebwah (the lioness),[25] which
boasts of a fine fountain; its three sources are divided into five leats of high and low levels, all
feeding the Orontes, except the easternmost spring.
The latter is said once to have watered Palmyra;
but we could not trace it beyond El Ká'ah. At
Lebwah the Orontes Valley, which we saw to the
westward as we travelled above it, is already deeply
cut and well defined; the popular name is El Ma-
jarr, or the Place of Draught. Travellers and consequently maps the more easily confound influents

---

the Canaanites spoke a Caucaso-Tibetan or Palæogeorgian language of
the earlier stage, ' when there were several types of the same root, and
when the radical letters were susceptible of permutation at will.' The
' river-term,' for instance, contained the radicals *d r n.* In the modern
Georgian and Mingrelian dinare, a river, the *d* and *n* or *n* and *d* represent water, and the *r* gives the idea of running. But it was indifferent
to the Canaanite how he placed the letters: thus in Jordan the *r* is in
the beginning; it is in the middle of Kedron and Orontes.

[25] The modern name is sometimes pronounced Lebu. It is the
Lybo or Lybon of the Antonine Itinerary, evidently derived through
Arabic from the Hebrew Labi or Labiyah, ' an old lion,' ' a lioness' (supposed to be a Coptic root), whence Beth Labaoth, or Lebaoth, the house
of lionesses.

with source, as after heavy rains all the gorges discharge surface water. The word Wady[26] is usually
translated by us ' valley,' instead of Fiumara or Nul-
lah : nothing, in fact, is less like our English valley
than a Syrian Wady: the former word would be
more fitly Arabised by Sahlah or Watá. The Wady,
almost all the year round, is a winding broken line
of bleached and glaring white, of lamp-black or of
brown-gray rock faced with slime-crusted and water-
worn pebbles, and scattered over with large angular
stones. It becomes a storm-brook or rain-torrent; a
raging, foaming, muddy débâcle, which for a few days
or hours dashes the boulders together, hurries down
tree-trunks, and is certain death to man or beast that
would cross it. Few travel in Palestine during the
hot season ; and we saw the country at a time when
the real and perennial river-sources are best shown.

[26] In Hebrew nachal (נחל), and in Greek χείμαῤῥος, storm-brook
or rain-torrent. It is opposed to the Hebrew Ge (גי — for instance,
Geben Hinnom) and the Arabic Fijj, a ravine *praeruptum eoque neglec-
tum*. About a score of years ago, when I ventured to translate Wady
by Fiumara, objections were raised to naturalising the latter term : it
was local, incorrect, unintelligible. But let the traveller in Southern
Italy and in Sicily declare whether the mountains are not streaked with
true Wadys, and whether the latter are not called Fiumare. The incon-
gruity of such expressions as the Brook Kedron and the Brook Cherith
(Wady el Kalt)—bone-dry lines of rock—must be palpable to all who
see nature as it is.

Although Pliny (v. 19) expressly tells us that the Orontes takes its rise near Heliopolis (Bá'albak), its origin has suffered perversion in books as well as in maps. Abulfeda derives it from the Ra'as Bá'albak, one of its minor influents. Mr. Porter (*Five Years in Damascus*, p. 315, 2d edit.; repeated in Murray, 541) makes the Lebwah fountain the 'highest source of the Orontes.' Mr. W. A. Barker (*Journal of London Geographical Society*, vii. of 1837, p. 99) follows the still popular opinion, and derives it from the eastern foot of Libanus, under the caverned hill known as Dayr Már Márún (Convent of Saint Maro): yet in the same page he mentions the small spring from Lebwah, which, after flowing several hours through the plain, falls into a basin, whence rises the Orontes.

This Dayr Már Márún, well known to travellers, is a mere summer-place hewn in the rocks, like the Lauræ of modern Coptic fraternities; in fact, a Chaitya or Church-cave, as opposed to a built Vihara or monastery; and from the hands of the holy men it passed into those of bandits, rebels, and goatherds. The true convent, the old head-quarters and cradle of the once heretic sect, which is still remembered as the 'Maradat Jebel Libnán'—the contumacious of

Mount Lebanon — is now the site of Khán Rastan (رستن), vulgarly pronounced Restan. As late as A.D. 1745 the 'ruins of a very large convent' were here noticed by Pococke; it lay upon the right bank of the Orontes, and it supplied materials for a huge fortified caravanserai, which also is rapidly falling to decay. Rastan[27] is the Arethusa of Seleucus Nicator, whose King Sampsiceramus (Shams el Karam, the Sun of Generosity?) was conquered by Pompey. Though fortified, provisioned, and strongly garrisoned, it was easily taken by Abu 'Ubaydah and his men in boxes. But if the Laura does not deserve its title of Dayr, nothing can be more charming than the view which it commands over the deep and tree-lined gorge below—nothing more refreshing to the eye than the gushes of liquid crystal pumping out of the living rock into basins shady with tender-leaved planes and strongly-scented wild vines; nothing, in Palestine at least, more memorable than the succession of huge arteries worked as if by hydraulic pressure, and at once forming with their blue waters a river some sixty feet wide, brawling down

[27] The plan of the Greek city is admirably plain, and there is, I should say, no more promising digging-ground in North Palestine. Mr. Porter (Murray, p. 589, sub voce *Rastán-Arethusa*) gives ten arches to the Rastan bridge; I counted eleven and a bittock.

the rocky and tortuous conglomerate bed. I could not wonder that the imaginative Hellenes made its beauties the scene of a marvel; and although the Ayn el Zarka (the Blue Spring), and the Naba' el Asi, its more copious neighbour, are not the true fountains, they are at least the main sources. They seem to explain the two rocks from which, according to Nero's travelling captains, the vast force of the river Nile issued forth.[28]

Three reasons are given for the epithet 'El Asi,' or the Rebel. Popularly, the injurious term alludes to the belief that the Orontes never faces the Ka'a-bah, flowing north, contrary to the rule of all waters in Cœlesyria: hence, according to Pococke (chap. xii.), it is also called by some the Makloub — El Maklúb, or the Inverted. Abulfeda (*Syria*, p. 149) makes its rebellion consist in refusing water for the fields, unless compelled by the Na'úrah, or mighty box-wheels — one of them, El Mohammediyyah, is said to be forty metres in diameter—which travellers going northwards see at Hamah for the first time. I am disposed, however, to agree with Volney (p. 155, ii. English translation) and many others that the

[28] 'Ibi, inquit, vidimus duas petras ex quibus ingens vis fluminis excidebat' (L. Annæi Senecæ *Nat. Quæst.* lib. vi. cap. 8).

Rebel is so named from the swiftness, the windings, and the turbulence of its upper stream. All who have forded it will carry away the same impression: the least curious about what the wild waves are saying might ask:

'Qual diverrà quel fiume
Nel suo cammino
Se al fonte si vicino
E tumido così?'

It is a rebel to the last: the gusts of the Asi gorge, where it falls into the Gulf of Antioch, are, as sailors well know, fierce, furious, and unmanageable as are the head-waters.

We inspected the Christian villages Ra'as Ba'al-bak and El Ká'ah, where the Cœlesyrian valley becomes unusually barren, and presently flares out into the rolling ground-waves—often divided by valleys so deep, that from a short distance the rider will fail to catch sight of them—stretching from the northernmost block of the Anti-Libanus to Hasyah, Sadad, and Hums (Emesa). After crossing the Já-dah[29] westwards and south-westwards, we made for

---

[29] The word Jádah (جَادَه) is here applied to flattish ground, especially opposed to Saniyyah (ثَنِيَّه), a Col or Pass. I have explained the latter to mean 'Winding Pass' in *Pilgrimage to El Medinah and Meccah* (vol. ii. p. 147, 2d edit.). Murray (p. 509) makes the road to

the Wady Fárih. This distinctly-marked lateral gorge, which has a namesake in the 'Eastern Mountain,' separates the barren crest of the highest Libanus—whose two southern prolongations are the gray walls of Jebel Sannín and Jebel Kafr Salwán, 'of the Siloam Village'—from its eastern outliers; the latter, a distinctly-marked lumpy mass, is called the Sha'arat Ba'albak, in order to separate it from a similar extension to the north known as the Sha'arat 'Akkár. The surface of reddish humus, dotted over with trees, explains its name, the 'hairy,' popularly applied to such features.[30] The undergrowth is mostly of Suwwayd (the little black), not unlike our blackthorn, and of Unnayb (the little grape), a bilberry (*vaccinium*), whose gratefully acid currant-like fruit is here used for pickles. The trees are the Sindiyán (*Quercus pseudo-coccifera*), vulgarly termed ilex, or native oak, and forming an extensive scrub; the

---

Palmyra skirt the base of ' a rounded barren peak called Jebel Tiniyeh, 'the hill of figs.' The peak in question is the celebrated Abu 'Asá (عصا), pronounced 'Atá, and the Pass to the east is called Darb el Saniyyah, or Road of the Col. Van de Velde, probably led into it by his predecessors, makes the same mistake.

[30] Some etymologists recognise the word in the Hebrew Seir (שעיר), popularly termed ' rugged,' the ancient term for the country about the Gulf of Akabah. Others hold the derivation inadmissible. Similarly Josephus (i. 18, i.) interprets Esau by 'hairy roughness.'

Mallúl, another kind of oak, whose wood does not decay in water; here and there a Ballút, or cocciferous oak, which upon these heights produces the 'Afs or gall-nut; the Za'arúr (a hawthorn); the Kaykab or maple; the wild pear and almond; the arbutus and the Butm, or terebinth.[31] The principal growth is the Lizzáb, a juniper[32] with blue berries, of which only one specimen was seen upon the valley plain. Its foliage, though not the bole, from afar resembles cypress; hence Van de Velde (ii. 475) terms these juniper barrens ' cypress groves.' The tree is nowhere so plentiful as upon the northern half of the

[31] It seems not settled amongst Hebraists following Celsius, that al (plural elím) is the oak; whilst alah (eloth and elath), popularly translated evergreen oak, is really the terebinth called by the Arabs El Butm. Even in these days the two trees are confused, *e.g.* the Bálut Ibrahim, ' Abraham's oak,' near Hebron. When Dr. Thomson (*The Land and the Book*, p. 243) tells the world ' there are more mighty oaks here in this immediate vicinity' [*i.e.* Mejdal el Shams, in the southern slopes of Hermon, where, by the bye, no mighty oaks are now preserved] ' than there are terebinths in all Syria and Palestine together,' he speaks from a limited experience. Towards Palmyra and the desert the terebinth becomes essentially *the* tree.

[32] The juniper of the English version is an error for the broom, in Hebrew Retem or Rethmeh (רתם, in Arabic Ratam (رَتَم), the Retama of Tenerife and the Andes, and the Ratam genista (monosperma?), of Forskål, the planta genista of popular travels. Dr. Robinson (ii. 806) makes the Arabs of Wady Músá call the juniper 'Ar'ár (the Hebrew aroer ערוער), translated ' heath' by Luther and in the English version.

Anti-Libanus, though it has been well-nigh extirpated from the southern parts.

Neither C nor D has any trace of this important Sha'arah. The former, however, calls the outliers a 'girdle of trees and brushwood ;' the latter, '*plateau boisé*,' whereas it is everywhere a slope. Dr. Robinson (iii. appendix, 183) mentions 'on the northern declivity of Lebanon a tract, El Sha'arah, which is a forest generally infested by robbers.' Wady Fárih is still celebrated in local tale and legend as the scene of conflicts between the Turkish Pashas and the turbulent feudal family of Harfúsh—a snake now scotched. He should not, however, have called it a forest, as does Mr. Porter (2d edit. p. 314). The only places in Syria and Palestine where I have seen anything worthy the name even of a wood are between Hasbeyyá and Kufayr, and about Kafr Shobah—all settlements upon the western slopes of the Hermon. For a few rods the head is in the shade, and the foot treads upon fallen leaves, a pleasing reminiscence of the far north. Tabor on its western side, and parts of Jebel Ajlún, are still tolerably tree-clad; but the former is a mass of craggy limestone, and short sharp earth-slopes, from which the ilexes grow like pines; and the latter has no charcoal market. Dr. Robinson (iii. 172) calls such growths 'orchards of oaks' (*Quercus ægilops*) ; and American travellers often compare the Sindiyán with their apple-trees. When *Tancred or the New Crusade* and *Five Years in Damascus* were written, Syria and Palestine appear to have been far better wooded than they are now. About Kunayterah, and in the Jaydúr district south of the Hermon, for instance, many such groves and woods have of late years completely disappeared.

We all remarked that the unmade road up the 'Glad Fiumara' (Wady Fárih), with its natural metal, was the best yet seen in the 'Holy Land;' and this afterwards proved to be the rule. Near the head of the course, where the trend was 260°, we found a succession of shallow swallow-holes, sinks or punch-bowls—hollows all without watershed—bone-dry at this season, but showing a pale green tint amongst the browns and yellows. After five hours of slow riding, a descent of thirty minutes placed us in an oval basin, bounded on the east by the 'Sha'arah' outliers of the Jurd el Gharbi, or Western High-lands—a term presently to be explained—and west by what we afterwards called the 'Cedar Block.' The latter is here faced eastwards by a sharp slope with sundry slides. In places it is not impracticable; but now and then the natural macadam appears almost too loose for a safe footing. Looking up from this basin, it is difficult to determine which point of the Libanus is the highest. The north-eastern head, a buttress known as ' Jebel 'Uyún Urghush,' being the nearest, appeared to rise a little above its fellows; whereas, afterwards seen from the true apex, from Mount Sannín, from the Hermon, and from the northern Anti-Libanus, it proved itself to be of secondary importance.

The basin merits attention. It is known as the ' Wady 'Uyún Urghush,' which, as His Eminence the Maronite patriarch afterwards informed us, is a corrupted translation from the Greek ' Eyes of Argus.' The name is explained by the number of little sources rushing, bubbling, and springing from the stony feet of hills, often as if a pipe or a conduit had just been broken: the valley is said to water 15,000 goats and sheep per diem. Examining it narrowly, we found that although D drains it to Orontes it has absolutely no slope, being subtended on all sides by higher ground. C is more correct, showing this phenomenon in several places. We passed two sinks, into which the streamlets, bending

sharp round in a loop, disappear, absorbed by the
bowels of the earth, leaving, as if in a filter, super-
ficial brown scum. Here, for the first time, we
could account for the multitude of bright runnels
which, cleared and refined through the huge strainer
of mountains, everywhere in Cœlesyria—'a land of
brooks and fountains that spring out of valleys'—
gush quick from the stony edgings of the highlands, whose upper reservoirs are hidden from the
sight.

These reservoirs form an important feature in the
two Libani and the Hermon, together with the adjoin-
ing uplands; they are unnoticed by traveller or tourist, and I saw them for the first time on this excursion. The natives call them, when large, 'Júrah,'[33]
meaning a hollow or sunken plain: it is opposed to
Marj, a flat timberless meadow, and to Ghútah (غوطة),[34]

---

[33] The classical word appears to be Juwár, *spelunca montis*.

[34] Dr. Beke (*Origines Biblicæ*, &c. p. 19, Preface to 'Jacob's Flight,'
&c.) makes the Ghútah (more classically pronounced 'El Ghautah') of
Damascus, the Land of Uz, ' 'Ausitis.' The Hebrew 'Ayn has, it is true,
in many cases—some scholars say always—the sound of the Arabic
ghayn; Oreb, a raven, for instance, being pronounced Ghoreb, like the
Arabic Ghuráb, whence corvus and crow. But the early Hebrews may,
like the modern Egyptians, have softened the Ghayn by turning it into
'Ayn. In the case of Ghútah and Uz or Húz, I cannot see how my
friend etymologically gets rid of the Tá (ط), a characteristically ob-

a green and well-watered lowland with the addition of trees. When there is a distinct swallow,
the name is 'Bálú'ah' (بالوعة), meaning literally a de-
glutator, such as a house-sink, or sewer for offal, a
sun-crack, or a whirlpool: the word is particularly applied to what the Bedawin call El Hazúzah (حزوضة),[35]
a stony hill rising from a circlet of sand so fine and
loose that, like the dry Syrtis of Hazramaut, it
swallows up man and beast. I am informed that it
lies at a distance of four days' dromedary march
from Roman Bostra (Nova Trajana), in the Eastern
Hauran. The third kind is the large crateriform
depression in the limestone surface called Tallájah
(تلّاجة), because it acts as ice, or rather snow,
house.

In all three types the action is the same, and the
cause is evidently that very common phenomenon in
limestone countries, a fault in the strata. Similarly
the waters of Lough Mask do not pass into Lough
Corrib by surface channels, but by underground
chasms and rock arches. The inflow is generally

---

stinate dental. We want instances in which the Hebrew Tsade becomes not Sád (ص), nor Zád (ض), nor Zú (ظ), but Tú (ط).

[35] In classical Arabic Hazúz or Hazauzú is the name of a certain
mountain in the sea used by the Arabians as a place of transportation.

down a gentle slope of humus, towards a wall of calcareous rock that shows perpendicular fractures above the surface, doubtless continued below. In some of them there is a funnel-shaped hole, which remains open during the dry season, and an alpenstock can probe it, often returning wet. The only rule that could be laid down by us concerning these reservoirs was, the more stony the land the more frequent the sink. They vary in size from a yard to 250 yards in length, and each mountain block seems to preserve some characteristic Júrah: these will be noticed as we sight them.

From the 'Eyes of Argus' we rode in one hour and forty-five minutes down the Wady el Nusúr (of the Vultures), a common name in these highlands, where the birds are supposed to affect particular springs. An especially vile bridle-path placed us before sunset upon the highway for the crowd that crosses the Cedar Pass from west to east, and that strikes Ba'albak *viâ* the summer village 'Aynátá (عينيتا). This word is given in C, 'Ainat;' in D, 'Ain Aaata;' in Mr. Barker and his editor's paper, "'Aïn-net-e' (is the man writing Chinese?), or 'the forthcoming spring,' and ' Aïnete (perhaps Aïn Atá, *i. e.* gift spring);' Murray (540) finally gives 'Ain

'Ata: erroneous all. It is simply the Arabised form
of the Hebrew Anathoth (Josh. xxi. 18, &c.), except
that the latter is in the plural.[36] From our camping
ground, under a walnut clump on the eastern slope
of the Wady separating the bare and barren dorsal
spine of the Libanus from its lower heights and its
Sha'arah outliers, we could see, distant about one
hour and thirty minutes' ride to the south-west, and
apparently draining northern Sannín, El Yammúnah,
the blue sink resembling a mountain-tarn. Van
de Velde (ii. 476) calls it 'the small Lake Lemone
or Yemone;' travelling dragomans prefer Birkat
Yammúnah, which would mean 'tank-tarn.' Yamm
in Syriac, as in Hebrew and Arabic, is the deep, the
great sea; Yammúnah, its diminutive, a lake or
tarn—synonymous, in fact, with the modern and
popular Buhayrah (بحيرة), diminutive of Bahr.[37]
Near this lakelet is the intermittent spring called
Ayn el Arba'in, because it appears annually on
March 9 (new style), the Maronite festival of the
Forty Martyrs.[38] Similar features are El Mambaj,

---

[36] So in 'Ayn Hadherah' for Hazeroth, Ejnub for Ije-abarim, Tibnah
for Timnath, and in many other cases.

[37] The reader will find El Yammúnah again referred to, with fresh
details, in vol. ii. chap. ii.

[38] Murray (p. 425) calls it '*Beit Jann*, the House of Paradise,' and

near the Bayt Jann village at the eastern foot of Hermon, the well-known Pool of Siloam, and the Bir
Sittná Maryam (the Virgin's Well) below Jerusalem.

On Friday, July 29, we zigzagged up the mountain whose sloping crest forms the Cedar Pass (Zahr
el Kazíb, قصيب). The path is fitly termed a 'rod' or
'switch;' it is an ugly narrow track, where a false
step would insure a roll of some hundred feet. The
time occupied was one hour and thirty minutes,
and the general direction magnetic north. At the
first turn the thermometer showed 58° F., but the
mercury was still falling, and might perhaps have
reached 45° F. The height of the Cedar Col was
made by aneroid 7700 feet.

A few minutes more led to the Col; and the
panorama of the little but most interesting Syrian
world, at once so central and so isolated, viewed from
this summit, amply repaid my labour. All but the
foreground showed blue, bluer, and bluest; darkest
in the nearer ravines, palest upon the horizon. Looking westward, where now 'a mournful and solitary

---

observes that it deserves the name as contrasted with the wilderness
around, &c. &c. It simply means 'House in the Garden' (جن for
Jannat); and the villages have a legend about the origin of the name.
There is another Bayt Jann in the Druze country, near St. John of
Acre.

silence prevails along the coast which had so long resounded with the world's debate,' there was a fine perspective of mountain chain running north and south, with lateral offsets of craggy hill-ridge, broken by cañon and wady, ravine and gorge, all trending towards one common object—the profundity of shore and sea. Most remarkable here was the noble amphitheatre, which we called the Cedar-basin: it is precisely the Arco[38] of the Portuguese, and I had already studied its shape in the great Curral das Freiras at Madeira. The latter, however, wants the Valley of Saints,

> ' A cañon so cleft asunder
> By sabre-stroke in the young world's prime,
> It looked as if broken by bolts of thunder
> Riven and driven by turbulent Time.'

Inland, the whole of the Cœlesyrian Vale lay map-like under my eyes: the Hermon Mont running athwart the southern limit, with more of Easting than the Anti-Libanus; and the latter sinking into the upland plain about Katana, into the Ager Damascenus or Padan-Aram, and into the dreary tracts of desert extending far as the Euphrates. From

[39] Literally arch or bow; secondarily applied to a curved mountain ridge, and to the lands subtended by such curve, *e.g.* Arco de Calheta, de São Jorge, and others.

afar off we could distinguish the lay of the waters of
Merom, heading the huge and unique fissure which
is bisected by the rapid Jordan till it expires in
the bitter waters of the Asphaltite Lake. The whole
formed an epitome of Syria and Palestine, which
have been said to epitomise the habitable world.
Here we saw at a glance all the gradations of climate, from the tropical to the polar. We were
viewing from Alpine heights the plains of the temperate zone, falling into the torrid about Tiberias.
Our range embraced every form of ground, coast-
scenery and inland, volcanic and sedimental, mountain and hill, fertile plain, rich valley and garden-
land, oasis and desert, rock and precipice, fountain
and spring sweet and mineral, river, rivulet, and
torrent, swamp and lakelet and sea. There were all
varieties of vegetation, from the mushroom to the
truffle; from liquorice to rhubarb and sumach; from
the daisy, the buttercup, and the bilberry, to the mulberry, the grape-vine, and the fig; from the pine, the
walnut, and the potato, to the palm, the plantain,
and the jujube. A fair range of products—coal, bitumen (Judaicum), and lignite, iron, copper, and pyrites,
with perhaps other metals still unexplored—lies beneath its surface, expecting the vivifying touch of

modern science; whilst its gypsum, syenite, porphyry, pudding-stone, and building-material have been worked since the dawn of history. Thus the country was directly fitted for the three chief forms of human society—the pastoral, the agricultural, and the commercial, represented by the tent, the cottage, and the city on the shore. In its palmy days the land must in many places have appeared to be one continuous town; whilst even at the present time there is no country of proportional area which can show so many and such contrasts of races. Syria and Palestine, I may safely prophesy, still await the hour when, the home of a free, a striving, and an energetic people, it will again pour forth corn and oil, it will flow with milk and honey, and it will 'bear, with proper culture, almost all the good things that have been given to man.' Such also was the abode of the Peruvian Yncas; but, physically speaking, the latter was nobler far, as the Andes are to the Libanus.

Whilst I descended the sister-slope winding to the Cedars, the rest of the party struck off to the north-east. The surface was strewed with pierced and drilled, with ribbed and pointed calcareous stone, the horizontal striæ being regular, and the trans-

verse irregular—a form remarked by Mr. Tyrwhitt
Drake in the Valley of the Tih and about Sinai. The
alternate and excessive contraction and expansion, the
work of frost and thaw, of sun and storm, of exceptional siccity and of extreme dampness, have cracked,
split, and broken up the stone into cubes, which
farther degrade into flakes and fragments nearly
flat. This is the normal revetment of the Syrian
Jurd or highlands. The shingle, which somewhat resembles the burnt shale used to metal park-roads in
Lancashire, should not, however, be called 'gravel,'
with Mr. Porter (304, 2d edition); nor must this
sign of contemporary glacial action be confounded
with that of the true Frozen Age, as shown by the
polishing, the grooving, and the rasping of the rocks
above the cave whence issues the principal lower
influent, called Source, of the Nahr el Kalb (Lycus
River). The yellow interstitial soil which also underlies this natural macadam is swollen and puffed
up, especially after rains and thaws; and finally the
solar rays loosen and crumble it, rendering the surface easy to man and beast. When walking, the
mountaineers always prefer it to the stones, and
those who value their boots will do well to imi-
tate the native example. The round-topped hills

of the limestone formation, which look not a little like old contour-drawings in maps, are so easy and regular, that one can ride without dismounting to the very summits of the Libanus, the Anti-Libanus, and the Hermon ; whilst everywhere goat-paths streak the highlands. In fact, the only decent roads in Syria and Palestine, except that of the French Company from Bayrut to Damascus, and not excepting the Turkish Sultani (king's highway) from Jaffa to Jerusalem, and the ridiculous ' carrossable' from Iskanderún (Alexandretta) to Aleppo, are the nature-metalled Fiumaras and mountain slopes. Those of the Anti-Libanus are perhaps superior to all others : up many of them a carriage-and-four might be driven.

Skirting a mamelon on the left, the travellers followed a knife-board ridge ; its long lean flanks sloped gradually on the right (east) to the Wady el Nusúr on our road of yesterday ; whilst sharp slides, and in places sheer precipices, fell westwards to the Cedar Valley, whose great drain, the Wady Kadíshah, first showed its fine and bold proportions. This immense amphitheatre is undoubtedly the most characteristic feature of the Libanus. After one hour and twenty-five minutes of walking from the col, they

halted upon a rounded summit called by Fáris
Rufáil, Ra'as Zahr el Kazíb, the Head or Hill of the
Rod-back, to which the zigzag from the 'Aynátá
Valley is compared. The thermometer showed 53°
Fahr., the barometer 20·980, and the aneroid
20·870. Thus the Rod-back would be one of the
three highest peaks of the Libanus, and measure
10,077 feet in altitude.

Then, leaving their horses in a sheltered hollow,
they struck to the N.N.E., and after a stiff pull of
thirty minutes, they stood upon Jebel Muskíyyah
(مسقیه), here often pronounced Mushkíyyah and
Mishkíyyah. The term may be a corruption from El
Maskiyy, the saturated or the soaked. In the maps
it is not noticed even by name; and Mr. Tyrwhitt-
Drake, on a subsequent visit, found the people calling
it Naba' el Sh'maylah (the Northerly Spring). Van de
Velde, however (ii. 476), assigns to Jebel Muskíyyah
an altitude of full 10,000 feet. Here the hypsometer
gave absurd results: unfortunately, air had been left
in the tube, the column of mercury had split, and
being too fine and thread-like, it could not be re-
united. This sudden failure of instruments is always
a severe trial to the traveller's temper. He should,
before buying 'B.P.s,' carefully ascertain that the

glass tube has been exhausted of air, in which case the quicksilver moves freely to and fro. Throughout these countries also he must not forget spirits of wine, as the common 'Raki' will not burn.[40]

From Jebel Muskíyyah various compass-bearings were taken to places laid down on the maps. The northern apex of the Anti-Libanus bore 102°, a little south of east, whilst the Ra'as el Núríyyah (النوريه), upon the seaboard, was north of west (291°). This point is erroneously called in A, Ra'as ash Shakeh (Theoprosopon),[41] and in B, Cape Madonna. It lies about nine miles south of Tarabulus (Tripoli), and it is accurately given by Murray according to the hydrographic charts. I may here mention the difficulty to which travellers in these mountains are ever subject. The Wadys and the water-courses, like the wells, are known by name to everybody; but none save the goatherds see any use in applying specific terms to peaks and heights which they never visit. Consequently it often happens that an interesting and peculiar feature will be included under some general term, to the great detriment of maps. A committee of Ma'áz, or goatherds, is absolutely

---

[40] For other remarks on instruments, see Appendix No. I.

[41] Τὸ τοῦ θεοῦ πρόσωπον of Strabo (16—): the bold promontory which forms the north of the Libanus proper.

necessary, if the hills of Unexplored Syria are to be correctly named.

At this point the travellers left their guide and attendants, who showed signs of 'caving in.' Descending the northern slope of the Muskíyyah, walking along a dorsum occupied by moles—what can they find to eat there?—and bending north-east (47° Mag.), they mounted another eminence, which, as often happens, appeared to be of greater height. The aneroid, however, showed the same as before, and still 100 feet above the Ra'as Zahr el Kazíb. This apex is called by the people Jebel Makmal (مكمل); and the villagers of 'Assál el Ward have a tradition that the 'Perfect Mountain' contains a pit into which men have fallen. Seen in profile from the Anti-Libanus, it is rendered remarkable at this season by its long snow-line sloping to the north.

Amongst the angles taken from the Makmal was one to the Jebel Fumm (or Famm) el Mizáb, 286°. This headland forms a bluff upon the northern rim of the Cedar Valley, and it derives its name, 'Mouth of the Funnel' or 'Spout,'[42] from a gutter-like watercourse which opens upon the semicircle below. The

---

[42] The Persian Mizáb is naturalised even at Meccah (*Pilgrimage to El Medinah and Meccah*, vol. ii. p. 161, 2d edit., where Burckhardt calls it Myzab). The dictionaries, however, convert Mizáb to Mi'záb.

people corrupt the term to 'Tum el Mezíb.' In Syrian Arabic *f* and *t* are interchangeable, like *d* and *z* (ﺽ and ﺫ), *s* and *sh*—the latter a confusion old as the days of *sibboleth* and *shibboleth*. The 'Fumm' is popularly supposed to be the highest point of all the Libanus; whereas the eye, looking from the east, sees that it is not. Mr. Henry A. de Forest (Van de Velde, ii. 495) made by aneroid 'Fŭm el Mîzâb' 'just 9000 feet, or say 600 less than Major Von Wildenbruck found .some years since with his barometer;' and that officer had placed it only 100 feet or so below 'Dhŏhr el Kŏdhîb' (Zahr el Kazíb).

The next was a longer stretch of an hour and a half in a general direction of 15° (Mag.), but with many windings, chiefly to the west. Descending the slope of a little strath, the travellers found long narrow strips of snow disposed upon the levels, and upon the faces exposed to the south, whence the cold wind comes. Since the days of the Evangelists (Luke xii. 55) it is known that in the lowlands of Syria when the south wind blows, people say there will be heat: here, however, the reverse is the rule. In the Bukáʼa, as in western England, the south wind is essentially rainy, being probably a deflection from the west and the south-west caused by the mountain funnels. North, again, about the plains of Hamah, it becomes the warm wind.

These névés are called Manásif el Talj[43] by the people, who, curious to say, have no name for the avalanche; yet the latter is frequent, and does much damage amongst the mountain villages. They were found hard and icy only at the edges, where the soppy ground was puffed-up and swollen; the surface was not too soft for the tread; at the lower end, however, all formed a nearly upright wall, eight to ten feet high. Each névé was footed by a distinct moraine of large and small blocks, which were the worst of walking ground, and through the stone field trickled at the lowest level runnels of water set free by the sun — miniature copies of the impassable torrents which issue from the immense glaciers of the north. After flowing for a few yards into and down the valley, the streamlets disappeared in pits; some mere wells, not a little resembling the air-holes called 'Najmah' of the Kanáts, or underground aqueducts, common from Damascus through Sind and Afghanistan to Western India, whilst others measured forty feet across: a few were evidently

---

[43] Manásif is the plural of Mansaf, the place of Nusúf (نسوف) *i.e.* a long and difficult ascent.

artificial, the many were natural. This is the characteristic Júrah or sink of the Cedar Block. It is found
also on the western flank of the Hermon, above the
Ayn el Jarníyyah, its solitary fountain; and three
sunken holes occurring close together may be observed on the Arazí el Ghayzah, the rolling upland
plain south-west of Assál el Ward.

The locusts, which in 1870 had ravaged the
plains, left their scattered wings all around the
névés. The birds were mostly larks, and of these
chiefly the spur-lark. A small collection was made
of the Flora, which is here excessively stunted by
wind and frost, and it was deposited by Mr. E. H.
Palmer with Professor Babington of Cambridge.
Since that time Mr. W. Carruthers of the British
Museum has kindly undertaken to name them.

Of all growths the most remarkable was the
thorn, called in different parts of the country Billán,
Tabbán, Atát, and Kibkáb, which forms large green
prickly beds, shaped like giant mushrooms, pin-
cushions, and pillows, with a contrast of small ten-
der-coloured and delicately-shaped flowers profusely
scattered over its spiny surface. This growth is
nowhere more monstrous than over the upper slopes
of the Hermon; and in places it stands up as if

raised by a stem from the ground. It makes a hot
and sudden blaze like the *Quebra panella* of Brazil,
and the guides frequently amuse themselves with
giving to the mountains the semblance of volcanoes.

A steep ascent of thick Tabbán, and a long
néve with a bend to the right, placed the travellers
upon the summit of the third apex. It was called
by one goatherd Karn Saudá (the Black Horn); by
another, Jebel Akkár, evidently the general name of
the northern range; and Jebel Timárún by the father of the schoolmasters at Nabk and Yabrúd. The
thermometer showed 75° F., and the aneroid now
proved a descent of 0·30 from Jebels Zahr el Kazíb,
Muskíyyah, and Makmal; whilst a second visit by
Mr. Tyrwhitt-Drake gave it an altitude of 9175 ft.
Northward the mountains, denuded of snow by the
hot breath of the north, fell in folds towards the
river-valley of the Eleutherus (Nahr el Kabir), the
northern boundary of the Libanus, separating it from
the Jebel Kalbíyyah of the Nusayri race. From this
elevation it became evident that neither the Fumm
el Mizáb (as the people said), nor the Jebel 'Uyún
Urghush (as we had supposed) was entitled to hold
up its head with the highest. Unfortunately for farther observation, the sea-clouds, which in the forenoon

had flecked and mottled the horizon, gradually stealing an inch deep of sky, began about midday impudently to seethe up and to invest the mountains, which at 3 P.M. were obscured by drizzle and Scotch mist. The travellers congratulated one another upon finding themselves at home in the far north. July and August are not too late for surveying the highlands; but the wind, they say, blows regularly for three days from the west, which of course gathers the clouds ; during the next three, the norther and the easter sweep the firmament clean.

From Jebel Timárún the travellers had good sights to the rival Anti-Libanus. The Halímat el Kabú (bearing 111°) seemed to be, probably because the nearest, the very apex of the 'Eastern Mountain :' this was afterwards found not to be the case. It is remarkable for the sloping saddle-back which forms its summit, somewhat resembling the celebrated Gávia near Rio de Janeiro. By an extreme confusion the guide called it Jebel Mu'arrá[44] and Jebel Kárá: these mistakes will be cleared up in Chapter III. treating of the route survey of the Anti-Libanus.

[44] El Mu'arrá, meaning stripped, bald, denuded, is a common village name in Syria: two are found upon the eastern slopes of the Anti-Libanus.

After building, by way of landmark, a 'kákúr' (dead man or old man) of loose stones, the travellers returned to their men and horses : happily for the people, Mr. Tyrwhitt-Drake had taken exact bearings. The cloud-fog uncommonly facilitates losing oneself; moreover, as usual in calcareous formations, the outlines are uniform and monotonous, with a family resemblance resulting from degradation, disintegration, and erosion, which everywhere exert nearly the same force. They found no sign of granite or porphyry, nor even the tertiary trap and basalt which characterise the Hermon. Neither fossils nor moulds came to hand, not even the ammonites, the snakes of St. Hilda, so common on the Tau'amát Nihá. But the limestone was of many different kinds: the Jurassic (secondary and cretaceous) formed the base; there were also in sight dolomites (magnesian limestones); lime almost crystalline, in fact nearly marble; oriental alabaster (fibrous carbonate of lime); selenite; satin spar (a variety of the same); yellowish-white gypsum in small lumps (hydrous sulphate of lime); crystals of lime (often called diamonds by the natives, and probably the 'masses of quartz' mentioned by Van de Velde, i. 138); columnar crystalline carbonate of lime (sometimes mistaken for gypsum); bituminous limestones, and many others. As a rule, each mountain block of any importance has its own peculiar stone. That of Jebel Sannín, for instance, is a white nodule set in a yellow ring. About Abu el Hín in the Anti-Libanus we find the limestone stratified with bright red and tawny yellow; that about Nabi Bárúh is remarkably crystalline; on the counter-slope of the Tala'at Musa it is blood-red; that of the Halímat el Kabú is variegated pink and yellow. The stone about Ra'as Rám el Kabsh is of leaf-like thinness, and a little beyond, it splits into giant cubes like Cyclopean blocks, here paving the ground, there lying moraine-like below the cliffs; now it strews the hills in large slate-like slabs of an inch thickness, then it is rough as sandstone: the 'horse-bone' variety is common, and the holes drilled through the stones vary from the size of a pin's head to what would admit a man's shoulders.

Mr. Tyrwhitt-Drake's sketch-map of the Cedar Block shows a double line of four and three heads each, disposed north to south, with a deviation of about 35°. To the east rise the 'Uyún Urghush, the Makmal, the Muskíyyah *alias* Naba' el Sh'maylah, and the Ra'as Zahr el Kazíb; whilst the Karn Saudá

or Timárun, the Fumm el Mízab, and the Zahr el
Kandíl front seawards. A single reliable barometric
observation, almost coinciding with the aneroid,
enabled us to fix the altitude of the southern feature,
Zahr el Kazíb, at 10,018 English feet, whilst the
other peaks are almost upon the same plane. Thus
the highest points of the Libanus are the northern:
the contrary is the case in the hill country of
Judæa, Mount Ebal being 2700 feet high, and
Hebron 3029.[45]

The people call this group Arz (ارز) Libnán,
'Cedar of Lebanon' (mountain), thus preserving the
Hebrew name Arz (Cedrus Libani): we followed
their example in naming it the 'Cedar Block.' It
is evidently the Mount Hor[46] (Hor ha Har), which

---

[45] According to Lieut. Warren, R.E. (p. 210, No. V. *Palestine Exploration Fund*), the Hermon, which he makes 'a portion of the Anti-
Lebanon range,' was assumed to be 10,000 feet; but on September 14,
1869, we reduced it by aneroid to 8700 feet (p. 222), or, in round numbers, to 9000 feet, the height estimated by Lynch and Russegger.

[46] The Hebrew הור, an archaic form for Har, a mountain, or possibly an intensive form, a 'great mountain;' in the Septuagint τὸ ὄρος;
and in the Vulgate Mons altissimus. 'Hor ha Hor' (or 'Har') is rendered by some the 'Mountain of (or upon) the Mountain;' a good description of the barren Cedar Block based upon its lower story, the
wooded 'Sha'arah.' There is no reason for concluding, with Smith's
Dictionary of the Bible ('Hor'), that the whole range of the Libanus
is intended by the term. Nor can I agree with Mr. Porter, that the

formed part of the northern Israelitic border as promised to Moses (Num. xxxiv. 7-9), before it was extended eastward by Ezekiel.[47] The northern head, at whose feet flows the defining line of the Eleutherus, is, I have shown, the apex of the Libanus, and the wall droops with tolerably regular slopes and steps to the south. Here its boundaries are uncertain. Politically it ends with the Nahr el Awwali (Bostrenus river), so called because it was the first stream of Lebanon to those going northwards from Sidon: others prolong it to the Litání or River of Tyre. Geographically, there is no doubt that its southern limit is the Plain of Esdraëlon.

Volney in 1786 was therefore right in placing

'entrance of Hamath' (Numb. xxxiv. 8) should be confined to the ugly gorge (Wady Dayr Mar Jiryus) commanded by the castle El Husn, or Husn el Akrád. The traveller from Hums to Hamah will at once remark the depression forming a great highway between the Northern Libanus and the Jebel el Hulah, or southern section of the Jebel Kalbiyyah, the valley of the Nahr el Kabír (Eleutherus), up which the sea-breeze finds its way to the uplands — the line by which it is proposed to run the Euphrates railway, and along which the Circassian colonists have just driven their wagons. This has been, is, and ever will be, the true 'entrance to Hamath.'

[47] There are, in fact, three limits : 1. (Gen. xv. 18) from the Nile to the Euphrates; 2. (Numbers xxxiv. 4, 5) from the Nile to the entrance of Hamath—a mere section; and 3. (Ezekiel xlvii. 15-17) which includes the Damascene.

(i. 293) the most elevated point of all Syria 'on Libanus, to the south-east of Tripoli:' he gave it a theoretical altitude of 1500-1600 (French) fathoms, the computed point of perpetual congelation which Dr. Kitto here laid down at 11,000 English feet. By subsequent travellers, and especially by Dr. Robinson (iii. 440), the Cedar Block has been vaguely recognised as 'perhaps the highest summit of the mountain.'

The names, the heights, and the shapes of this great feature are variously given by geographers and travellers. A assigns to 'Dhahr el Khotib,' the 'highest summit of Libanus,' 10,050 feet. This is repeated by the Rev. Mr. Tristram (*The Natural History of the Bible*, p. 1), who makes the highest peak to be 'Dhor el Khodib, just above the famed cedars, 10,050 feet high, capped (?) with all but perpetual snow.' The American missionaries, quoted by Dr. Wortabet in an able paper ('The Hermon and the Physical Features of Syria and Northern Palestine,' *Journal R. Geog. Soc.* No. xxxii. of 1862, pp. 100-108), represent Makmal to be the 'highest summit of the Lebanon,' with 9200 feet absolute altitude, or 300 feet lower than the Hermon (9500). Some write the word Makhmal, which would mean 'velvet;' others Mahmal, a litter, a place of carriage : Mr.

Paton, however (*History of the Egyptian Revolution,*
i. 246), gives correctly the ' bare peaks of Sannin
and Makmal.' D allots to ' Jebel Makhmal' 12,000
feet—a slight exaggeration. C places ' Jebel Makhmal' south of the Cedar Pass, and proposes as the
' highest summit' the mountain ' Dhor el Khodib,'
which is probably the Jebel Ṭimárún of these pages.
It neglects the other great apices, the Muskiyyah,
the Fumm el Mízáb, and the Jebel 'Uyún Urghush;
it does not trace the noble Cedar Valley; in fact,
the map is a novelty to one who has travelled over
and studied the country. D, pretending to scientific
accuracy, has the proud preëminence of being the
very worst. After laying down the Cedars (usually
placed at 6500 feet) at the reasonable altitude of
1925 metres, he has been led by some wondrous
error of triangulation into assigning 6063 metres
(= 18,189 English feet) to ' Dahr el Khotib,' which
is, moreover, made the apex of ' Dj. Makmel.' It
shows to a certain extent, but without sufficient pre-
cision, the grand development of the Cedar Valley;
which, being by far the most characteristic feature,
has been the most neglected by the cartographer. On
the other hand, it supplies the highest levels of the
Libanus with a lateral fissure, long, broad, and shed-

ding to the north-east. Murray makes 'J. Makhmal,' the 'highest summit of Lebanon,' 10,050 feet; and accurately transcribes all the errors of the French map.

*   *   *   *   *

P.S. The following note upon the subject of the Ba'albak ruins lately appeared in the *Builder*:

Sir,—I am very glad to see that by quoting Mrs. Burton's recent letter you have called attention to the magnificent remains of the temples at Ba'albak, and to the precarious condition of some of the most striking features in what is perhaps the most beautiful group of classic ruins in the world. As you invite comment from those who have visited them, I will, in a few words, point out what are, in my opinion, the most pressing dangers; and offer a few suggestions as to the readiest and most desirable mode of meeting them.

Those even who know Ba'albak only by pictures will remember that, occupying the most conspicuous place on the great platform, six gigantic columns, surmounted by an entablature, tower high above all others, and stand boldly out in deep golden contrast to the lilac, snow-streaked range of Lebanon. These six columns are all that remain of the fifty-four which composed the peristyle of the Great Temple. Three fell in 1759. The columns have a height of 75 feet, and a diameter of 7 feet 3 inches. It will appear hardly credible that at the present time the shafts stand on but half their diameter. The Arabs *have cut away the other half to abstract the metal dowel* which joined the shaft to the base. In a district often affected by earthquakes it may be imagined in what jeopardy these columns stand.

Now, with careful workmen and skilled superintendence, considerable additional security might be given to the structure. There are some good Greek masons in Damascus, but as to competent superintendence available I have no information. To act without a skilled architect would be to imperil the group. But I regard the underpinning of these columns as by far the most pressing work.

The great portal of what is called the 'Small' Temple (it is bigger than the Parthenon) next calls for attention as described in Mrs. Burton's letter. This portal is 42 feet high by 21 feet wide, and has beautifully sculptured architraves. The dropped key of the lintel requires support, which might, I think, more readily be given by metal cramps, or by notching in stone dovetails, than by the granite shaft proposed by Mrs. Burton, which would obstruct the opening and deface the interesting sculpture on the soffit of the stone. To clear away the obstructive Arab wall, now built in between the antæ, as well as the accumulated rubbish, which work seems to have been commenced by Captain Burton, is an admirable step. Except here, however, I should discountenance demolition; especially *demolition paid for with the materials removed.* This is a most dangerous course in such a case; and, with such people as the Arab population of the neighbourhood, not to be thought of; not a stone in the place would be safe.

In conclusion, I venture to recommend the subject of the present condition of Ba'albak to the consideration of the Institute of Architects. Their committee might probably, without great trouble, gather together whatever information or suggestions are within reach, and found thereupon some simple recommendations. If these were forwarded to Captain Burton, I do not doubt that he would value them, and turn them to account as opportunity allowed.

For my own part I am delighted to find so energetic a man taking an interest in the subject, and I heartily wish him support and success.

(Signed)   J. D. CRACE.

PART II

FROM THE CEDARS OF LEBANON TO ZAHLAII TOWN.

THE day after our arrival at the Cedars (Saturday,
July 30) was idly spent in prospecting the valley,
and in counting the clump : superstition says that
this is impossible, and perhaps it is difficult to the
uninitiated in such matters of woodcraft. I fear it
will be considered bad taste to confess that none
of us fell into the usual ecstasies before these exaggerated Christmas - trees, which look from afar
like the corner of a fir plantation, and which when
near prove so mean and ragged that an English
country gentleman would refuse them admittance
into his park. Indeed many a churchyard at home
has yews which surpass the 'Arz Libnán' in appearance, and which are probably of older date. Volney
(ii. 177) is still correct in asserting, 'these cedars, so
boasted, resemble many other wonders; they support
their reputation very indifferently on a close inspection.' It is now emphatically incorrect that

'The mountain cedar looks as fair
As those in royal gardens bred.'

As a rule, the Cedars of the Libanus are a badly-clad, ill-conditioned, and homely growth; essentially unpicturesque, except, perhaps, when viewed from above. Especially these. All the elders are worried like Cornish cheese - wrings, hacked and stripped, planed into tablets, shorn of branches, and stained with fire, chiefly by the 'natives;' we found them burning their lime and boiling their coffee with the spoils of the 'Lord's trees.' There is an old man, entitled Wakíl el Arz, but, as usual, this 'guardian of the Cedars'—a Custos sadly wanting custodes—is the first to abet, for a consideration, all who would see 'Lebanon hewed down.'

The number of the trees is variously given by travellers: Mr. William Rae Wilson (*Travels in the Holy Land*, 1847), has taken the trouble to make a *résumé* of their statements, which will now bear an appendix. In 1550 the patriarchs were twenty-five, and the same total is given by Furer in A.D. 1565, and by travellers in 1575. The good missionary Dandini, in A.D. 1600, found twenty-three; in A.D. 1657, Thevenot, twenty-two; in A.D. 1696, Maundrell, sixteen; in A.D. 1737, Pococke, fifteen; whilst in A.D.

1786, Volney declared (i. 292), 'there are now but four or five of these trees which deserve any notice.' In 1810, Burckhardt mentions 'eleven or twelve of the oldest and best-looking Cedars;' twenty-five very large, about fifty of middle size, and more than three hundred small and young: of the latter some now remain. In 1818, Mr. Richardson reckons seven; in 1832, M. de Lamartine, who did not visit them, also seven; Van de Velde (ii. 478) found twelve oldsters surrounded by an after-growth of 400 youngsters, more or less, and he was told by the Maronites that the mystic dozen was planted by the Apostles. Madame Pfeiffer (p. 197, Eng. trans. *Visit to the Holy Land*) saw in 1842 'twenty very aged, and five peculiarly large and fine specimens, which are said to have existed in the days of Solomon.'

And the descriptions differ as much as do the numbers. The Rev. Mr. Tristram (p. 360, *Land of Israel*) declared the birds perching upon the tops 'beyond reach of ordinary shot'—where *did* he buy his powder? We could throw stones over the trees. Dr. Stanley found a dozen patriarchs, repeating Mr. Porter (p. 303, 2d edit.), 'only a few, about a dozen.' The former should have been more careful of his topography; he represents his 'apex of the vegetable kingdom'—whatever this may mean[1]—as 'huddled together on two or three of the central knolls.' We counted nine old trunks, whilst the grove was scattered over seven distinct ridges, four larger and three of smaller dimensions, the former disposed in cross shape. The base is of snow-white limestone, here covered with, there piercing through, the dark humus of cedar-needles and débris. The largest mound, to the north-east, and separated from the eastern ravine by a smaller feature, supports the miserable little chapel, where I was horrified to see the holy elements placed in a sardine-box; this has since been remedied by the piety of English Catholics and by the kindness of the *Tablet*. The oldest trunks are those which clothe the south-eastern ridge. There are no 'babies,' as the goats, now a standing nuisance in Syria, devour them at their birth, and mostly the conifer, like the orange family, is an aristocrat —intolerant of plebeian undergrowth and humble grass. The Reverend Mr. Thompson (*The Land and the Book*, which should have been called *The Book*

---

[1] Possibly alludes to:

> 'No tree that is of count in greenwood growes,
> From lowest juniper to cedar tall
>   *   *   *   *   *
> But there it present was, and did fraile sense entice.'

and the Land) declares that the true cedars grow only in this valley. They are doubtless a local type, probably part of the arctic flora, in which the Libanus, like the Anti-Libanus and the Hermon, abounds. According to Mr. B. T. Lowne,[2] the cedars of the Libanus moraines and the papyrus of the Jor-

[2] 'On the Flora of Palestine,' *Science of Biblical Archæology*, July 4, 1871. Mr. Lowne reduces the flora to eight distinct elements, each occupying its own region. Four of these are dominant existing types in Southern Europe, Russia, Asia, North Africa, Arabia, and Northwest India. The fifth is found in numerous examples of plants belonging to Palæarctic Europe; whilst the cedar and the papyrus form the sixth. Mr. Lowne, however, is in error when he confines the latter to the Jordan Valley. It is found near the Mediterranean shore in the beds of small streams; and the traveller going down the coast to Jaffa will pass through a miniature forest upon the River Fálik, near the Arsuf ruins and the sanctuary of Shaykh Ali ibn el 'Alaym el Fárúki (a descendant of Omar). *En passant*, I may remark that when Dr. Potter translates, in *Prometheus Vinctus*, βυβλίνων ὀρῶν ἄπο,

'Where from the mountains with papyrus crowned,'

he makes the poet utter an absurdity. The paper rush (*papyrus antiquorum*) may grow about the swampy feet of hills—not upon their summits. We should therefore read :

Where from the bases of the Bybline hills.

It would be curious to inquire what was the cedar (Psalm xcii. 13, 14) planted in the Temple of Jerusalem. For the traditional connection of Seth with the seeds of the cedar and the cypress, the pine and the apple, readers are referred to the *Legends of the Holy Rood*, &c.; Early English Text Society; edited by Richard Morris, LL.D.; London, Trübner, 1871.

dan are traces of the two ancient and almost extinct floras descending from old geological periods. But the existence of the true cedar in other parts of the Lebanon has been known since the days of Seetzen (1805), and the next few hours' march showed us another cedar grove, within a few miles of whose shades Mr. Thompson must have ridden. He also declares, that 'at night the trees wink knowingly, and seem to whisper among themselves you know not what.' I am pleased to be able to report that these venerable vegetables neither winked at me nor whispered aught that all the world might not hear.

> ' The cedars wave on Lebanon,
> But Judah's statelier maids are gone'—

is not topographically correct of this, *the* Cedar Clump. It is rather *in* than *on* the Libanus. The site is an amphitheatre of imposing regularity and dimensions, being some five miles in diameter, gapped only on the west where the Kadíshah, a gorge-valley deeply cut in the rent strata — the valley smiling above with village and hamlet, with orchard and terraced field; the gorge grim below with stony cliff, precipitous shelf, scattered boulder, and sole of sheet-rock—conducts at times a furious torrent to the 'Great Sea,' alias the Little Mediterranean.

The general conformation is that of a bow and arrow, the bow being bent almost to a circle, and this shape is not uncommon in the Anti-Libanus as well as the Libanus. From a ship's deck we see only the mouth of the gorge and a shallow spoon-shaped depression below the mountain-crest.

The modern version of the old Syriac is Wady Kadíshah, in Arabic Wady Kaddísín (Fiumara of the Holy Men,[3] Cœnobites whose convents and her-mitages are scattered in all directions. The cedar knolls stud a half-way plateau, a step comparatively level, backed by the large yellow-brown rim of bare rock and débris which we had ascended and de-scended on the yesterday; they are fronted, a few hundred feet below, by a white semicircle of creta-ceous formation, cut and carved into ribs and pinna-cles, walls and castellations, of singular wildness. This forms the true head of the Wady Kadíshah, which in many points resembles the Wady el Nár (Kedron), to whose eastern cliff-bank clings the ce-lebrated Greek convict-convent of Mar Sabá. But whilst the latter is harsh, rugged, and desert, burning

---

[3] The name corresponds with the Hebrew Ha-Kodashim 'of the Saints.' The Hebrew, Syriac, and Arabic roots are to be found in קדש, viz. puer mollis, that is to say, consecrated to Astarte or Venus. The feminine is קדשה, a harlot, one dedicated to the Dea Syra.

in summer and cold as death in winter, the Kadíshah, bare and stony itself, runs through a riant land. It is a question whether the Kadíshah, like the Wady el Nár, be not formed by glacial action; a modern popular traveller terms the latter, a 'glacial valley,' but in a very different sense. Unable to praise the cedars, I may say in favour of their 'park,' that it affords the only tolerable mountain view hitherto seen in the Libanus—I may say in Syria and Palestine, with the exception perhaps of the fair region about Náblús. Here there is something like variety, like outline, and it revived faint memories of romantic Switzerland's humbler beauties. When Van de Velde (ii. 490) ranked the latter after the tame and uninteresting Libanus, he must have been labouring under a more than usually severe attack of ' Holy Land on the Brain.'

I was fortunate enough to secure, with the permission of Murray's Handbook, sundry of the small valueless cones which are used chiefly as charcoal for application to wounds. But who will absolve me from the ' sacrilege' of carrying off a large block as a present for my cousin B——? Protestant writers are very severe upon this point. 'The cedars of Lebanon,' we are told, 'are not merely interesting

and venerable—they are " sacred,"' and 'deliberately
to use knife or saw is an act that would disgrace
a Bedawy;' yet the same writer in another place
assures us that Christianity is not a religion of Holy
Places; and if so, we may be certain that it utterly
neglects Holy Trees. There is nothing more curious
in the Reformed Faith, and in the multiplicity of
wild sects which have branched from it, than the
ever-increasing respect and even veneration for all
things Jewish, from the institutions of the Hebrews
to their material remains. It is an unconscious
reaction from the days of the Crusaders, when even
the Templars looked upon Solomon's Temple as a
something impure.

At the Cedars, Messrs. Drake and Palmer, greatly
to our regret, proceeded direct *viâ* Tripoli to Beyrout.
On the same day (July 31) we travelled over a
truly detestable short-cut, when we should have
passed through Bisherri town to Dímán, the summer
residence of 'his Eminence' (Ghabtatuh) the Maronite 'Primate of Antioch and of all the East,'
Monseigneur Bulus Butrus Mas'ad.[4] We were
charmed with the reception given to us by this

[4] The Petro-Pauline prænomen is assumed by every patriarch;
Mas'ad is the family name.

prelate, of whom his flock says, 'the Patriarch is
our Sultan,' and for once we saw the simplicity and
the sincerity of the apostolic ages.   Since our visit
I have frequently corresponded with his eminence,
who is a secular author as well as a theologian, and
his letters, it may be remarked, are as edifying as
his manners are plain and dignified.

From Dímán we resumed our way through the
Jibbah Bisherri, the 'village land of Bisherri,' which
lies on the western or seaward face of the Libanus.
This is the heart of the Maronite or purely Christian
region; and this district, like Jezzín farther south,
and Sadad (the ancient Zedad?) to the north-east,
produces a manly independent race, fond of horses
and arms, with whom I am not ashamed to own
community of faith.   Undisturbed by the defiling
presence of Rashid Pasha, the people are happy and
contented; their industry has converted every yard
of rock-ledge into a miniature field; they show a
steadily - increasing population, resulting from the
absence of the tax-gatherer and the recruiting officer;
and their only troubles are those bred and born of
Ottoman intrigues, of that barbarous policy which
still says, 'Divide and rule them all.'   Long may the
Règlement de la Montagne reign ! may Moscovite lord

it in Stamboul ere a Moslem governor is suffered to rule the land of the Maronite! The words applied by Dr. Hooker to Marocco are perfectly descriptive of unhappy Syria under her present affliction. 'The government is despotic, cruel, and wrong-headed in every sense; from the Sultan to the lowest soldier, all are paid by squeezing those in their power. Marocco itself is more than half ruinous, and its prisons loaded; the population of the whole kingdom is diminishing; and what with droughts, locusts, cholera, and prohibitory edicts of the most arbitrary description, the nation is on the brink of ruin; and but that two-thirds of the kingdom is independent of the Sultan's authority, being held by able mountain chiefs, who defy his power to tax or interfere with them, and that the European merchants maintain the coast-trade, and the consuls keep the Sultan's emissaries in check, Marocco would present a scene of the wildest disorder.'

The Jibbah road is not so execrable as might be expected, because it runs along the upper flank of what is properly called El Wusút. I may here explain that the Libanus and its neighbours are divided, according to altitude, into three portions. These zones, which, seen from the highest elevations, appear clearly defined, correspond with the fertile, the woody, and the desert regions of Etna and the mountains of Southern Europe, and with the Tierra caliente, templada, and fria of Mexico and Spanish America. Beginning from the seaboard, there are three steps, namely—

1. Sáhil.
2. Wusút; and[5]
3. Jurd.

The Sáhil, shore or coast,[6] opposed to Aram, the upland plateau which may be said to form Syria and Palestine, is a strip of ground, here flat, there broken, at this part barely exceeding two miles in breadth, and extending from the lower slopes of the Libanus to the sea. In pre-classical and classical times it was densely inhabited, as extensive ruins, often within bowshot, prove; and the mildness of the climate, combined with facility for traffic, render it still

---

[5] Volney (i. 190) mentions only Nos. 1 and 3, ignoring the Wusút.

[6] It is the ancient Kanaan (Canaan), and the Palesheth (Philistia), and Shephelah (שפלה, Josh. xi. 16) of the Hebrews, whence the Arabic Sofalah, the Greek Paralia (παραλία), and especially the Macras and the Macra-pedium of Strabo. 'Aram,' in its widest sense, includes all the uplands lying between the Mediterranean and the middle course of the Euphrates, from Phœnicia and Palestine to Mesopotamia, Chaldæa, and even Assyria.

a comparatively populous district, the number of settlements being determined by the water-supply. The climate is distinctly sub-tropical, and the damp relaxing heat of summer reminded me of Rio de Janeiro. It is, however, for a few days, a pleasant change, after the too dry and attenuated air of the uplands. The formation is mostly secondary Jurassic limestone, which renders the water hard and unwholesome, alternating with chalk, homogeneous as well as blended with bituminous schist, and banded with flint, chert, and other varieties of silex; whilst conglomerates of water-washed pebbles, and in places breccias, almost invariably clothe the sloping sides and the floors of river-valleys and ravines. The sandstone, which is so important a feature in the upper heights, is rare in the lowlands; trap and basalt may exist, but I have never seen a trace of igneous formation in the Libanus proper: it abounds in the southern Anti-Libanus, it is more plentiful still in the Hermon, and it is the only material of the Druze mountain (Jebel Durúz Haurán) to the east. In these levels the roads are incomparably the worst, and the people will not make or mend carriageable lines, for the same reason which prevents the African negro felling the dense jungle

around his village.   The salts and the potashes
washed from the higher sections give the lowlands
their admirable fertility.   Every stranger remarks
that crops are grown, and probably have been grown
year after year for the last forty centuries, without
any of the appliances which most other lands find
necessary.

The Wusút, as its name imports, is the middle
region.   Here towns and villages are perhaps not
so numerous as near the coast; and like the upper
heights, it still lodges a scatter of tented Bedawin.
This zone, however, is extensively cultivated by the
lowlanders with tobacco, cereals, and vegetables, especially the potato; rye would probably flourish, but
it has not yet been introduced.   The chalky soil,
locally called Howára, or the floury ground, is excellent for vines, besides producing the true hard
asphalt: the latter, when found in chalk capped with
limestone, melts in the sun.   The characteristic formation of the Libanus Wusút, however—the Anti-
Libanus will show other varieties—is a sandstone of
either hard grit or soft substance easily disintegrat-
ing into a 'Rambla' (Ramlah, or arenaceous tract).
Here overlying, there underlying the calcaires, it is
easily distinguished, at considerable distances, from

the blue-gray or glaring rust-patched limestones of
the upper and lower regions by its colour, now a
warm ruddy brown, then a lavender, like the Brazilian Tauá, and often by its dark purplish red, the
Sangre de Boi of Portuguese America. Exceptionally rich in trees, it is the only home of the pine
(locally called Sinaubar, *P. pinea*), whose light evergreen scatters—so different from the barrens and
slashes of the Southern United States—at once attract the stranger's eye. They are found clustering
upon a mound of sandstone protruding from the
lime, as in the celebrated Wady Hammánah, and they
conscientiously eschew the calcaires, which is not the
case with the Shamm or sapin (*P. halepensis*) of the
northern ranges about Alexandretta. Frequent landslips disclose at considerable depths (say sixty feet
below the present surface) the indurated resin—one
of the least perishable of substances—passing into
a fossiliferous state, like copal. This sandstone formation supplies the only muscatel grapes ever seen by
us in the mountains; it is the great storehouse of
the valuable metallic formations of the Libanus—
iron, pyrites, and copper. I do not despair of other
metals being discovered in it. It is rich in crystalline
hornblende, and in essonite where the garnet stands

out brightly from the hornblende. An important feature, as regards the cereals, it supplies them abundantly with phosphoric acid and with oxides; hence in the Wusút we never see the anæmia which affects those living in the purely calcareous and cretaceous districts; for instance, about Damascus. The sandstone region is, as a rule, far easier for horses than the limestone. It abounds in humidity, resembling in this point the strata about Liverpool, where the blow of a pick has more than once drowned out a coal-pit; hence its chief advantage—the abundance of excellent water, slightly, and in some cases abundantly, flavoured with iron. Yet almost all the principal springs of the Libanus and of Northern Palestine flow from the limestone formation. For instance :

The Ayn el Asáfír, the source of the river Ibráhím, and the Naba' el 'Afká, forming the Adonis River.

The Naba' el Hadíd (of iron); the Naba' el Laban (of soured milk) ;[7] the Naba' el 'Asal (of honey) ; the

[7] The natives say of the mountain, ' Yadur 'asalan wa laban'—' It flows soured-milk and honey.' Not a few suppose that this spring has given its ' meligalac' name to the Libanus, and assert that it was itself so called from its snowy pebbles; whilst those of the 'Asal (flowing honey) are of a bright yellow hue. The distinction is utterly fanciful.

v

Naba' Sannín : forming the Nahr el Kalb (Lycus River). I did not visit the Naba' el 'Asal spring, but all assured me that it is no exception to the rule.

The Barada and the Ayn Fíjah, forming the Abana(?) and the Pharpar(?).

The Ayn Már Márún, the Ayn Lebwah and the Ayn el Tannúr, feeding the Upper Orontes, whose western bank, however, is purely basaltic, whence the celebrity of its waters.

The Ayn wady Dulbah, the Ayn wady Hasbání, and the Ayn wady Banyás, feeding the Upper Jordan ; whilst the two influents from the Tell el Kádi are the produce of basalt.

On the other hand, the lower valley of the 'Awaj, or Crooked River, generally, but I believe erroneously, identified with the Pharpar,[8] and running parallel with the calcareous plain of Damascus,

---

[8] Murray's Handbook (p. 426) tells us : 'A short distance north of Wady 'Awaj is another wady, through which a small tributary flows into the 'Awaj. The name of this wady, *Barbar*, is the Arabic form of the Hebrew *Pharpar*.' This is a fair specimen of the carelessness with which these volumes have been compiled, and the recklessness with which important deductions are drawn from imperfect premises. There is absolutely no Wady Barbar: the name of the Fiumara (not in Van de Velde) is Wady Buhayráni. But there is a Jebel Barbar, which may be seen from Damascus. Its tall crest and sturdy sides have

is wholly basaltic, being in fact the beginning of
the trap region, which extends southwards to the
end of the Haurán, and eastwards as far as the
Euphrates desert. Thus the waters of Syria, not including the mineral, are the produce of basalt, of
sandstone, and of secondary limestone; the first being
the best and the last the worst.

The Jurd, a word which we recognise in Guardafui
—properly Jurd Háfún, the barren, open highland of
Háfún—includes the remainder of 'the Mountain' to
its crest, and may begin about 4000 feet above sea-
level. The aspect from below appears bleak and barren; the mountain limestone, of a fawn-grey sometimes
darkening to blue, often stands up bristling in crags
and backs of fantastic shape, in regular courses like
walls, or in huge blocks whose perpendicular cham-
fers and flutings, the work of time and weather,
are supposed by the people to show treasure buried
beneath them: where the disintegrated rock falls,
deep - red stains of iron oxide show the fracture

---

given a rough joke against the inhabitants of B'ka'asam, who are held
to be of the Bœotian kind. 'Shiddí ya mara, taktak Barbar min
saubih !' ('Haul away, good wife; Barbar hill has cracked and clat-
tered at his side!') is the address of the husband who, assisted by the
able and energetic partner of his bed, had fastened a rope round the
offending mountain, and was trying to pull it down.

from afar. Roads cannot run along the cliff-sides
on account of their sharp pitch, except where projecting ledges divide the height into gigantic steps; the
rounded crests, however, are almost always 'Mar-
kúb' (rideable), and they are often the best because
the only natural highways in the land. The water—
here abundant, there rare—is at all seasons icy cold.
From December to early April these upper heights
are swept by furious winds, drenched with torrential
rains, and covered with snows whose depth renders
them impassable; avalanches are common, and
moraine is strewn under the 'teeth of the cliffs.'
In summer, however, despite a sun of fire and the
thin air, a plentiful though stunted vegetation enables the large flocks of sheep and goats, especially
the latter, to exchange their Kishlák (قشلاق) or
winter quarters for the fresh and pure Yaílák
(يايلاق). This atmosphere, 'smelt' for the first
time by the traveller who crosses the Libanus between Beyrout and Damascus, is a cordial enjoyed
even by the lazy peasant of the plains, who finds
his appetite increased three-fold, and his slumbers
deep and dreamless. I never saw on the Jurd a
case of goître. Much cultivation is found in the
gorges and sheltered plains; it will extend to 6000

fect above the sea-level, and even higher. The
village-paupers raise temporary sheds whilst watch-
ing over their untithed wheat and tobacco, and
when grazing the horses and the neat cattle intrusted to them by their wealthier neighbours. The
growth of the Libanus Jurd consists of the Sindyán
oak (two species), whose acorns are enormous in
proportion to the tree, the terebinth, the Kaykáb or
maple, the Anjás barri or wild pear, the Za'arúr or
hawthorn, the Lauz el Murr or bitter almond, and
the Lizzáb (Juniper), a slow and secular growth, capri-
cious withal. The Anti-Libanus is affected chiefly by
the Butm, Kaykáb, Anjás, Lauz, Lizzáb, and Díshár
(ديشار) or wild honeysuckle. In olden times most
parts of the Jurd were doubtless wooded with thick
clumps, thin scatters, and long single lines of trees:
the people still preserve the tradition of forests
and groves—in classical times a favourite feature—
and at the base of Jebel Sannín we heard of petri-
fied trunks and branches of the 'Afs or gall-oak
(*Q. coccifera*). The want of fuel about the Jurd
renders the local deposits of poor coal doubly valuable, and the rich iron ores, found only in the rare
places where a line of sandstone divides the calcaire,
quite useless, at least in these days.

Having now ridden over the Libanus from north to south, I can supply travellers of my own sex with hints about mounting themselves. Riding-mules are rarely to be had. The best *monture* is the ugly, thickset, ambling pony from Hindustan, Persia, and Bokhara, known as Rahwán, Yábú, and Chehár-gúshah (the four-eared), from its split ears. The highest price should be twenty napoleons. Its plates, its girths, and its barley, which the 'natives' are uncommonly addicted to stealing, or rather to administering the 'horse-sandwich'—an ear of barley between two wisps of grass—require being looked after; and that is all. For riding it is safe as any mule, and it picks its way with almost asinine circumspection. The very worst animals are the valuable blood-mares of the plains, and these, till trained to hill-climbing or to skating over the ice-like pavement of the towns, are really dangerous. The poorest Kadísh (nag) is unusually surefooted throughout Syria and Palestine; and the timid must remember that the horse has four legs, and that it can easily be kept under the rider. In dangerous places let me advise a long arm and a short bridle, giving head freely, so as never to shorten step or stride; at the same time ever ready to support the mouth. In risky descents I lean a little forward where others bend backward, the object being to steady the horse's hands by additional weight.

The roads, or properly tracks, may be divided into four kinds. The most reprehensible are the hard, white, yellow, and reddish limestone - slabs and sheet-rocks, known as Balát or paving-stones: they are bad when flat, worse when rounded, and worst when inclined. In the water-worn channels and courses a hoof is sometimes jammed, and if the animal be not stopped at once, an ugly laming fall is the result: I have seen this happen three times. When descending the smooth steps and ramps, often foot-holed, channelled, guttered, and polished like glass—for instance the ladders near Tyre, and the Lycus River[9]—it is as well to dismount, especially if the attendants set the example. Next come the close conglomerates and compact chalks, the latter especially heating and dazzling when the sun in front makes them resemble the gleaming surfaces of streams. The hard and often crystalline clay-slates being jointed are not so slippery; they often, however, form very rough and unrideable ascents and descents. The fourth and the safest are the

[9] Both of these dangerous passes have lately been repaired.

sandstone grits, the basalts, and the loose stuff, over which the horses walk as they would upon metalled highways. Here a man clears his garden by throwing the rubbish into the road; and *en revanche*, since the most ancient days the invader, after cutting down the enemy's fruit-trees, strews the finest land with stones : this practice has entailed even modern and present difficulties upon cultivation. A practised ear can tell by the sound, even at night, what kind of ground is below; for instance, lime-stone by its clink and tinkle, and sandstone by its gritty crunch.

Complaining loudly of the roads beyond the Jib-bah traversing Kasrawán—high-sounding name of an ancient king—which may be the 'rampart and fortress of religious liberty in the East,' but which is certainly and proverbially the worst travelling country of the Libanus, we rounded the heads of the Nahr Ibrahim, near Akúrá (a source called preëminently El M'árah,[10] *the* Cave), and we halted at the glorious Afká influ-

[10] Syrians often slur over the guttural 'Ghayn' in this word; and thus assimilate it to the Hebrew מערה, concerning which I have spoken in part i. (*sub voc.* Ghutah *versus* Uz). Popularly Maghárah is applied in Syria to a small-mouthed cave; 'Arák or 'Irák (literally, the courtyard of a house) to one with a large aperture, like those of Bayt Jibrín (Dr. Robinson's old Horite city) and Dayr Dubwán, which the

ent, nobler than Vaucluse, with its crystal stream and
its green kieve—a mirror fit for Adonis; no wonder that Venus here chose a home! We crossed the
Naba' el Hadid, which C converts into El Hadis
('iron' into a 'traditional saying of the Prophet'),
and finally the upper valley of the Nahr el Kalb.
Upon the precipitous northern or right bank of
the Lycus, and about one mile west from the May-
rúbá village, my husband was shown a ruin of large
stones—as a rule, the bigger the stones the older
the ruins—some squared, and others part of the live
rock, with signs of mortise and tenon along the
coping for roof or ceiling-joists. The people believe
this 'Kharbat el Záhir' to have been a Dayr or convent. We were curious to ascertain if the Assyrian
tablets at the Lycus mouth, and said to date from
Sin Akki irib (Sennacherib), 2570 years ago, were
the memorials of armies marching by the short cut

---

people pronounce Dayri Dibbán, or Dubbán (of bears). The term
Khaymah, tent or pavilion, is also applied to the largest of these colum-
baria and matamors, probably from its modern appearance. Throughout Syria and Palestine there are undoubtedly many caves originally
formed by the escape of gases; others show traces of water and of
weathering in the softer parts of the rock; whilst not a few have been
made, or have at least been enlarged, by troglodyte man.

to the coast, from Ba'albak *viâ* Zahlah and down
stream, or if they followed the road preferred by the
moderns, through El Bukay'ah, 'the low plain,' the
'entrance to Hamath,' which separates the Libanus
from the Jebel el Húlah, to the port of Tripoli
(Tarabulús el Sham), and thence down coast. We
carefully inspected every ruin and remarkable rock,
hoping, but in vain, to detect corresponding sculp-
tures. Until these be found, we must believe that
the invader took the longer route, by the original
Iron Gate of Syria.

Ancient Ba'albak, I may remark, owed all its vast
importance to a central position, almost equidistant
from Damascus and its great ports, Tripolis, Berytus,
and Sidon. This advantage, we may safely predict
—in the long run site is sure to tell—will raise it
once more to high commercial rank, when the coming railway shall connect it with the Mediterranean
and with the Indian Ocean. The line to be taken
is still under dispute, and each writer seems to
propose his own. Alexandretta is . at present the
favourite terminus; but Suwaydíyyah, Tripoli, and
Beyrout all have special pleaders. The route advocated by my husband begins at Tyre or Sidon, and
runs through Ba'albak and Palmyra to Hit on the

Great River. It is certainly, although the Libanus
is a serpent in the path, preferable to that which
would connect pestilential Iskandarún *viâ* the difficult Baylán pass, the Lamk swamps west of Aleppo,
and the barren lands to the east, with the River
Euphrates at a section where the stream is not
navigable throughout the year. And, unless our
political status in Syria and Palestine, or rather, I
should say, in Turkey, be much changed, we need
not think of a railway to carry any one belonging
to our generation.

After a cool and comfortable night under canvas
at the Naba' Sannín, I rode direct to Zahlah: meanwhile my husband made two ascents of the mountain,
whose western walls, stark and horizontally stratified, and whose bluff southern buttress are so conspicuous from Beyrout, whilst its knobbly sky-line
renders it an equally good landmark to all Cœlesyria.
Sannín is also, like the Jebel Libnán,[11] a milky
mount, a White Mountain, a Mont Blanc, a Hæmus, a
Doenyo Ebor. But its whiteness arises from its walls
of glaring limestone, from its bare slides of chalk,

---

[11] In the Latin translation of Ptolemy by Bilibaldus Pirkimerus,
a quaint derivation is given (margin lib. v. chap. xv. table 3): 'Libanus,
a thure nato λίβανος dictus, Arabiam contingit.'

and from its big glistening outliers reflecting the light; its pearl-gray also becomes a brighter tint by its backing of black-blue sky, and by the foreground of dark pine-scattered sandstone and iron clay. Dr. Robinson (iii. 440) justly observes that the perennial snow does not exist in sufficient quantity to name it like Ben Nevis, Snowdon, or Himalaya; and we may extend his observation to all the mountains of Syria and Palestine.

The exaggerated description of the Arab poet, who makes that 'ruinous heap,' Damascus, a pearl set in emeralds, and sterile Sannín bear about his person the four seasons, is quoted by all travellers, from Volney to Wilson and Paton. The former terms this buttress (i. 295) the 'very point of Lebanon;' and in one place he seems to explain the word, 'the Sannín or summit of Lebanon.' Yet it certainly does not measure 9000 feet above sea-level. We were unable to trace the origin of the term, which is neither Syriac nor Arabic, unless we derive it from 'Shinna,' which, in the debased Arabo-Syriac of Ma'alúlah, still signifies a tall fort-like rock. Volney suggests (ii. 221) that it may represent Senir of the fir-trees (Ezekiel xxvii. 5). Senir, however, is usually made to be the Hermon, or a part of it—the fortress of Sinna named by Strabo (xvi. 2. q. 17). We also read of the 'Valley of Senyn' (*Pilgrimage of Johannes de Solms*, 1483), or 'Sennin' (Le Tresdevot, *Voyage de Jeruzalem*, Anvers, 1608), both quoted by Van de Velde (i. 260). According to Monseigneur Ya'akúb, Bishop of the Syrian Catholics at Damascus, 'Tor Saníno' takes its name from the 'Saníno' spring, which we saw issuing from its western base; and this is a noun proper, without other sense. I fear that the origin of the word is irretrievably lost.

Captain Burton's first ascent was from a dwarf, well-watered hollow on the Kasrawán-Zahlah road, known as the Jurat el Mahkam (Sink of the judgment-place?). The riding was not so good as up the Cedar Block; the hill-sides were studded and sprinkled with larger and rougher stones, and the natural macadam of shingle before described did not show in force till near the summit. Here the characteristic stone consists of chalky nodules of snowy-white limestone, often cube-shaped, and set as it were in a frame-block of yellow chert—the converse of what is so common in all other places, namely 'Biz,' or nodular and often kidney-shaped concretions of chert bedded in limestone. Reaching the

conical head of El Sughrat (الصغرى),[12] the Big Pit,
not to be confounded with Sughrat el Bunduk, the
Big Pit of the Filbert-tree, he rode along a knife-
board to the foot of the rounded head known as
Jebel el Mazár (of the Visitation place). Leaving
the horses in a hollow, after one hour and fifty
minutes of moderate walking he stood upon the
base of the little sun-temple, whose ruins crown
one of the summits. From this point there is a fine
bird's-eye view of the western Libanus, whose features are marked and peculiar, if not picturesque.
Eight main ribs, the first and northernmost of which
sets off at Jebel 'Uyún Urghush and the Cedar Block,
separated by valleys of erosion, which the torrents
have deepened to chasms, trend from north-east,
bending to south-west, and connect the highest
chine, here almost meridional, with the lowlands
bordering upon the Mediterranean. South-east-
wards, the Kubbat el Sayyáh, the little dome that
overlooks Damascus, and about which such wild

---

[12] Capt. Warren (p. 294, No. VI. *Palestine Exploration Fund*) finds
the word Sughrat, which he writes 'Thogret,' very common about the
hill-country east and west of Amman; and he explains the prefix by
remarking that the ruins (T. Tusora, T. Tasin, and T. Umm Ramadán)
were standing upon a watershed.

stories have been written, places Sannín *en rapport* with the capital.

On the 3d of August Captain Burton made a second ascent of Jebel Sannín; this time he struck the great southern buttress, which lies north of, with a little westing from, Zahlah. About half way he came upon the first of the Talláját (ﺕﻼﺠﺍﺕﻟ) or hollows, which are filled with snow between November and March, and which, assisted by the early and the later rains, gather and distribute the crystal springs, gushing out upon and making a garden of green in the Buká'a. As the heat increases the snow-labourers must go higher for their harvest, and they have run a decent bridle-path along the western flank almost to the summit of Jebel Sannín. It would hardly be advisable to ride an untrained beast up this line with a clean slide of 200 fathoms almost underfoot. There is the usual local tradition of a Harfúshí horseman having dashed down it to escape the avenger of blood; and, as usual, the man escaped, whereas the mare was killed.

The mule-path is headed by a Névé, and thence a stiff slope to the right leads to the apex of Jebel Sannín. Here also are two Júrahs, swallow-holes, crateriform hollows in the limestone surface; one lying to the north-north-east of the other, and each measuring about 100 feet in diameter. From this spot a specimen of the 'Ud el Khull (vinegar wood) was added to our little collection, intrusted to Mr. Palmer. The aneroid made Sannín 1·60 lower than the apex of the Cedar Block, or 8895 feet. D gives the height 2608 metres; Murray, 8555 feet. The difference of altitude is visible to the eye, looking from the Buká'a plain at the outline of the Libanus clad in winter suit. When the Cedar Block, like the Hermon, is purely ermined with virgin snow, Jebel Sannín is more thinly robed in a lighter white, and its southern continuation, Jebel el Kunaysah (of the Chapel) and Kafr Salwán, show merely powdered heads. These three chief snow-caps are faced by an equal number upon the Anti-Libanus range: the northern Haláim near Kárá; the central or Fatli Block near Mu'arrat el Bashkurdí; and the southern, Jebel Ahhyár, fronted by the cliffs popularly known as the Jebel el Shakíf, north-east of Zebedání.

The descent of Sannín is down the southern face. Though practicable, it is steep, and it lasts less than half the time (17:40^m) which the ascent will occupy.

At Zahlah we were hospitably received by Miss Wilson, superintendent of the British Female Syrian

VOL. I.   K schools; and we met with nothing but kindness and attention from the authorities and notables of that energetic and somewhat turbulent Christian town. Here ended the geographical interest of our tour, which had lasted a fortnight, from July 31 to August 3, 1870. I venture to hope that our humble gleanings will show how rich is the harvest of information awaiting the traveller who has time and opportunity for reaping it; and that I may have contributed my mite towards promoting a more critical examination of this young-old land.

ISABEL BURTON.

CHAPTER II.

PRELIMINARY TOUR IN THE JEBEL DURUZ HAURAN—EX-
PLORATION OF THE UMM NIRAN CAVE AND THE
TULUL EL SAFA—THE VOLCANIC REGION EAST OF
DAMASCUS.

PART I.

BEFORE the traveller in Syria and Palestine can explore, he is compelled to wander about the country
far and wide, in order to find out what remains to
be done. This information he will vainly seek from
the citizens and from the caravan-dragomans, who
love the beautiful simplicity of the highway, and
who hate nothing more than to face the discomforts
and the insecurity of the byway. Moreover, it is
ever difficult in the extreme to gather exact topographical details amongst a people who require truth
to be drawn from them 'by wain-ropes.' 'Le paysan
interrogé,' says the astute M. Lecoq, 'ne répond
jamais que ce qu'il pense devoir être agréable à qui
l'interroge ; il a peur de se compromettre.' This is
true of Syria with a shade of difference, for here we
are Europe reversed : the interrogated peasant wishes,
if possible, to compromise his interrogator. We were
living, for instance, some six months at the foot of

that eastern spur of the Anti-Libanus upon whose south-eastern slopes lies the large northern suburb of Damascus, El Sálihíyyah (of the Saints),[1] facetiously changed, on account of its Kurdish population, into El Tálihíyyah (طالحـيّة), (of the Sinners). As we called it the Sálihíyyah Hill, so of course did all those around us. Presently I found it laid down in all the maps as Jebel Kasyún, and adopted by Captain Warren (p. 240, No. V. *Palestine Exploration Fund*). On inquiry, this proved to be a mistake for Kaysún (قيـسون); and conversation with a peasant-guide of B'lúdán presently taught me that the word, though not admitted into the common Arabic dictionaries, is universally used to signify yellow chamomile, a weed plentiful upon the slopes, and much used as a simple. Here, moreover, the name is not unusual : there is a ruin in the 'Aláh known as Shaykh Ali Kaysún, and a Kaysún village near Safet. The people have, in fact, a marked objection to correct the traveller's mistakes. I was allowed to call Kasr Namrúd

---

[1] This is the popular derivation ; but I much suspect that it took its name from the Kurdish Sultan Saláh el Din (better known as Saladin). All the rulers of that race naturally enlisted their countrymen, who acted as Mamlúks before the days of the Circassians; and it is remarked of the Kurds that they always prefer for their quarters the highest ground in a city—' Like the English,' add the natives.

in my diary ' Kasr 'Antar;' and but for a second visit
to the place, the mistake might have found its way
into print.   Again, nothing is more common, and I
may add more mortifying, after you have ridden an
hour or so from a village where you have spent the
night, than to be asked whether you were shown
such and such a ruin, of which you have never heard
till too late.   Incurious about the past, or rather
about everything which does not immediately affect
the interests of the present, the Syrians are pro-
foundly ignorant, and even disdainful, of archæology.   There are few men in Damascus who can
point out the site of the Ommiade Palace, the tomb
of the great Caliph Muawiyah the First, or even the
last resting-place of Saláh el Din, the fearless and
irreproachable knight of El Islam.

Again, most travellers, before entering upon exploration in Syria, of course determine to inspect
places of general interest—Jerusalem and Damascus,
for instance—otherwise, when studying the unknown,
they will feel somewhat like the modern Englishman
(by the bye, there are not a few of them), who has
visited most of the European capitals, but who has
not seen all the three chief cities of the United Kingdom; who is familiar with Switzerland and with the

Italian lakes, without ever having visited Westmore-
land and Killarney; and who is at home on the
Pyrenees, whilst he would be thoroughly abroad in
Derbyshire and the Hebrides. But to visit carefully
the beaten tracks in the Holy Land occupies some
six months, and few can afford leisure, not to speak
of health, beyond that time. Besides, no new-comer
would suspect that so many patches of unvisited, and
possibly at the time unvisitable, country lie within a
day or two's ride of great cities and towns such as
Aleppo and Damascus, Hums and Hamáh; and where
the maps show a blank of virginal white around El
Harrah, for instance, which should be black enough,
students naturally conclude that the land has been
examined, and has been found to be without interest,
—the reverse being absolutely the case. Moreover,
there are not a few who will scarcely have stomach
for the task, when they learn the reasons why these
places have escaped European inspection; namely,
that they will not afford provisions, forage, and
water; that they are deadly with malarious fever;
or that they are infested by the Bedawin. The
latter, indeed, compare favourably with the Greek
Klephts; they have not yet learned to detain you for
ransom, or to threaten you with excision of the nose

and ears, unless your friends consent at once to pay the exorbitant demand. They will spear you a little, as they did M. Dubois d'Angers, French Secretary of Legation at Athens, who, by firing a revolver, expected to put a razzia to flight like monkeys; but they will not kill you in cold blood, except according to the strict *lex talionis*—the Sár, or blood for blood. Still, even under these mitigated circumstances, travellers, certain that an escort, unless of overpowering numbers, will at once turn tail, hardly care to expose themselves, their attendants, and their effects to a charge of Bedawin cavalry. And, curious to say, this backward movement of the guard is the traveller's safety: the plundering tribe — which, if it could seize the whole party, might at times, more or less rare, remember that dead men are dumb — knows that it has been recognised by the fugitives, and that before evening the tale will be bruited abroad through the length of the land.

'Our visit to Ba'albak and the northern Libanus, related in the last chapter, was followed, in October 10th to the 31st, by a sister excursion to the southern parts of the mountain, the home of the Druzes, better watered than that of the Maronites. We visited, at her palace of Mukhtárá (the Chosen

One), the Sitt Jumblát, now the head of that great Druze house (properly written Ján-pulád, or Life of Steel); and we passed a morning with his Excellence Franco Pasha, Governor of the Libanus, who was busily engaged in restoring Bayt el Dín (in our books Ibteddin and Bteddin), the ruined castle of the late redoubtable Amír Beshír Shiháb. Thence we ascended the Hermon, to whose summit I had accompanied Captain Warren, R.E., on October 29th, 1869; and I succeeded in shipping off to England the stone with a fragmentary Greek inscription discovered by that officer. The excursion concluded with a gallop to the Waters of Merom —the 'pet lake' of a certain popular author — a hideous expanse of fetid mire and putrefying papyrus; with a call upon the only Bedawi 'Emir' in this region, the Amir Hasan el Fá'úr, of the Benú Fadl tribe; and with an inspection of the romantic and hospitable Druze villages, Majdal el Shams, 'Arnah, Rímah, and Kala'at Jandal, which cling to the southern and the eastern folds of the Hermon.

The winter was now setting in apace, suggesting repose, or at least short excursions to those who can rest only by change of exertion. About the middle of January 1871, escorting an old Brazilian friend,

Mr. Charles Williams of Bahia, I rode out with the Meccan caravan as far as Ramsah, its third station; wrote an official report upon its organisation; and returned to Damascus *viâ* 'Izra'a, the Edhr'a of the Handbook,[2] and the celebrated Haurân valley-plain, inspecting the chief settlements, and making acquaintance with the principal Shaykhs. An important inquiry concerning the interests of a British-protected subject made me set out on February 22d for Hums (Emesa), and Hamâh (Hamath, Epiphaneia), on the northern borders of the consular district of Damascus. At the latter place—both will be found alluded to in the Appendix—I examined and sent home native facsimiles of the four unique basaltic stones, whose characters, raised in cameo, apparently represent a system of local hiero-

---

[2] Pp. 502-3. The author contends that this is the Edrei of the Pentateuch (Numb. xxi. 33), and founds his third argument upon the similarity of the modern Arabic Edhr'a. I can assure him that no Arab either writes it or pronounces it otherwise than Izra'a (اِزْرِع), slightly corrupted to Azra'a. On the other hand, Dera'âh (دَرَعاه), evidently alluded to by Eusebius, is a far more suitable site for the ancient Bashanic city. There is much to 'attract special attention in this place, which the author of the Handbook apparently never visited. Otherwise he would not have described the mosque to the north as a large rectangular building 'at the southern extremity of the town;' nor would he have converted its common Hauranic minaret into a 'high tower.'

glyphics peculiar to this part of Syria, and form the connecting link between picture-writing and the true syllabarium. My host, M. F. Bambino, Vice-consul de France, was kind enough to give me, amongst other valuable papers, two maps which he had traced by aid of native information, noting the most important of the 360 villages—this favourite number is also given to the Lejá—which stud the upland plain known as El 'Aláh (علاه) or 'Aláwát, sometimes pronounced 'Ulah and 'Uláwát. This high rolling ground, beginning at Selamíyyah, the well-known ruin and outwork of Palmyra, six hours' ride from, and bearing E.S.East (118° Mag.) of the Mound of Hamáh (the 'Mother-in-law'), extends some five days' journey, they say, to the north, and from east to west two or three days. The surface is not unlike Upper Norwood, if the latter wanted hedges and trees. Mr. Hughes marks it the Great Syrian Desert, forgetting that the Seleucidæ here kept their immense studs of elephants and horses. The whole is virgin ground, and the same may be said of the eastern slopes of the Jebel Kalbiyyah on the left bank of the Orontes, and of the country extending from the parallel of Hums to that of Selamíyyah. M. Prosper Bambino had the goodness to accom-

pany me during a day's ride, and after some five
hours we had examined no less than five ruins,
namely Tell Jubb el Safá, Marj Húr, Tell Iznín,
Khirbat el Tayyibah, and Shaykh Ali Kaysún.   The
settlements are all provincial townlets of the Lower
or Greco-Roman Empire, and the basaltic buildings
exactly reflect the 'Giant Cities of Bashan;' that is
to say, show Christian architecture of the first to
the seventh century.   The inscriptions which I saw
were invariably Greek, and mostly in cameo or raised
characters, some of them admirably cut.   This *trou-
vaille* was, I have said, bequeathed by me to my
friend and fellow-traveller, who, in view of the Circassian colonisation which had then already begun
in this new and highly interesting region, lost no
time about copying the inscriptions and sketching
the buildings, whose destruction is now so imminent.

I returned to Damascus on March 10th, *viâ* the
northern Jebel el Húlah ('that which intervenes'),
studying on the way the fine crusading castle Husn
el Akrád, and the plain of the Nahr el Kabír, the
Eleutherus river.   The hardships of this march
were considerable; most of the country was under
water, and the rushing torrents and deep ditches
caused long detours.   Heavy and continuous rains

KALA'AT EL HUSN, ALIAS HUSN EL AKRAD.

began shortly after we left Hamáh, accompanied by furious blasts, and ending in snow and sleet which approximated the climate of Syria to that of Norway; the weather suggested the 'Alpinas, ah! dura, nives' of Virgil, and it did damage. A Jew servant of my companion, M. Zelmina Füchs, soon afterward sickened and died; and I still bear the marks of frost-bite, an accident which also happened to Captain Wilson, R.E. The people of Damascus call the last four days (o.s.) of Shubát or February and the first three of Adár or March El Mustakrazát, the 'borrowed ones,'

and Ayyám el 'Ajúz, the 'days of the old woman;'
because February becomes a borrower from March
in order to kill off the old men, and to make the
old women break up their spinning-wheels for fire-
wood. This week, which ends in fact the later
rains, is supposed to be the most fatal of the whole
year. We also make March come in like a lion.

All my excursions were strictly within the
limits of the consular district of Damascus. Not
a little business was managed during what appeared to be mere trips and 'perpetual peregrina-
tions.' On returning to head-quarters we resolved
to avail ourselves of a short leave granted by her Majesty's Secretary of State for Foreign Affairs, and to
examine the Holy Week at Jerusalem. I rode down
the country by the vile Kunayterah road *viâ* Tiberias,
where the Hebrew subjects protected by Great
Britain were complaining that Rashid Pasha, then,
but happily no longer, Wali or Governor-general of
Syria, had taken from them and had sold to
the Greek bishop, Nifon of Nazareth, a cemetery and
a synagogue which for the last 400 years had be-
longed to their faith ; and *viâ* Safet, where men
held passports which ought to have been annually
changed, but of which sundry, by peculiar imbecility,

had not been renewed since 1850. Thence I gal-
loped down the coast to Ramlah, and reached El
Kuds *alias* Bayt el Mukaddas on Palm Sunday, April
2d, 1871. The Holy Week is the very worst time
for studying the topography and antiquities of Jerusalem, especially if the varied and complicated cere-
monies of Latin and Greek, Armenian and Copt—
some of them lasting through the night, and none
of them worth seeing after an Easter in Rome—
must be 'done.' There are also certain Moslem
rites well worth seeing, and the Jewish passover fell
at the same time; whilst in 1871 the feasts and
fasts of the Latin and Greek Churches happened to
be synchronous—a combination which will not re-
occur for many years. However, we laboured hard,
and we brought away our pilgrims' diplomas duly
signed and sealed.[3]

---

[3] The following is the form of certificate usually supplied to *viator*
when not *vacuus:*   Ducal Crown.
     Ducal Crown.   Dove.   Ducal Crown.

✠

    ARMS OF ST. FRANCIS—PLAIN CROSS SURROUNDED BY CORD.

In Dei Nomine, amen.

Omnibus et singulis præsentes literas inspecturis, lecturis, vel legi
audituris fidem notumque facimus, Nos Terræ Sanctæ Custos Devotum
Peregrinum.

Illustrissimum Dominum Capit. R. Burton, Consulem Anglum Jeru-

Bethlehem, which supplied some silex-instru-
ments hitherto rarely met with in the Holy Land;
Hebron, where an especial order from Damascus
had been sent directing the Shaykhs of the Haram
(Sanctuary) to be more than usually fanatical; and
a short tour in the direction of Beersheba, where
we found the ancient Horite dwellings of Dr. Robinson, cut with Greek crosses, and rich in rude
modern and Coptic inscriptions, concluded the journey south. We then returned by the banale route
viâ Jericho and Bethel, Náblús and Nazareth, Tiberias and Safet, to Damascus. Of the events which

salem, feliciter pervenisse die 3 mensis Aprilis anni 1871, inde subse-
quentibus diebus præcipua Sanctuaria, in quibus mundi Salvator dilec-
tum populum suum, immo et totius humani generis perditam congeriem
ab inferi servitute misericorditer liberavit, utpote Calvarium ubi Cruci
affixus devicta morte, Cœli januas nobis aperuit, SS. Sepulcrum, ubi
sacrosanctum ejus corpus reconditum, triduo ante suam gloriosissimam
Resurrectionem quievit, ac tandem ea omnia Sacra Palestinæ Loca
gressibus Domini, ac Beatissimæ ejus Matris Mariæ consecrata a Reli-
giosis nostris, et Peregrinis visitari solita, visitasse.

In quorum fidem has scripturas officii nostri sigillo munitas per
Secretarium expediri mandavimus.

Datis Jerusalem ex venerabili nostro Conventu SS. Salvatoris die
10 mensis Aprilis 1871.

Secretarius Terræ Sanctæ,
(Signed) Fr. ANTONIUS DE TYBURE, Ex. Prov.

Seal of the Guardian
Reg. *of the Convent of*
Mount Sion.

rendered the last journey memorable to us I shall have more to tell at a future time.

Reaching head-quarters on May 19th, I found the season far advanced. During the winters of 1869-70 and 1870-71 rain had been unusually scarce throughout the seventy-nine direct geographical miles between Sanamayn and Hasyah, including the Damascene, mountains and plains. It is mostly a limestone country, interposed between two great basaltic surfaces; and while the Neptunian was dry, the Plutonian was exceptionally well watered—the igneous formation, as has been remarked, begins south of the Damascus plain, about the valley of the 'Awaj River distant some five direct geographical miles. The rapidly-increasing heat also made me the more anxious to finish my visits in the lowlands, and again to find myself in summer quarters at cool, if not comfortable, B'lúdán.

During upwards of a year and a half's sojourn at Damascus, I had been tantalised by the sight of the forbidden Tulúl el Safá, the Tells[4] or hillocks of

[4] The word must not be written, with Capt. Wilson, R.E., 'Tel' (p. 123, No. IV. *Palestine Exploration Fund*). It corresponds with the Greek Μαγούλα and Hebrew Gibeah, a hill—a term once so common in the topography of Syria and Palestine. Safá, plural of Safát, means large smooth stones, and is the well-known name of a sacred eminence in Meccah.

the Safá region. These pyramids, hardly bigger than baby finger-tips, dot the eastern horizon within easy sight of the city, and thinning out northwards, prolong the lumpy blue wall of the Jebel Durúz Haurán, which appears to reflect the opposite line of the Anti-Libanus. Many also were the vague and marvellous reports which had reached my ears concerning a cistern, tank, or cave, called by the few who know it Umm Nírán, the Mother of Fires; that is to say, the burning; probably so termed from its torrid site, the great basaltic region of the Eastern Damascene. It is alluded to in 1860 by the excellent Dr. J. G. Wetzstein, formerly Prussian Consul at Damascus (note 1, p. 38, *Reisebericht über Hauran und die Trachonen;* Berlin, Reimer, 1860), an official whose travels and whose writings, not to mention his acquirements as an Orientalist, have perpetuated his name in Syria. After a journey through the Safá and the Haurán mountains, peculiarly rich in results, he was prevented by the imminence of the Damascus massacre of '60 from exploring Umm Nírán. It also escaped, in 1867, Mr. Cyril Graham, whose adventurous march is too little known. A collection of his papers, scattered throughout various periodicals — for instance, the *Journal of the Royal*

Geographical Society, vol. xxviii. of 1858—and published in a handy form like the *Reisebericht*, would be
a valuable addition to modern travel-tale.

Perhaps the most interesting discovery made by
Mr. Cyril Graham in the Eastern Haurán is the 'writing which, though not purely Himayaritic, is nevertheless very much allied to it.' I am far from answering in the affirmative to his question, ' May we not be
guided by this to the fact, that the Himayarites originally came from much farther north or north-east
—perhaps from the Euphrates or Mesopotamia —
and then gradually worked their way down into
Central and Southern Arabia?' It appears to me
that he has unconsciously hit upon one of the great
stations made by the Benú Ghassán (Gassanides),
' that powerful but almost unknown people, of direct
Himayarite extraction,' when emigrating from Yemen, after the bursting of the Marab dyke, of disputed date,[5] to the Damascene, where they are known
to have long reigned, and where they became some
of the earliest converts to Christianity. In this
matter they followed in the steps of the Phœnicians,

---

[5] There were two traditional ruptures of this stone embankment,
so celebrated in Arab history : the first took place about A.D. 100 ; the
second shortly after the time of Mohammed.

who, according to Herodotus, also came from the
south; and we may remark that these fertile and
populous regions, 'Arabia Felix,' translated from the
Semitic 'Yemen,' has ever been the Cunabula gentium.

The difficulty and the danger of visiting these
places arose in my time simply from the relations
between the Serai or Government-general of Damascus and the hill-tribes of Bedawins ('Urbán el Jebel),
who, mixed up with the Druzes, infest the Trachonic
countries. The hill-tribes proper ('wild-ass men'), all
descended from a common ancestor, are the 'Agaylát
(written 'Ajílát), the Hasan, the Shurafát, the 'Azám-
át, and the Masá'id. The Safá, or eastern volcanic
region, is tenanted by the Shitayá, the Ghiyás, and
the Anjad, also connected; whilst the Lejá (or Le-
jáh, *i. e.* the Refuge) belongs to the Sulút, in conjunction with, or rather as clients of, the Druzes.[6]

---

[6] In 1857 we are told by Mr. Cyril Graham (p. 283, vol. xxviii.
Journal of the Royal Geographical Society) that 'Es-Solút' have almost
always blood-feuds with the Druzes. Mr. Porter, in a footnote, adds:
'There are four other small tribes in the Léjah—namely, El-Medlij,
Es-Selmán, Ed-Dhohery, and Es-Siyaleh. I am informed that all these
are sub-classes of the Sulút, and that there are about a dozen other
divisions.' Burckhardt, in 1810, found that the 'Arabs who inhabit
the Leja pay some deference to the Druzes, but none whatever to the
Turks or Christians of the neighbouring villages.' He names these
tribes Sulút (100 tents), Madlej (120), and Salmán Dhoherah and Siya-

These nine hordes are individually of small importance; but as there has been a certain amount of
intermarriage amongst them, all readily combine,
especially when a Razzia comes upon the tapis. They
are the liege descendants of the refractory robbers of
the Trachonitis, who, to revenge the death of their captain, Naub or Naubus (El Nukayb, diminutive for El
Nakib, *the* Leader?), rose up against the garrison of
3000 Idumæans, stationed in their country by Herod,
the son of Antipater. Wonderful tales are still told
of their prowess as plunderers in the last century;
for instance, how one of them, swarming up the
mainstay, and cutting a hole in the canvas, entered
by night the pavilion occupied by the Pasha of
Damascus, a dignitary who in those days had the
power of impaling or flaying alive; and how, having
invested himself in the Káuk and Farwah—the melon-
shaped cap and the fur pelisse of office—he quietly
waddled, Turk-like, out of the entrance, and disappeared beneath the nose of the sentinel.

Several of these refractory tribes, however, especially the Shitáyá and the Ghiyás, had submitted

---

lah (50-60 each). Of the mountain tribes (Ahl el Jebel) he enumerates
the following: Esshenabele, El Hassan, El Haddie, Ghiath, Esshere-
fat, Mizaid, El Kerad, Beni Adham, and Szammeral.

themselves, and had given to the Government of Damascus hostages, who were periodically changed. Yet, to the scandal of every honest man, their brethren at large were allowed to scour the plains, to carry off the crops, and to harry the flocks and herds of the peasantry. Each successful outrage encouraged another outrage, and a deaf ear was officially turned to every complaint. The fact is, the Bedawin made profitable work for the tribunals, and they served as the ready implements of revenge against all those disaffected to, or disliked by, the petty autocrat who then disgraced the land by his rule.

These Bedawin show no peculiarity of type. They are small and slightly-made men, notably different from the sturdy and stalwart peasant-class, and still more from the pale and etiolated citizens and burghers. The face is remarkably oval; the eyes are bright brown, with the restless roving look of the civilised pickpocket; the features are high and well formed, and the skin is clear olive-yellow. They wear the usual Jedáil, or long love-locks, well buttered and of raven's-wing tint; whilst their dress is conspicuous by its scantiness and irregularity. The action, like the expression of the countenance, is wild and startled, and the voice is a manner of bark.

They would make an excellent light infantry, and
their pitched battles deserve a professional description. When attacked, they place the women, children and cattle in the rear, form a rude line, which
they carefully guard against being outflanked, and
advance file-firing with considerable regularity. They
never hesitate to attack a stranger who enters their
lands without the guidance of a fellow-tribesman;
and their ideas of hospitality have been considerably
modified in the presence of semi-civilisation. For
this reason, it was not decently safe to ride three
hours beyond the eastern gate of Damascus. The
day before we set out for Palmyra, a Ghazú (plundering party) had murdered an unfortunate peasant
near Kutayfah. Shortly afterwards, a troop of five
Benú Hasan did considerable damage in the Ghútah
villages; two of them lost their heads, but Mustafa
Bey, then Chief of Police, and now deservedly disgraced, considered it barbarous to expose *in terrorem*
Moslem pates over the Serai at Damascus. The Subá'a and other 'Anizah ruffians thereupon made the
Ager Damascenus a battle-field; whilst the Wuld 'Ali,
under the leadership of that notorious villain, Mohammed el Dukhí, were permitted to graze their
herds—that is to say, to levy black-mail—in Cœle-

SYRIA. Such a laxity of rule has never yet been
remembered. In December 1870 a mixed mob of
twenty-five Arabs, Kurds, and Maghrabis (Algerian
Moors), firing their guns, and freely using their sabres, rushed into the Tahún el Zelay, a mile from the
eastern outskirts of the capital, and wounding eight
men, of whom six were Druzes, carried away grain,
weapons, and whatever they could loot. This offence
was also unnoticed by the local government. Early
in January 1871 the hill-tribes drove off some 32,000
head of sheep and goats from the Jebel Kalamún (the
Chameleon); and the offence was repeated on February 13th by the Subá'a and the Sawa'al, sub-tribes of
the 'Anizah. Since that time, hardly a week passed
without some such event being recorded. Yet the
Hadíkat el Akhbar, the French and Arabic paper
highly salaried to wear the rosiest of rose-coloured
spectacles, had the audacity to publish, 'Le désert est
cultivé, les Bedouins sont soumis, et le brigandage
anéanti.' And thus dust was thrown in the eyes
of the civilised world, whilst the Government-general
of Damascus employed hordes of banditti to plunder
its own hapless subjects. Did the Emirs of Sind or
the Nawwáb of Oude ever attempt aught more pre-
posterous? It is fervently to be hoped that the

excellent orders issued to the Jurnaljis (newspaper
editors) by Mahmúd Pasha, who, happily(?) for the
empire, succeeded Ali Pasha of pernicious memory,
will be strictly carried out; and if the proprietor of
the Syrian *Moniteur* passes a few months in gaol, the
example will be as beneficial to future libellers as
the punishment is merited.

So it came to happen that all the broken-down
Gassanian convents called El Diyúrá (the Dayrs)
had never, to my knowledge, been visited by a European traveller.[7] The Rev. Mr. Porter often alludes
to them as the 'ruins said to exist in the untrodden
regions dimly seen on the eastern horizon;' and he
was told (chap. ix. 2d edit. *Five Years in Damascus;*
London, Murray, 1870) that a hundred horsemen
would not attempt a journey to the 'Diûra.' I was
fortunate enough to inspect the three. My first excursion was in December 1869, when we—that is to
say, M. Piochard de la Boulerie, a French entomolo-

---

[7] Mr. Cyril Graham visited the square tower of basalt called by the
Arabs Dayr, or Kasr Kasam, and the two 'Dayrs' to the north; but
he seems to have missed the northernmost near Dhumayr (vol. xxviii.
p. 31, *Journal of Royal Geographical Soc.*). Curious to say, he believes
them to be 'evidently castles, the three forming most probably a line
of border fortresses to protect the country against the incursions of the
Arabs.' Had that been the case, their cisterns would not have been
outside the walls—to quote only one objection.

gist, who spent three months in Syria making an
immense collection, and myself—escorted by a very
slender and timid party, pushed along the Robbers'
Road, and succeeded in reaching the two northern
ruins. My companion was not a little surprised to
find under the basaltic stones the coleopters of the
Sinaitic desert; and he will doubtless give an interesting account of this curious fauna. On that occasion we nighted, without receiving or doing damage,
at Harrán el 'Awámid, the old Sun or Ba'al Temple
said to contain the well of Abraham, so accurately
described by my learned friend Dr. Beke.[8] The
second trip, in early December 1870, led me to the
third or southern building. On this occasion I had
less luck. The Ghiyás ruffians, not so much startled
by our sudden appearance as acting upon a concerted
plan, formed a line of some forty skirmishers, and
advancing steadily as if on parade, treated us to a
shower of bullets, severely wounding in the leg my
gallant companion Bedr Bey, son of the deceased
Kurdish chief Bedr Khan Pasha. Intending afterwards to visit their country, and knowing how fatal
to such enterprise would be a blood feud, we did not

---

[8] *Origines Biblicæ* (vol. i. p. 10, &c. &c.) treats of Padan-Aram; and
Jacob's Flight (passim) describes 'Rebekah's Well.'

return their fire, although, being well mounted, and the riding-ground being good, we might have brought down as many of them as we pleased. It was a fiery trial to us both; and we afterwards bitterly repented our forbearance, when we found out that the ruffians were to remain unpunished, and that after answering our message by a declaration that some other tribe must have attacked us, the cowards openly boasted of the outrage. After the degradation of Rashid Pasha, the mystery was cleared up. We found nothing remarkable in the Diyúrá except their excellent state of preservation where man has left them uninjured. Their site is the Lohf,[9] the Hebrew Chabal, the raised and rope-like edge of the lava torrents poured out by the volcanic Tulúl. The lip forms a true coast to the beds of the Damascus lakes, more properly called swamps, the *Fanges* of Spa, a salt clay-flat in the dry season, and a draining-ground for the Barada and the 'Awaj, when they have any water which the irrigated fields can spare. The style

[9] Murray's Handbook (p. 471) translates El Luhf, confounding it with 'Luhuf,' the 'Coverings.' It is a local word, and it certainly does not mean 'a narrow strip of the plain extending round the Lejah.' This is apparently taken from Burckhardt, who repeatedly uses the word 'Loehf,' but confines it to the 'borders of the Ledja.' We heard the people apply it to the lip of the Safá as well.

of building, similar to that of the Haurán mountain and valley plain, and to that of the 'Aláh or uplands north-east of Hamáh, is old Christian, dating probably from the days when the Benú Ghassán (Gassanides) of Yemen ruled the Damascene. The material is basalt, generally porous; the stones are for the most part rudely trimmed, and the shape of all the buildings is parallelogrammic. No. 1, the northernmost, has round towers at the angles; the western wall is on the ground, and the entrance is by the south side. North of this is a large impost of white limestone, the lintel of a gate leading to the cells, and the outlines of the church may still easily be traced. Below the south-eastern tower is a well, now dry, but showing long use by a deeply-grooved kerb-stone, and hard by is a sarcophagus used as a trough.

A ride of forty-five minutes leads to the central Dayr, which is made conspicuous bv a coat of dingy plaster revetting the lower third: from afar it looks more complete, but it is even more ruinous than the first. The large enceinte has fallen on the north-eastern corner, and the southern wall is hardly in better condition: the church on the north-west angle shows a cross cut in the stone, and remains of stucco

tinted green and red, both colours remarkably fresh,
like the Phœnician mason - marks found upon the
subterranean walls of the Jerusalem Haram. The
cells are on the south of the church, and to the
east is a small alcoved building partly fallen—it may
have been a refectory. The third Dayr lies some
two hours' ride from the second, and three from the
villages of the plain west of the Swamps. It is much
broken on the south and east; the south-western
wall may be climbed, and gives a fine view of the
'Lake Region.' A rough cornice runs outside the

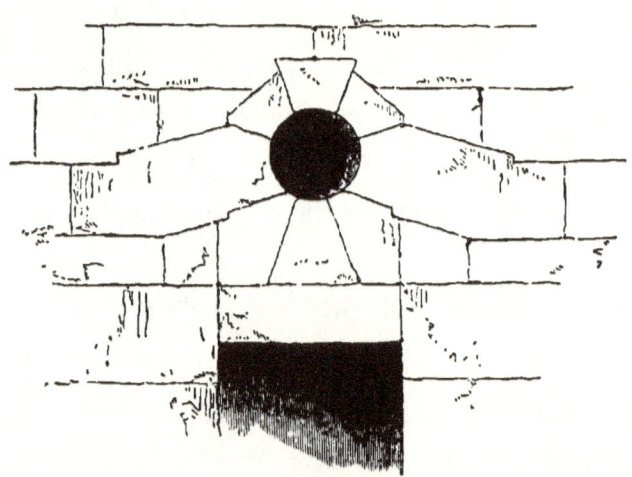

SPECIMEN OF RELIEVING ARCH WITH WINDOW (DAR EL HALIS, JENAYNAH).

building: the south-eastern door has a basaltic impost six feet six inches long by one foot two inches
deep; at each end there is a Greek cross, and in the

centre I fancied might be traced the letters K Y P
(Agios Kyrillos?).[10] The impost is relieved by another basaltic block forming a shallow false arch;
a favourite form in these regions, apparently derived
from local Greek architecture, which possibly borrowed it from the Hebrews. Inside the southern
door of the south-eastern room are three crosses,
and outside, on the north-west, are two red crosses
on a white ground, which might have been painted
a year ago. From this Convent the Kasr Kasam, by
some called the fourth Dayr, bore 189° (Mag.).

The Cœnobites who owned these religious houses
doubtless converted into smiling fields the now deso-
late clay-flats which separate the swamp beds from
the true coast of basalt. In the present day the
ruins might be utilised as guard-houses and dépôts
for irregular cavalry; and the latter, when happier
times come to the province, will patrol along this
line between the villages El Hijánah and Dhumayr,
so as to bar the Bedawin bandits from their occupation of driving the fertile Marj or Ager Damascenus.
To conclude this part of the subject: in Mr. Keith
Johnston's map accompanying these pages the

---

[10] The light was peculiarly unfavourable. Perhaps the letters in
question were merely faults in the basalt.

Diyúra will be found accurately laid down by com-
pass observations from various points north and
south; they are erroneously placed in the maps of
Van de Velde, Kiepert, Wetzstein, Porter, and others.

On Wednesday, May 24, 1871, we—that is to say,
Mr. C. F. Tyrwhitt-Drake and I, left Damascus, intending to crown a tour through the Hauran Mountain (Jebel Durúz Haurán) by an exploration of the
Tulúl el Safá. Little need be said concerning our
first eight days of travelling over a well-worn line,
except that we found the mountain, like Syria
and Palestine generally, explored as to the surface
in certain well-worn lines, and elsewhere absolutely
unknown, whilst the known part bore the proportion
of a single seam to the rest of the garment. My
fellow-traveller's map of our tour will be a considerable addition to our scanty geographical knowledge
of the Trachonitis. Its correctness will be vouched
for by the fact that his unbroken series of compass-
bearings through the Badiyat el Tíh (Desert of Wandering) and the rest of the Sinaitic Peninsula, which
' covered 600 miles of country, shows an almost
unappreciable error on subsequently joining a place
the latitude of which has been ascertained' (p. 7,
No. I. June 1871, *Palestine Exploration Fund; The*

Desert of the Tih and the Country of Moab, by E. H. Palmer).

We collected during that week some 120 inscriptions: of these some proved to be new, and after having been submitted to the Palestine Exploration Fund, they now appear for the first time ushered into the world by my old friend W. S. W. Vaux. They include the three lengthy copies of Greek hexameters and pentameters from the Burj or mortuary tower at Shakkah, a ruin long since identified as the Saccæa of Ptolemy.[11] The subject is a certain 'eutyches Bassos,' whose wife and family and concubine are duly mentioned with all the honours: only one of the three, that on the left hand, and five lines out of the eleven on the right, had been copied by Burckhardt and by the Rev. Mr. Porter (chap. xi. *Five Years in Damascus*),[12] who makes the era ' 71 of the city'= A.D. 176. The building was a reduced copy of the old sandstone

[11] The skulls and other remains taken from the basement will be found described by Dr. C. Carter Blake in the Appendix I. of Vol. II.

[12] But Mr. Porter has carelessly applied this era to an inscription at Burák (which he writes Brakh), where one of them begins with ΕΤΟΥΣ Ē ΤΗΣ ΠΟΛΕΩΣ. The months are Macedonian (Peritius and Apulcius); but, as Mr. Freshfield remarks (*Athenæum*, No. 2237, Sept. 10, 1870), they are used by Josephus, and consequently they might have extended to the Bostran era (A.D. 106).

tomb-towers on the Necropolis road of Palmyra, one
of those Viæ Appiæ which exist in all ancient Syrian
settlements. The inscriptions are incised over the
doorway of the first floor, which opens to the east;
and they are contained in three tablets, the centre
one large and the two side ones small. The framing
is the usual 'Lauh' or writing-board, everywhere used
in the East: and the triangular handles of the *car-
touches* are ornamented with flowers like roses, showing four, five, and six petals, that with four being
double. On the left handle of the large *cartouche* is
a scroll.

On Friday, May 26, we ascended the quaintly-
fashioned tumulus of clay, or rather indurated sand,
suggesting that volcanoes like those of Krafla may
here have existed : the surface was sprinkled over
with scoriæ. It is called by the people Tell Shayhán, from the Wali[13] or Santon, equally respected

---

[13] Usually written Wely. A curious misuse of this word has crept
into general Anglo-Oriental use. It literally means a favourite, or a
slave; hence, a slave of Allah, a saint. Saints are mostly buried under
buildings of four walls, supporting a dome : the splendid building which
covers the Sakhrah or rock in the Haram Sherif of Jerusalem is a well-
known instance. The traveller would point to such a structure and
ask its name. Hâzâ Wali—that is a Santon!—would be the native
answer. Hence, we read of a 'little white-washed Wely,' the receptacle

by Druzes and Moslems, whose rude conical dome of basalt, carefully whitewashed to resemble a pigeon-house, and springing from an enceinte of the same material, natural colour, crowns the summit. Here, when taking a round of angles, we remarked for the first time that local influences greatly affected the magnetic needle; and subsequently, on the Tulúl el Safá, one reading showed an error of ten degrees. I could only regret that the Committee of the Palestine Exploration Fund had refused the loan of a theodolite to one of their best observers, simply because his name did not conclude with the mystic letters R. E.

The ridge-like summit of Tell Shayhán—whose altitude is 3750 feet, and whose trend is north to south, with a slight deviation from the meridian—shows no sign of crater. In this matter it contrasted sharply with the neighbouring features—mere barrows pierced at the top, truncated, straight-lined

---

being confounded with the inmate, who probably never required such civilised operation. I observe that ' Nabi' (prophet) is about to share the same fate, the *contenu* being confounded with the *contenant*. Similarly, a popular modern book on Syria explains Tell (mamelon, hill, or hillock) by an 'Arab village,' because in Syria villages are usually built upon mamelons, hills, or hillocks.

cones, like the 'Bartlow Hills,' and similar formations in England. It was not till we had ridden round to the south-west, the route for Kanawát, that we

TELL SHAYHAN FROM THE NORTHERN GHARARAH.

sighted the huge lateral gash, garnished with stones, bristled with reefs, and fronted by heaps and piles of broken and disjointed lava, whence all the mischief had come. From the road its general appearance was that of a huge legless armchair. The first glance showed us that the well-known Leja, the Argob of the Hebrews, and the western Trachon of the

Greeks and Romans, famed in these later days for the defeat of the Egyptian Generalissimo Ibrahim Pasha, is mostly the gift of Tell Shayhán. It is, in fact, a lava bed; a stone-torrent poured out by the lateral crater over the ruddy yellow clay and the limestone floor of the Hauran Valley, high raised by the ruins of repeated eruptions, broken up by the action of fumaroles or blow holes, and cracked and crevassed by contraction when cooling, by earthquakes, and by the weathering of ages. This, the true origin of the Leja, is not shown in the maps of Mr. Cyril Graham and of Dr. Wetzstein (*ll. cc.*); and where they nod, all other travellers have slept soundly enough. In *Jerusalem Recovered* (p. 413), however, the Count de Vogüé, who visited Si'a *viâ* Kanawát, suspected the source of the Leja to be from a mountain near 'the city of Schehbah;' the name is not given, but it is apparently Tell Shayhán. 'Tel Shichhan' is distinguished by Burckhardt from 'Tel Shohba,' but he does not perceive the importance of the former. Dr. Wetzstein, on the other hand, rightly defines the limits of the pyriform 'Mal paiz,' placing 'Brâk' town (Burák, the Cisterns) on the north, at the stalk of the pear; Umm el Zaytún on the east; Zora' (Dera'áh, before alluded to), at the westernmost edge; and to the south, Rímat el Lohf[14] (Hillock of the Lip), a village visited by Burckhardt. His Leja receives a 'grosser lavastrom,' proceeding in an artificially natural straight line from Jebel Kulayb, and flowing from south-east to north-west. We therefore determined to inspect that feature. How far 'abroad' other travellers have been in the matter may be seen by the example of the Rev. Mr. Porter (*Five Years in Damascus*, p. 282). 'The physical features of the Lejah are very remarkable. It is composed of black basalt, which appears to have issued from pores in the earth in a liquid state, and to have flowed out until the plain was almost covered. Before cooling, its surface was agitated by some powerful agency; and it was afterwards shattered and rent by internal convulsions and vibrations.' The author, however, probably thinking of the Giants' Causeway, 'did not observe any columnar or crystallised basalt;' whereas both forms are common; the former imperfect, but the latter unusually well marked.

Two whole days (May 27, 28) were spent in studying the remains of Kanawát—the ancient Canatha and Kenath, a 'city of Og'—meaning the under-

---

[14] It is thus distinguished from Rímat el Hezúm (of the Girdles), Rímat el Khalkhal (of the Bangle), and a dozen other Rímats.

ground aqueducts : these bald ruins[15] are intricate, and they have been very imperfectly described. Burckhardt found only two Druze families in the place; now there are as many hundreds. We here, for the first time, remarked the 'beauty of Bashan,' in a comparatively well-wooded country, contrasting pleasantly with treeless plains and black cities of the Haurán. We copied many inscriptions, and found a few broken statues in the so-called Hippodrome : Mr. Tyrwhitt Drake fortunately secured a stone, which is evidently the head of an altar, with central bowl for blood, small horns at the four corners, and holes in the flat surface for metal plates. Upon opposite sides appear the features of Ba'al and Ashtarah of the 'two cusps' (Karnaim),[16] boldly cut

[15] The traveller fresh from Europe is immediately struck by the absence of ivy, which beautifies decay as far south as Portugal; and on his return to England is agreeably impressed by the difference. The plant is once mentioned in Scripture (2 Macc. vi. 7); but is it the true Hedera helix? I have nowhere seen it in Syria or Palestine, except at B'lúdán, where Mr. Consul R. Wood planted two stems near the western wall of his summer quarters. The plants did not die; but they would not grow; the cause might have been the normal pest, goats; or possibly a northern instead of the western presentation would have given better results. As will be found, however, in Vol. II. Chap. II., my friend and fellow-traveller found ivy growing in wild luxuriance upon the northern slopes of the Libanus.

[16] Murillo's celebrated Virgin absolutely reproduces the idea of

in high relief upon the closest basalt, with foliage showing the artistic hand, here unusual. We then

CHRISTIAN ALTAR AT-TELL MEFA'LANAH, NEAR KANAWAT.

travelled along the western folds of the celebrated Jebel Kulayb, and visited the noble remains of Si'a (ﺳﻌﺎ flowing—water or wine), a temple whose acanthus capitals, grape-vine ornaments, and figures of gazelles and eagles, all cut as if the hardest basalt were the softest limestone, showed the ravages of Druze iconoclasm. The blocks reminded me of the huge cubes of travertin, said to be entirely without

Ashtarah Karnaim. This fine relic was deposited at the Anthropological Institute, exhibited at the Society of Antiquaries, and forms the frontispiece of this volume.

cement, which mark the arch of Diocletian at Rome, ruined in A.D. 1491 by Pope Innocent VIII. Here we met with three Palmyrene inscriptions, which were sent for decipherment to Professor E. H. Palmer: it is curious to find them so far from the centre, and they prove that the Palmyrene of Ptolemy, and other classical geographers, extended to the south-west, far beyond the limits usually assigned to it by the moderns. Otherwise, as a rule, these Tadmoran remains are not very ancient, and they have scant interest. The name of an Agrippa occurs in the Greek legends at Sí'a.

Travelling from Sí'a to Sahwat el Balát, the village of my influential friend Shaykh Ali el Hináwí, a Druze 'Akkál or Illuminatus of the highest rank, we crossed three considerable 'Stenaás'—stone floods, or lava beds—whose rough and rugged discharge glooms the land. The northernmost flows from the Tell el Ahmar, a fine landmark; and the two others trend from the western slopes of Jebel Kulayb; all three take a west-south-westerly direction, and end upon El Nukra; for an explanation of which term see Dr. Wetzstein (p. 87): this flat bounds the southern and the south-western lips of the Leja. Thus we satisfactorily ascertained that the 'grosser lavastrom' is not in existence. Had it been there, we must have crossed it at right angles.

On the next day we ascended Jebel Kulayb, for the purpose of mapping the lay of many craters which appeared to be scattered about, inextricably confused. Viewed from the heights of the Libanus, the Anti-Libanus, and the Hermon, this mountain appears like a dwarf pyramid studding the crest of a lumpy blue wall, and it is popularly supposed to be the apex of the range which palæogeographers have identified with the Ptolemeian 'Alsadamus Mons.'[17] The name has been erroneously written by Burckhardt and others, Kelb, Kelab, and Kulayb (كليب), meaning 'Little Dog,' and is mispronounced Kulayyib: the orthography, as pointed out by Mr. Porter, is Kulayb (قليب), 'Little Heart,' or 'Turn-ing-point;' and the latter is doubtless the correct sense, as the central ridge of the Jebel Haurán here droops southwards into an upland valley. On a nearer view, El Kulayb has one peculiarity: where all the cones are barren heaps of red and yellow clay and scoriæ, it is feathered with trees up to the

---

[17] See, however, Dr. Wetzstein (p. 90). I avoid making extracts from his excellent *Reisebericht*, as my leisure moments at Damascus were employed in translating and in annotating it.

summit. The vegetation does not, however, as is the case in other parts of Syria and Palestine, interfere with the view.

At the village El Kafr,[18] south of 'Turning-point Mountain,' we found large flakelike slabs of fine compact crystalline greenstone, the first and last seen in this purely volcanic region. They are brought from a Júrah, or pit, known as Bátt (Settlement) Marj el Daulah, lying half an hour's walk to the east of El Kafr, and this is said to be the only quarry in the land. The exceptional outcrop may be connected with the greenstones, which in the northern part of the Sinaitic Peninsula overlie the true granites; and it will be remembered that these volcanic formations play an important part about the newly - discovered Diamond - fields of South Africa. Columns of granite and syenite are found profusely . scattered about the ruins of Syria, extending even

[18] M. Charles Clermont - Ganneau, Chancelier Dragoman of the French Consulate, Jerusalem, a man of singularly original mind and a conscientious student, suggested to me that Kafr and Kufr (a village and heathenism), being the same root, may bear the same relationship as pagus and paganus. It will be remembered that our heathen and the German heiden, to mention no others, are palpably derived from heath and heide—synonymous words showing that when Christianity became a state religion, the 'professors' of the earlier faith fled the cities and retired *in rus.*

as far as Palmyra. The modern inhabitants invariably declare them to be Masnú'a—of made stone:
similarly the Lyonnais, we are told, determined that
the pillars of the Athenæum or Augustan Temple,
built at the confluence of the Rhone and the Saone,
were artificial, because they were spotted red and
white. Those on the coast, as at Kaisáryah (the
Augustan Cæsarea Palæstina, the old Tower of
Strato), where they have been strewed to make modern jetties, were doubtless shipped from Egypt:
in the southern interior, the material was probably
conveyed from the Sinaitic regions *viâ* Moab and Ammon, even as in these unmechanical days basaltic
millstones are rolled into Damascus from the Hauran.
I found no traces of granite or of syenite in any part
of the Holy Land proper; but, as will presently
appear (Vol. II. Chap. III.), the northern cities, such
as Hamáh, were supplied with syenite by the 'Aláh,
where it exists *in situ.* This is ending at a point
where other men began. In the days of my earlier
residence in Damascus, however, the people had declared that they could show me the quarries; the
latter proved to be a reddish porphyry, and a pudding-stone, which, somewhat like the Giallo antico
of Egypt, takes a high polish. It is locally called

Shahm wa Lahm ('Fat and Flesh'); and at Ba'albak many of the well-educated applied the term to the true granitic and syenitic columns.

We rode from El Kafr through heaps of ruins and a tract of mulberry plantation to the Hísh Hamáh,[19] large vineyards whence the vine sacred to a goddess has departed, leaving only long broad ridges and occasional cairns of rough stone, like the débris of Cyclopean walls; over these in days of old the genial plant was probably trained, and they still serve to protect the country from the wild horseman and from civilised cavalry. ' Dousaria' is usually supposed to be 'a deity who patronised the cultivation of the vine.' I would suggest that the root may be the Arabic ' daasa,' whence the back-treading ceremony usually called ' El Doseh' at Cairo and in the Bukâ'a: thus the goddess would preside over the treading down and trampling upon the grape for wine. Farther south, my fellow-

---

[19] In Syria and Palestine a difference is made between Hishsh and Hísh (حِيش.), which will not be found in the dictionaries. The former is applied to a volcanic cone almost bare of vegetation in the Jebel Durúz Haurán; the latter means a ragged bush, as in the Jebel el Hísh, which continues the southern Hermon. Of the word Hirsh I shall presently speak. Burckhardt, noticing Hísh and Hirsh, says that both are applied to ' forests' where the trees grow twenty paces from one another.

traveller had remarked a scene somewhat similar. 'Among the most striking characteristics of the Negeb, or South Country of the Bible, are miles of hill-sides and valleys covered with the small stone heaps in regular swathes, along which the grapes were trained, and which still retain the name of Telcilat el 'Anab, or grape-mounds' (*Desert of the Tih*, &c. p. 21). In other places they were called 'Rujúm el Kurúm, or vineyard (vine?) heaps' (p. 45). The stranger who passes through beautiful Jaulán on the high-road from Banyás to Damascus first sees these cairns and swathes.

The broken ground at the foot of El Kulayb was bright with the Kiskays, a species of vetch; the Sha'arari, or red poppy; and the Sha'arari el Hamír, 'donkey' or yellow poppy; mistletoe, with ruddy berries, clung to the hawthorn boughs, as has been observed upon the olives in the highlands of Judea and in the regions east of the Jordan; and the vivid green of the maple and the sumach, whose berries are here eaten, contrasted with the dark foliage of the ilex-oak scrub, and of the wild white honeysuckle. Cultivation extended high up the southern flank, and the busy Druze peasantry was at work, the women in white and blue (Argentine colours),

each, like the Tapada of the last generation in
Peruvian Lima, sedulously veiling all but one eye.
Half an hour led us from the village to the base;
after eight minutes we left our horses upon a
sheltered strip of flat ground, and seventeen minutes
placed us upon the summit. The slope varied from
21° to 25°; the surface was strewed with light and
well-baked scoriæ of the usual red and yellow hues,
especially the former, and a little south of the apex
was a diminutive crater opening eastwards. The
aneroid showed 4·18 lower than the summits of the
Cedar Block, giving an altitude of 5785 feet.[20] The
hygrometer supplied by M. Casella stood at 0°.
The air felt colder than on the heights of the Hermon in June 1870, and the western horizon was
obscured by the thickest of wool-packs.

Amongst the thin shrubbery of Sindiyan - oak
which capped and dotted the western or rainy wind-
ward slopes of El Kulayb, whilst the eastern was
bare like its brother peaks, we traced on the summit
a line of cut and bossed stones set in Roman cement
and bearing 195°. We then visited three remarkable caves in the descent below the crater, and

[20] Mr. Cyril Graham computed it to be about 6000 feet above the
level of the Mediterranean.

opening between south and south-west. All are
evidently hand-hewn in the conglomerate of hard
red scoriæ; probably intended for rain-cisterns, they
have become of late years dens of Arab thieves.
The uppermost had an outer and an inner arch,
with a barrel-roof and a kind of Mastabah or bench
at the farther end. The second was double and
supplied with two entrances, the western semicircular, and the other square: in the inner north-
western wall of the latter was a cut lamp-niche,
and at the bottom appeared a recess resembling a
loculus. The third cave lay a few paces to the
south-south-west; the outside slope on the western
side showed a flight of steps much injured by wind
and weather. The ceiling, like those of the other
two, was arched, and the dimensions were 30 feet
deep by the same width, and 45 feet in length.
Light appeared at the northern or farther end,
admitted by a small shaft, and a rude pier supported the wagon-tilt roof. The walls were white
with etiolated moss which never saw the sun, and
we found nothing inside these cool quarters but
gnats and fungi.

The summit of El Kulayb gave us two important observations. The apparently confused scatter

of volcanic and cratered hill and hillock fell into an organised trend of 356° to 176°, or nearly north-south: the same phenomenon will be noticed in the Safá, and in its outliers the Tulúl el Safá, which lie hard upon a meridian. Thus the third or eastern-most great range separating the Mediterranean from the Euphrates desert does not run parallel with its neighbours the Anti-Libanus and the Libanus, which are disposed, roughly speaking, north-east (38°), and south-west (218°).

The second point of importance is, that El Kulayb is not the apex of the Jebel Durúz Haurán. To the east appeared a broken range, whose several heights, beginning from the north, were named to us as follows:

1. Tell Ijaynah, bearing 38°, and so called from its village: though not found in Dr. Wetzstein's map, it is rendered remarkable by a heap of ruins looking from afar like a cairn, and it is backed by the Umm Haurán hill, bearing 94°.

2. The Tell, rock, and fountain of Akriba[21] (Dr. Wetzstein's Akraba), bearing 112° 30′.

[21] In Syria and Palestine there are many Akribás, two villages of that name lying within a few hours of Damascus. The most celebrated of all is that built six miles south-east of Náblús, identified with Ekrebel (Judg. vii. 18), and afterwards capital of the Acrabattine district.

3. Tell Rubáh, bearing 119°; and

4. Tell Jafnah (Hillock of·the Vine), a table mountain with a cairn at the north end, bearing 127° 30′.

During the course of the day we passed between Nos. 1 and 4, and we assured ourselves that an observation with a pocket clinometer and spirit-level taken from the summit of El Kulayb was not far wrong in assigning 300 feet of greater altitude to Tell Ijaynah; that is to say, in round numbers 5780+300 6080 English feet. But though the Turning-point Mountain is not the apex of the Haurán highlands, it conceals the greater elevation to those looking either from the crest of the Hermon, or from any part of the Auranitis Valley; and while one standing upon the plateau which forms its base considers it a hillock, it appears from the lowlands and from the opposite highlands a mountain of considerable importance. Still it is hard to identify it, as Mr. Cyril Graham appears inclined to do, with the 'God's high hill, even the hill of Bashan,' spoken of by David.

A visit to the eastern settlements facing the Euphrates Desert—Sailah (Sâlâ, which Mr. Graham writes Sáli, and Mr. Porter Saleh); Bosán (Busán);

Sa'nah, Rámah, El Mushannaf,[22] Kariyat el 'Agaylát
('Ajílát), Tarbá, and Nimrah—convinced us that
the Jebel Durúz has greatly changed since it was
described by travellers and tourists. In these days
it becomes necessary for those who would enter
into the architectural minutiæ of Syria and Palestine, to carry with them the words of Burckhardt,
Buckingham, and Lord Lindsay; the old plans will
help to distinguish ruins which almost everywhere
during the past half century have been so damaged
as hardly to be recognisable. The general style
of building much resembles the 'View of Chamber
in Maes-Howe,' drawn by Mr. Farrer (No. 88, Fergusson's *Rude Stone Monuments*). Here the land until the last 150 years was wholly in the hands of
the Bedawin, especially of the Wuld Ali branch of
the great 'Anizah family, and of the hill-tribes 'Agaylát, Shitáyá, and Ghiyás, together with the others
included under the generic name 'Urbán el Jebel.
About that time it began to be occupied by the
Druzes, whom poverty and oppression drove from
their original seats in the Wady Taym, and upon

---

[22] This is apparently Mr. C. Graham's 'Beshennef' on the wild glen
that heads the 'Wádi en Nemárah.' In 1857 he found it, like Bosan
and Sailah, freshly colonised by the Druzes.

the slopes of the Libanus and the Hermon: Burckhardt found them settled here in 1810.[23] During
the last five years of Rashid Pasha's reign, not less
than seventeen mountain villages have been re-
peopled, and in the autumn of 1866 some 700-800
families· fled to this ' safe retreat.' We can hardly
wonder at the Exodus when we are told that nearly
half the settlements of the Jaydúr district, the ancient
Ituræa[24]—eleven out of twenty-four—have been with-

---

[23] In 1812, when he was at 'Arah, he was informed that one hundred
and twenty Druze families had exchanged the western mountains for
the Haurán.

[24] The classical Ituræa seems to have extended eastward of the
modern Jaydúr (Jedúr). St. Luke makes Philip tetrarch of Ituræa,
and of the region of Trachonitis—that is to say, of the two Trachons.
We also read (J. de Vitry) that the former bounded or adjoined Trachonitis on the west, and Gaulanitis on the north. Possibly it then included the Iklim el Billán (the Camel-Thorn region), which occupies
the south-eastern and eastern slopes of the Hermon; but it could
hardly ' lie along the base of Libanus, between Tiberias and Damascus.' In these days it is a tract of fertile but deserted country,
separated from Jaulán (Gaulanitis) by the southern continuation of
the Hermon range, a versant known as Jebel el Hísh (scrub-moun-
tain). Its *chef-lieu*, Kunayterah, is completely abandoned, though inhabited in the days of Burckhardt. I need hardly record my disagreement
upon this point with this traveller. He makes Jaulán a plain (?) south
of Jaydúr, and west of the Haurán, comprising part of Batanæa, Argob,
Hippene, and perhaps Gaulanitis. But I agree with him when he remarks that the maps of Syria are incorrect regarding the mountains of
his ' Djolan.' To the east, the Awwal Haurán, or northernmost extension of the Haurán Valley, divides it from the Leja (western Trachon).

in twelve months ruined by the usurer and the tax-
gatherer. The fugitives find in the Jebel Durúz
Haurán a cool and healthy though somewhat harsh
climate, a sufficiency of water, ready-made houses,
ruins of cut stone for building their hovels, land
à discrétion awaiting the plough, pasture for their
flocks and herds, and what they most prize, a rude
independence under the patriarchal rule of their
own chiefs. There is, it is true, a nominal Kaim-
akam, or Civil-governor, stationed by the Turks
at Suwaydah, with a handful of foot-police and a
few mounted irregulars. But the Nizam or regular
troops do not extend here; the imposts are moderate, the Bedawin cannot harry the people, and
Sergeant Kite is unknown. Hence, as has before
been remarked, the only peaceful and prosperous
districts of Syria are precisely those where exist
the maximum of home-rule and the minimum of in-
terference by the authorities.

It is hardly necessary to dwell upon the short-
sighted and miserable management which drives an

How small this is, and how densely populated it once was, requires but
a glance. The tetrarchs Herod of Galilee, his brother Philip, and Ly-
sanias of Abilene—not on the middle course of the Barada, but on the
western limits of the Haurán—had frontiers distant from one another a
single day's ride.

ROUND TOWER AT KANAWAT.

industrious peasantry from its hearths and homes
to distant settlements where defence is much more
easy than offence, and where, as Cromwell said of
Pease Burn, 'ten men to hinder are better than an
hundred to make their way.' This upon a small
scale is a specimen of the system which keeps down
to a million and a half the population of a province
which, though not larger than Lancashire and
Yorkshire united, in the days of Strabo and Josephus
supported its ten millions and more. The European
politician is not sorry to see the brave and sturdy
Druzes thrown out as a line of forts to keep the

Arab wolf from the doors of the Damascene. On the other hand, the antiquary finds to his regret the statues and architectural ornaments broken up, the inscribed stones preferred as being the largest and smoothest for building rude modern domiciles, and the most valuable remnants of antiquity whitewashed as lintels, or plastered over in the unclean interiors. Similarly in Ireland those venerable piles the Catholic abbeys were mutilated by the people for the benefit of their own shanties. Many cities of the dead, described by the guide-books as utterly ruinous, have now become villages which do not date from more than eight or nine years. The next generation of travellers will see nothing like the tasteful house of basalt, in fact a 'mansion of Bashan,' sketched by Dr. Wetzstein (p. 54); and the sentimentalist will no longer 'find the perfect stillness and utter desolation very striking and impressive.'

On the evening of Wednesday, May 31, we reached Shakkah, the old Saccœa, still showing extensive ruins and sundry fine specimens of Hauranic architecture; especially the house of Shaykh Hasan 'Brahim, with its coped windows and its sunken court. The chief public buildings will be alluded to in the Appendix. Here we were received by the Druze chief Kabalán[25] el Kala'áni, who, meeting us at Kanawát, had promised an escort to Umm

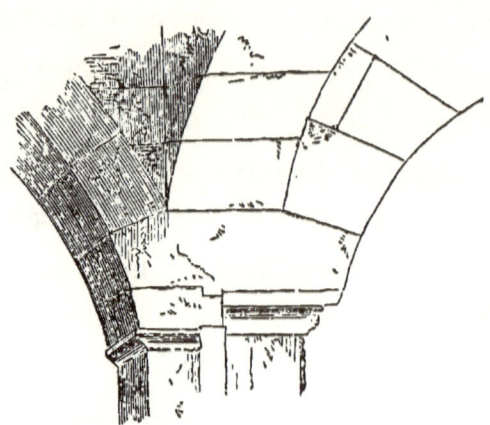

SPRING OF ARCHES IN ' EL KAYSAN,' SHAKKAH.

Nírán: he had, however, warned us that his people were on bad terms with the Ghiyás Bedawin, who were now in their summer quarters, the Wady Ruhbah (Spacious Valley), distant only about fifteen geographical miles from the cave. We were greatly disappointed in this man. He had travelled with Dr. Wetzstein, from whom he had received for a trip of fourteen days 365 napoleons, besides sundry rich presents, a sword, and a pair of pistols—and so say-

[25] Mr. E. H. Palmer has, I believe, suggested that this word may be a corruption of the Turkish Kaplán, a tiger. I have an indistinct memory of its being used as a name before the Turkish or Turkoman period. The Arabic signification would suggest ' acceptance,' *i.e.* from Allah.

ing he lied. After putting us off with the usual excuses, he fixed—or rather, after the fashion of the Druzes, he caused to be fixed—as his ultimatum forty napoleons for ten horsemen; a lesser number could not go for fear of the Ghiyás. We simply refused, and the ruffian then hung out his true colours, declaring that we should not leave his house before signing a paper to show that we had set out in safety and that he was not answerable for our future; that is to say, he was to be allowed to plunder us, and to produce satisfactory testimonials that he had stood our friend. We laughed in his face, told him to stop us if he dared, sent for our horses, and at once made for the little village of Taymá, lying about eight miles to the south-east. It was out of our way; but the Shaykh Yusuf Sharaf, the brother of one Hamzah Sharaf, a Druze, who had accompanied us and who is domiciled at Damascus, showed far more good-will.

The first necessary step before venturing into a fighting country was to dismiss all the *bouches inutiles.* I sent back to Damascus my good old Kawwás Amín Agha, who had brought no weapon but his water-pipe, together with the muleteer-lad Ali Shadádat el Halabi, and his two mules carrying

impedimenta not required for the desert. Old Hamzah Sharaf was also returned into stores (Bayt el
Mauni): a few years' residence at Damascus had
converted him to the most timid and feeble of men.
This change is often seen amongst the Druzes, a
brave and even a desperate people in their own
mountains, where they are 'everybody;' a residence
in or about the capital, where their numbers are
insignificant, appears utterly to demoralise them.
We engaged as guide the Zabtiyah or policeman
Ahmad el Shamí, who knew every inch of the road,
who had travelled over it twelve years ago, who had
never travelled it at all. During the night he was
begged by Kabalán el Kala'ání to leave us in the
lurch; but his hungry sense had scented bakhshish,
and he pooh-poohed all threats even mortal. He had
no gun, and evidently he never intended to use his
two rusty single-barrelled barkers. It was a treat to
see him doubled up—stockingless toes almost touching proboscid nose—bestriding his scurvy old gray
mare, a vicious Rosinante which he had bought for
a few measures of grain, and to hear the boastful
'cracks' about himself and his exploits, prolixly nar-
rated in the corrupt Damascus jargon so grating to
the ears after the pure speech of Nejd and El Hejáz.

We also managed to secure the services of a queer
old Bedawi, who answered to the name of Ráhíl.
Rachel—like Marie in France and Evelyn and Anne
in England, to mention no others—is not unusually
adopted by the wild men as well as by certain
Syrian Christians. Of course we did not ask his
tribe, for fear of being answered 'Ghiyás.' Talji
(Snow-ball),[26] an assistant Bedawi, was also hired to
lead the two mules which carried grain and water
for our horses and the scanty rations which we had
reserved for ourselves. The only attendant was
Habib Jemayyil, a Syrian youth of good family
from about Bayrut, who had during a year and a
half more than once proved his pluck. This poor
lad wept bitterly when he heard of my intended
departure from Damascus, although he knew that I
had provided for him. He was inconsolable because
he was too late to wish me a final farewell at Bayrut.
I do not imagine that the feelings of the Englishman
are less warm and acute than those of the Syrian;
but the former struggles to conceal his tenderness,
he hates 'scenes,' and he has had considerable experience in painful hours stoically endured. The

---

[26] The polite Arab version of our rude address 'snow-ball' is 'Y'abú
sumrah' ('O father of brownness').

1 7

latter has no object, natural or artificial, to hide his
heart. This is probably one charm which attaches
for life the memory of those dwelling in the chill
and misty north to their few weeks of Syrian travel,
despite the dragoman, the muleteer, and other in-
conveniences. They have gathered wild flowers in
mid-December—that is to say, they have for once
seen and felt the sun—to the benefit of the physical man, whilst the moral man has seen and felt
what attention and affection the people have to
bestow.

On the morning of Friday, June 2d, we quitted
the inhospitable Shakkah, leaving the churl Kabalán,
too surly even to return a parting salute, squatting
baboon-like outside the Kaysariyyah, a fine old ruined
pagan edifice converted to a Christian church, in
which he and his had built their wasp-nests of clay.
But we were not fated to set out for the wilderness
so slenderly escorted. A late feud amongst the
Druzes, wherein the villages of Dumá, Ruzaymah,
and Junaynah had united against Shakkah, Taymá,
and Nimrah, led to a conflict at the latter place, in
which fifteen men were killed and a considerable
number were wounded. The Druzes make their
own gunpowder—it may be known by the smoke

clinging to the ground and hanging long in air—
of the saltpetre which they scrape from the sides and
floors of their caverns,[27] of holm-oak charcoal, and
of sulphur bought in the towns. The Turkish authorities are as jealous about admitting ammunition as
arms to the mountain. The consequence is, that
the old long-barrelled guns can do little beyond
some 250 paces, and that an ankle-bone will stop,
instead of being broken by, a bullet. We had
prescribed for three youths, of whom one, Mahmúd Kazamání, had a shoulder-blade pierced clean
through : his style of treatment was inserting a
Fatílah (a wick or long pledget of cotton), which
perfectly well acted as perpetual seton. They were
ashamed of their kinsman's conduct, and like the
policeman, without dreaming of asking leave, they
mounted their best mares and dropped in to Taymá
by little parties, till at length we had a tail of six
men. During our first march they were reinforced
by an attendant who brought their rations, and thus

---

[27] It is also supplied by earth taken from ruined cities. The stuff
is first placed in large wooden colanders, with another vessel below ;
water is added, and after a single straining it is drawn off into copper
caldrons. It is now boiled for a day and a night; and then, on exposure
to the open air, impure crystals, which require washing, form round the
sides of the boiler.

our total amounted to the respectable figure of ten combatants—without paying forty napoleons.

We rather regretted than rejoiced at this act of supreme civility. It wasted our time in getting in forage for the quadrupeds; the barley required husking, and the peasant was busy with his harvest-home. Moreover in the short space of two or three days such a party cannot, without great violence, be duly disciplined. Each man carries out his own ideas: obstinate as a mule, he guides the guides; he squabbles to water his own mare first; he rides off the road, perhaps losing himself for hours; and he sings his war-song where he should be silent. Finally, the general object is to finish the distasteful, profit-less task as quickly as possible, without any regard to the leader of the expedition. There was scant chance of fight being shown by seven youths against 200 or 300 Bedawin, a force which the bandits can generally muster; and the value of the mares suggested that the tactic would be the Parthian, without however the firing *à tergo*. Still it was intended as an act of civility, and we could not refuse it without seeming ungracious.

The youths escorted us during two day marches; and on the second evening, bidding us adieu at the

Bir Kasam, they wended their way home. These
Druzes are, as the natives say, Shátcrin (clever) upon
their own mountains; beyond them they will hardly
house themselves, and they are as fish out of the sea.
'Their gods are gods of the hills.' Unable to walk,
our friends ascended hardly a single volcano with
us. They called for water every half-hour, pitilessly
draining our scanty Zemzemiyyahs.[28] They ate every
hour, and they clamoured for rest every two hours,
and for sleep every four hours. They complained
of the heat and the cold; of the wind and the scirocco; of the dust, the mist, and the dew. They
declared the fatigue of a half-night journey to be
intolerable; and often they would throw themselves
in the shadow of a rock, pitiably sighing forth the
words, 'Mayyat laymún'—lemonade! After the first
day's work, they turned black with sun-burning;
and one of them actually made for himself an um-
brella of leaves, fastened to a long stick. On the
march they were the most unmanageable, and at
the halt the most unhandy of Eastern men; in fact,
they were far more like fractious children. The

[28] The word is explained in my *Pilgrimage to Meccah and El
Medinah*, vol. i. p. 24. Damascus does not make the neat crescent-
shaped goatskin water-bags, which hang so handily along the saddle:
its highest art resembles an old leathern fire-bucket.

mares were as soft and lazy as their masters; they dropped their plates, and after the second day half of them were lame. Only one Druze youth, Mahmúd Kazamání, accompanied us to Damascus; and he received a five-shot revolver as an acknowledgment of his services. A similar weapon was also sent to the civil Shaykh Yusuf of Taymá—I only hope that it reached his hands.

Before leaving the Jebel Durúz Haurán, I can hardly refrain from giving my witness in the case of Porter *versus* Freshfield, which came on in the *Athenæum* Court about July 1870. Plaintiff had asserted that he was the undoubted possessor, in virtue of discovery, presumption, and occupation, of certain giant cities, belonging not to Fin M'Coul, but to one Og King of Bashan;[20] and he demanded an injunction against the defendant, who, wilfully mistaking sneering remarks and cynical allusions for logical arguments—ignorant moreover of the ethical law that 'criticism, to be effectual, must be honest' —had wilfully, scandalously, and injuriously asserted that most travellers in the aforesaid giant cities will be reminded, 'not of Og, but of the Antonines; not of the Israelitish, but of the Saracenic conquest.' The

[20] See preface, 2d edit. *Five Years in Damascus.*

suit ended *magno cum risu* by a verdict of the jury
of Reviewers, duly charged by Mr. Chief-justice Fergusson, that defendant and his party had 'disproved
the existence of any such giant cities whatever;' and
furthermore, that 'the so-called giant cities of Bashan were in fact no giant cities at all, but mere
provincial towns of the Roman Empire.'

To speak seriously, if it be possible upon such a
subject: my conviction is, that Messrs. Freshfield
and Fergusson, when assigning a recent origin to
the Hauranic ruins, are thoroughly justified, if we
assume the 'early date' to extend from the first to the
sixth or seventh century of our era. We cannot in
these days rank the Emim, the Rephaim, the Anakim,
and the Zamzummim with the Titans, the Goet-
magogs, the Corinæi, the Adamastors, and the Brob-
dingnagians, by translating the racial names 'physical giants.' They may have averaged a Patagonian
stature, say from five feet ten inches to six feet four
inches—the latter represented by the largest bones
which I brought from the Palmyran tomb-towers.
But the *charpente osseuse* of man is as unfit for
gigantic height as his digestive organs are to endure
through 600 to 930 modern solar years. All the
European and United States giants personally known

to me have been, with one exception, mild and
melancholy men — somewhat dull withal — afflicted
with weak knees and often with chronic diarrhœa.
'Whilst the dwarf struts the giant stoops.' When
skulls and bones, weapons and implements, of the
Emim, Rephaim, &c. shall have been produced into
court, and submitted to competent scientific authority, it will be time to believe that there were
physical 'giants' on the earth. Ewald is not justified in asserting that a primitive race possesses
gigantic stature more frequently than the advanced
nations; the contrary is, if anything, the fact. Barbarism stunts, civilisation favours, the growth of
man physically as well as morally. Privations and
penury are adverse to, comfort and luxury increase,
the development of human nature. Wealth prolongs, want shortens, the life of man. The process
of deducing the antiquity of a people from architecture assumed to be primeval is merely begging
the question; and the attempt to establish the
gigantism of a race from the height of its doorways,
or from the area of its halls, is hardly worthy of a
modern observer. The old Conquistadores of Bolivia,
finding the native huts provided with pigmy doors,
called the tribe Los Chiquitos, whereas the 'little

ones' proved to average above the ordinary stature of the so-called 'Red Man.' But to argue thus in the present age of the world is an anachronism. We want material proof to wait upon faith. To the iron bedstead of Og, which some have rendered a 'sarcophagus of black basalt,' we oppose the great bed of Ware.

MM. de Vogüé, Duthoit, and Waddington have published well-known plans and elevations of the chief Hauranic buildings. My fellow-traveller and I, thinking it just possible that the foundations might have escaped their observation, made a point of carefully examining them, and we found little, if any, difference between the groundwork and the superstructure. In buildings of undoubtedly high antiquity, such as Ba'albak, there is, I need hardly say, a notable contrast between the basement and what it supports. The point under dispute is simple, but it is not to be settled by an *argumentum ad verecundiam*, by the authority of Messrs. Graham and Robson. Let those who believe that any Hauranic building dates before the days of the Greeks and Romans, the Gassanides and the Palmyrenes, point out a single specimen of 'hoar antiquity;' show a single inscription, produce a single 'relic of the primeval Rephaim.' If Mr. Porter would draw or describe any building of the kind which has come under his observation, he would confer a lasting benefit on students, and he would offer a tangible opportunity of discussing the subject: at present there is none, nor can there be any whilst mere assertions and authority occupy the place of proof.

Finally, it appears to me that our visits to the 'Aláh district, lying east of Hamáh, have brought to light the existence of an architecture which, though identical with that of the Hauran, cannot in any way be connected with that of Og and his days. Separated by barely seventy miles of latitude from the southern basaltic region, the northern has also its true 'Bashan architecture;' its giant cities; its Cyclopean walls, and its 'private houses, low, massive and simple in style, with stone roofs and doors,' and huge gates conspicuous for 'simplicity, massiveness, and rude strength.' Throughout Moab, again, we find the same style, only modified by limestone being used instead of basalt. Did the Rephaim and Co., then, extend from the southern parallel of the Red Sea to within a few miles of Aleppo? Did a Turanian race in the trans-Jordanic regions stretch from north lat. 31° to north lat. 36°, through 300 direct geographical miles, leaving Damascus to average humanity? Evidently such an architecture is the work of necessity: stone rafters must be short, and they require supporting arches as well as large projecting cornices and corbels; we can hardly expect a sloping roof without wood for framework, or great height of wall where the ceiling is necessarily limited. Hence the 'simplicity' of the architecture; hence also its 'massiveness and its rude strength.' And, it must be remembered, these buildings are the reverse of gigantic. The temple of Bassæ shows stone rafters fifteen and sixteen feet long, whereas in 'Bashan' and the northern sister-region a stretch of eight feet is exceptional.

PART II.

DUMA and Taymá were visited by Mr. Cyril Graham (*loc. cit.*), who writes the latter word Theimeh, whilst Mr. Porter suggests that it is 'probably the Bezeine Burckhardt heard of.' It is described as 'presenting some of the most perfect examples of the old houses of Bashan.' We searched the village carefully, but we could not find a single specimen now remaining. The photographer should lose no time in visiting these lands.

A stiff scirocco began at 9 A.M. (Friday, June 2), blurring the outlines of the far highlands, before beautifully crisp and clear, and feeling at this elevation—4400 feet—exceptionally cool. During the day it worked round, as we had so often observed at Jerusalem, by the south to the west, probably the effect of the heated basaltic region on the east, which would make room for the sea-breeze. Clouds also appeared to the north-east and the north-west, and a distant rag or two of rain—at this season not unusual, we were informed—trailed upon the head of Jebel Durúz Haurán.

After a copious breakfast with Shaykh Yusúf we resolved to waste no more time, and at 1.50 P.M., though the water-skies were deplorably tearful, we rode down the hill-side upon which, like a Morean or rather Pelopónnesan township, the little Taymá is situated. Travelling toward the north-east, we passed on our left the Bir Arází, where the goatherds were watering their charges. It is so called from a village now ruined by the seizure of its lands, and lying à cheval upon both sides of the (Wady) Ghabíb el Jahjáh (غبيب الجهجاح): of these words the first is meaningless; the second, signifying a chief or an unworthy fellow, is sometimes used as a proper name.[1] Farther afield lay Dumá, Ruzaymah occupied by three Buyút (great houses where there are no small), and the Junaynah hamlet. We had visited the latter, which is still, as in 1810, 'the last inhabited village on this side towards the desert. We

---

[1] It was a favourite with the Harfush family, the feudal heads of the Metaweli or Shiahs of Syria.

were obliged to give up the two former, owing to the 'blood' between them and to our escort; these youths gave Ruzaymah the worst of bad names.

Our route now lay down the well-defined Wady Jahjáh, which after rains discharges eastward into the basaltic country known as El Harrah, the hot or burnt land.[2] To the right was the Tell el Barakah (of Blessing), a regular earthwork mound, with a quaintly-shaped mass of basalt, probably the top of a crater, hanging to its western flank. Beyond it rose the Tell el Hishsh, a truncated cone of bright red scoriæ regularly shaped as if heaped up by man. An hour's ride over rough but not difficult ground placed us at the Krá'a (القراع), the 'hard' or the 'firm,' which is simply a lava-torrent showing volcanic dykes, secondary craters, and blow-holes, with barrows arbitrarily disposed at all angles. The

---

[2] Dr. Wetzstein (p. 98) explains the term, which is applied to many similar features; and I have alluded to it in my *Pilgrimage to El Medinah and Meccah* (ii. 230-5). Burckhardt's editor confines the term too much when he hints that to the west of the Safá proper is a district called 'El Harra—a term applied by the Arabs to all tracts which are covered with small stones, being derived from Harr, *i. e.* heat (reflected from the ground).' This Harrah must not be confounded with that south of Damascus—a hitherto unvisited region, said to abound in ruins and 'written stones.' I have committed it also to the charge of my friend and travelling companion.

two normal types, the long barrow and the round
barrow, are sketched by Dr. Wetzstein (p. 13).   He
considers them to be big bubbles whose surface,
reticulated like the armadillo's mail, is almost invariably blown off at the top or split along the ridge
by the bursting of the gases which elevated them.
In some cases, however, the narrowness and sharp-
ness of the gashes at the summit and of the cleft
which bisects the length seem to argue that the
mere contraction of the cooling mass was sufficient
to part it; moreover, not a few have cross cracks
as well as longitudinal fissures.   This may especially
be remarked in the mounds or round barrows: where
the gases had been actively at work the whole head
had been heaved off as if a mine had been sprung
within the mound, and only a circle of stone remained visible upon the ground.

The basaltic formation of the Anti-Libanus, the
Hermon, and the Jebel Durúz generally may be
divided into five kinds : compact, porous, ropy,
crystalline, and subcolumnar.   As a rule, it is
quadrangular; in some places we found five angles,
but never more.   The pores are not rarely filled with
an opalline substance, like that of Aden, and with
that crystallised calcareous spar which has been

noticed between basaltic pillars by travellers in volcanic regions, and which forms a remarkably white
deposit in the black Wadys. Externally the colour
is a dull red, the effect of iron oxide; often it is a pure
lamp-black, which appears extra dark when parts
are overgrown with the hard and persistent white
cryptogams that make their base resemble calcareous
stone. This lichen is very difficult to remove, and it
renders many inscriptions more or less illegible. My
fellow-traveller, after long taking thought, hit upon
the common currycomb as the best remedy, and he
found it completely successful. Some men waste
much trouble and more time in cleaning before they
venture to copy inscriptions; we could almost always
tell by the look of the stone when it had been han-
dled by some such 'slow coach.' The basalt in the
classical buildings, when spared by vegetation, has
often assumed by age the mellow cream-colour which
we admire in the marbles of Tuscan Pisa; but the
fracture is invariably black; at first I often mistook it for reddish-yellow sandstone. The ropy
variety either stands up like a shield with concentric
circles of metal, or it lies upon the ground like trea-
cle freshly poured out. Nowhere in the Trachonitis
did we see the old and degraded material of a dull

French gray, and simulating slate, which is met upon the slopes of the Hermon; for instance, about the Kataná village.

Evidently the basaltic formation of the Trachons is of younger date than that of the Hermon. An active volcano always presupposes the neighbourhood of the sea or of some large lake.[3] This outbreak

[3] Upon this subject I venture to subjoin a correspondence which took place in the *Field*, Dec. 16 and Dec. 23, 1871.

The reviewer of the discussion about the 'Lake Victoria Nyanza' remarked, in two bracketed paragraphs, of which it is enough to quote one: 'It is a somewhat curious circumstance, that in the Royal Geographical Society Captain Burton made his assertions at two following meetings, and it was only at the second of these he was reminded, in a rather timid way, that what he supposed to be new was known before. So well known is the fact, that, when Humboldt supposed two active volcanoes to exist in the Thian-Shan, geographers were obliged to cast about for the sheet of water which was considered essential to be found near volcanoes, and adopted Lake Balkash as not too far distant. When the two Thian-Shan volcanoes of Humboldt, Peshan and Ho-chew, were shown by a Russian geographer, M. Semenof, to have no actual existence, there remained no exception to the well-known general rule as to the proximity of active volcanoes to water. Lyell has a theory about it which will be found fully detailed in his *Principles of Geology*; and, in fact, the statement is constantly repeated in manuals of physical geography. It is, therefore, not easy to understand either why Captain Burton should have claimed the idea as one specially his own, or why geographers were so slow and timid in reminding him that he advanced nothing new—unless, indeed, they imagined that he had something quite fresh to bring forward, which he would develop in. process of time.'

My text is left as I wrote it in September 1871—it does not seem

probably belongs to the days when the Eastern Desert—a flat stoneless tract, extending from the Trachonitis to the Euphrates—was a mighty inlet of the Indian Ocean. The northern limit of this

---

to claim any idea as my own — and the following copy was at once addressed to the editor of the *Field :*

'*To the Editor of the "Field."*

'Sir,—Perhaps you will allow me to notice in a few lines certain remarks which appeared in your last issue : I allude to two bracketed paragraphs—one long, the other short—in your correspondent's report of our third session of the Royal Geographical Society, when the discussion concerning the existence of the so-called "Lake Victoria Nyanza" took place.

'My attention has been strongly drawn to the fact that the existence of an active volcano presupposes the vicinity of a large sheet of water, salt or fresh, by my last two years' residence in Syria and Palestine. The Hermon, for instance, which I propose to place in a separate orine system from the Anti-Libanus, is distinctly basaltic to the south, to the east, and to the west. The lava evidently issued from the mountain-tarn known to Josephus as Lake Phiala, and to the moderns as Birket el Ram, or Tank of the Highland. On the other hand, as history tells us, the now shrunken " Waters of Merom," still subtending the southern flank of the Hermon, extended far to the north of the present site, and occupied, indeed, the whole southern third of the noble Cœlesyrian Valley proper.

'Again, when travelling about the trachytic region known as Jebel Durúz Haurán, which is to the Anti-Libanus what this is to the Libanus, and when inspecting the multitude of little volcanic cones called the (Northern) Tulul el Safá, I remembered my journey to Palmyra—that wondrous city built upon the very shore where the last waves of the wilderness break upon the easternmost outlines of the northern Anti-Libanus. It became apparent that the desert, a flat

extinct Mediterranean may be found in the range of limestones and sandstones, the farthest outliers of the Anti-Libanus, upon whose southern and eastern feet Palmyra is built, and which runs *viâ* Sukhnah eastward to the actual valley of the Great River.

---

and mostly stoneless tract, rich in salt-diggings, and showing maritime fossils, was the bed of an extinct Mediterranean — an arm, in fact, of the Persian Gulf, which during geological ages—before it was raised, not by a catastrophe, but by secular upheavals—occupied part of what is now the lower valley of the Euphrates.

'Returning to England, I spoke upon the subject with sundry geographical friends, two of whom were named at the meeting—Mr. John Arrowsmith and Mr. Trelawney Saunders. Both told me that they had not given the subject that attention which it merits. Mr. Saunders, indeed, quoted Thian - Shan as an exception. Mr. John Ball afterwards named Cotopaxi, distant about two direct degrees from the Pacific, but possibly connected by a tunnel, whose spiracles are the great cones to its west. Others have since pointed out Jorullo. In fact, I have never found my friends " slow and timid" when differing from me in opinion.

'The " somewhat curious circumstance" alluded to by your able correspondent loses all its " curiosity" when accurately stated. I have no right to originality of idea in the matter, after reading Humboldt and Lyell like most other men. I did not propose the theory as new, but rather as one still deserving our attention, and at any rate far from hackneyed even to professed geographers. I regret having conveyed a " wrong impression ;" but we are all liable to be misunderstood. I hope it is not my habit to claim what is not my own. And, finally, the *naïveté* with which a very serious charge is insinuated, if not advanced, argues either some hastiness of composition, or a somewhat lax morality in the larger sense of the term.

'RICHARD F. BURTON, F.R.G.S.'

At the ruin known as Kasr el Hayr (الخير, of the lowland where water lodges), in the Jayrud-Palmyra Valley, I found the stone composed mainly of pectines so loosely agglutinated, that the fingers could pick them out.

We crossed the K'rá'a in fifty-five minutes, and entered the Naka' (النقع) : the word, meaning a flat country where rain stagnates, is here applied to rolling ground of loose ruddy-yellow soil, the detritus of basalt, which during wet weather balls the feet so as to prevent walking, and in which during the dries horses sink up to the fetlock. This is the staple material of the Haurán Valley, and the Anti-Libanus shows it especially in the little basins, such as that which faces the well-known classic temple Dayr el 'Asháyir. The Naka' is distinguished by thin yellow grass and a scatter of stones, with here and there a deep hole dug by the rain-water, and enlarged in some cases by animals. We started two hares—an ill-omened move. The *Lepus Syriacus*, very little bigger than a young rabbit, has remarkably long cars, possibly developed by the perpetual necessity of being vigilant, and the coat is pale ash, very well suiting the ground. The rotten surface is dotted with Rujúm or stone-heaps, placed as landmarks, and there were not a few graves and Maráh (مَراح), where goats are herded during the spring. Here the Bedawin distinguish between the Rasm (رَسْم) or winter place, and the Maráh or Makíl used during the rest of the year. In the Libanus and the Anti-Libanus, 'Maráh' and 'Makíl' are most used; and the building may consist of dry stone walls, or of well-made and carefully-roofed huts, like the Greek καλύβια.

About 4 P.M. we halted to await the camels at a Rajm whose name was unknown. The shadow of the cloud crept over us like the beginning of an eclipse; a few drops of rain fell, and we were never without gnats or mosquitos, whilst fleas seemed everywhere to grow from the ground. The aneroid corrected showed 26·26, the thermometer 85° Fahr., showing that we had descended to 3780 feet; and the hygrometer stood at 13° dry. Our passage of the Naka' occupied two hours. Then ascending a hill-brow, which in Spain would be termed a Loma, we fell into El Hazir, 'the Hollows.' The only difference in the aspect of the land was a trifle more of stone, whilst the basalt was either lamp-black or snow-white with the usual cryptogam. These people borrow from the Bedawin a special term for every modification of terrain, however trifling. The lands to the north, a mixture of clayey soil and

stone, are called El Hármiyyah; the stony ground
to the east is El Wa'ar, the usual generic word;
and still on our right ran the stony Wady el K'rá'a,
which we had crossed and left southwards.

The term Wa'ar is explained by Dr. Wetzstein
(p. 15). It is not a little singular that the three
Hebrew words signifying forest—namely, Jear (Kir-
jath-Jearim, City of Forests), Chôresh, and Pardês,
a forest, a wood, and a garden—are all preserved
in Arabic, and are intelligible in Syria, with some
changes of signification. Wa'ar is rocky ground
especially hilly, with or without trees: Burckhardt
explains it as an appellation given to all stony soils,
whether upon plains or mountains. Hirsh, from a
root that means 'scratching,' is a scrub; and Furaydís
(παράδεισος, opposed to κῆπος, an orchard, and often
confounded in the English Version) is what our
imaginative travellers insist upon dignifying by the
name of a 'garden:' correctly speaking, it is a hunting-park.

From the Loma we had our first fair view of the
Safá. The little volcanic block, with its seven main
summits, is well laid down in outline by the Prussian
traveller (p. 7); to its south is an outlying scatter
of cones and craters, which the Druze youths called

Tulúl el Safá,[4] a term naturally confined at Damascus, where no others can be seen, to the northern offsets. A deeper blackness made the Safá stand conspicuously out of the Harrah; here the latter is a rolling waste of dark basalt, broken by and dotted with lines, basins, and pans of yellow clay, bone-dry at this season, and shimmering in the summer sun. These veins are generically known as 'Ghadír,' or hollows where water stagnates. The general trend is north-east to the Ruhbah, a long waving streak of argillaceous formation. In the far distance, extending from east to south-east, and raised by refraction above the middle ground of flat basalt, which lay beyond and below our rolling volcanic foreground, glittered the sunlit horizon of the Euphrates desert— that mysterious tract never yet crossed by European foot.

The Ruhbah was afterwards described to me by Daúd Effendi, Governor of Yabrúd, as a clay plain, dotted with stones (basaltic?) of egg size, gradually becoming larger as they neared the enclosure of mountain, but in shape always three-cornered. To the

---

[4] Mr. Cyril Graham (*loc. cit.*) prefers Safáh to Safá. But the names of regions terminating in Alif often take and reject indifferently a terminal Ha (ء) : cases in point are Leja or Lejah, and 'Ala or 'Alah.

north of the Kasr or Khirbat el Bayzá is a valley, upon whose stony sides are cut figures of men and beasts, and cuneiform perpendicular tracings which appeared to be inscriptions. Copies, he said, had been sent to Berlin, but they had not yet been deciphered. This account reminds us of Mr. Cyril Graham's 'written plain' in the Harrah, where he found hosts of stones covered with inscriptions in a character resembling the Sinaitic, accompanied with hundreds of such figures, representing horsemen, camels, leopards, deer, and asses. These 'writings' are reported to be scattered all over the Harrah, frequently where no traces of ruins remain. We here began to find out the right names of the several features, which had been changing ever since we left the Hijánah village, and to appreciate the precautionary measures by which the old Roman soldiery kept the Bedawin at bay. Far to the east, and in the heart of the Harrah, which is bisected by a military road, are shown their outstations, Khirbat el Bayzá, El Odaysiyyah, and Nimárah,[5] which must

---

[5] All visited by Mr. Cyril Graham. The word may be translated 'panthers' (Nimárat, not 'tigers,' as Burckhardt has it, p. 45); but the usual plural of Namir, popularly pronounced Nimr, is ' Numur.' He is, I imagine, in error when he writes for Odaysiyyah ' Tell 'Odza.' Dr. Wetzstein has, after the German fashion, ''Ode'sije ;' whilst Burckhardt gives ' Oedesic.'

have been impregnable to the wild man, and behind
which lay the waterless waste moating the fertile
regions of Syria.   But whilst civilisation in these
regions flows and ebbs, Bedawi barbarism exerts a
constant thrust and pressure from without: the moment he finds a weak place, he rushes at it with ruin
in his van and with savagery in his rear.   Hence,
according to no less an authority than Napoleon the
Great, the ephemeral tenure of empire in olden West
Asia.   As has been shown, under modern Turkish
rule the Bedawi is lord of the land, and he will
remain so till some strong European power revives
the strong system of the Romans.

At 6.20 P.M. we halted for a few minutes near
the Mintár el Kharúf (Look-out Place of the Lamb),
upon the borders of the stony black Wa'ar; a distorted and devilish land.   Here we remarked, for the
first time in Syria and Palestine, that the secondary
limestone, over which the basalt had been poured out,
was baked to a drab colour, and crystallised by the
heated contact.   In a subsequent page the reader will
find that parts of the 'Alah show basalt deposited
in shallow strata upon limestone.   As the shadows
of night deepened around us, and the clouds, which
at times shed heat-drops, obscured the moon, though

near its full, we could see nothing but the wild ink-tinted stone region, now in front, then on either side, and we could distinguish only that we were following—now crossing, and then recrossing—the course of a Wady which had become so winding that at times it ran south-east and even south, instead of north-east. We almost repented not having made the Bir Kasam, where we were sure of a full well, and having trusted to the Ghadír Abú Sarwál, the 'near' water of an Arab guide, whose 'karíb' may mean half a day's march. The young Druzes insisted upon hurrying on and chattering with old Ráhíl, who, mourning for his water, and unaccustomed to be flurried, more especially to be conversationised with, on the line of march, lost his way; consequently our small party of three was obliged to creep in the rear alongside of Talji and his camels.

At last, after two hours and forty-five minutes of this weary work, we called a halt, determined not to exhaust for the next day horses already thirsty. Our escort wasted enough water for a week, and were more utterly helpless than European children would have been under similar circumstances. The stallions had their usual stand-up fight, which injured the accoutrements much more than the wearers; and the camp, reckless of watch or ward, slept the sleep of the weary. Our day's march had been a total of six hours and forty minutes, which may be assumed at seventeen indirect geographical miles.

We left our hard beds at four A.M. on Saturday, June 3, and a few yards of advance showed us the Ghadír where we had been promised water. It is called Abú Sarwál (of the Man in Drawers); which, not having been used by the sansculotte Prophet, are 'un-Arab,' as a beard was 'un-English' in the year of grace 1830. This dwarf depression in a shallow Wady underlies a mass of rock which forms the right bank, and the yellow surface of caked and curling silt proved to us that it had been bone-dry for the last six weeks. Here we again fell into the 'Sultání,' or main track, which we had lost during the night; and after half an hour we struck El Nabash, a depression in the slope, thinly clothed with light green; it is said to reach the Ghadír el Ka'al (القعل). The name was not intelligible to our Druzes, and the dictionaries offer the usual extensive choice of significations common to Arabic triliterals: 'El Ka'al' may mean a miser, (a man) short of body, debased or unfortunate, and the forked stick that props young vine-branches, especially

about Hebron. Limestone appeared once more *in situ,*
and the surface was scattered with the normal snail-
shells: at this season the tenements were all 'to let.'
On the right of the Wady lay the shapeless ruins
of the village El Nabash—meaning a camel whose
sole is so marked that its footprint is at once known:
—the Bedawin had long ago caused the place to be
deserted; the left bank showed dykes and piles of
rough stones, which may have been homesteads or
graves. Ráhíl with his beasts, intending to cut off
the projecting corners of the Lohf, had pushed for-
wards to the north-east, the straight line for Umm
Nírán, whilst the Druzes had ridden eastwards to
see if the second Ghadír was also waterless. Presently a shot recalled us; and we bent south-east to
a point where a network of paths converged through
a stony tract, upon whose wave-crests appeared ruins
of small towers and look-out places. At six A.M. we
reached the Ghadír el Ka'al, thus expending a total
of eight hours and forty minutes upon a march which
all assured us may be covered by laden camels in
six hours to six hours and thirty minutes.

The Ghadír el Ka'al is, according to our guides,
the drainage basin of the Wady el K'rá'a; at this
season a mere sink without watershed; trending east

to west, it is about 90 yards long, and some 4 feet deep. It does not outlast the year, and its highest watermark never exceeds four feet above the actual level, when it would flood the eastern clay-plain. South of the pool rises a bank of basalt, showing two artificial watercourses, which may have been made by the now ruined village, El Hubbayríyyah ; and on the north is a narrow line of basaltic gravel and mud, like the floor of the Ghadír, here and there garnished with heaps and ribs of volcanic stone. The water was yellow, forming a green slime round the twigs which had fallen into it, and it abounded in small diatomaceæ. The birds were Katás (*Pterocles alchata*), a white-and-black duck, and the desert partridge; we saw tracks of waders, and we heard of wild pig. The vegetation was composed of the perfumed Shíh (*Absinthium*), the alkali plant, and salsolaceæ, whose lower growth was almost of mauve colour; a shrub with a mimosa-like leaf, and known as El Kharayríyyah (الكَّيَريَّة); together with the conspicuous blue-flowered 'Ghár,' so common to the Wadys of these regions.

We spent an enjoyable fifty minutes at the water, which lies 3290 feet above sea-level, and when the watch showed 7.15 A.M., we began to retrace the ground already covered. Presently we fell into the Saut (الصوط), or Scourge,[6] a line of drab-coloured clay which subtends the Western Lohf, or rim of the Northern Tulúl el Safá region, and which sheds to the south-south-east; the mud dries as the basalt splits, in lozenges and in five-angled flakes. The same phenomenon was remarked by Captain Forbes when travelling about Ellborg. 'The mud, in many cases, had separated itself into perfect basaltic forms, not always regular in their number of sides' (*Iceland*, chap. x.). According to Dr. Uno von Troil (*Letters on Iceland*, p. 283), this distinct and peculiar appearance has been noticed by him, not only in dry clay, but 'even in starch when dried in a cup or basin.' Here the country was good travelling; we saw many old footmarks of sheep, goats, and shod horses; overlying them, however, was the fresh spoor of a dromedary, which still bore the sign of last night's heat-drops. The rider was evidently bound, like ourselves, from Shakkah, or an adjacent village, for the north-eastern regions, where the Bedawin dwelt; but not on a visit of curiosity, nor for the

---

[6] It may also mean a place where water collects: Arabic contains several hundred terms which express every possible modification of this common geographical feature.

purpose of exploration; and we gave the ill-omened
footprints all the significancy which they deserved.
We had set out on a Friday, we had seen a crow,
and two hares had crossed our path.   Hard on our
right hand rose the Lohf, a crusted embankment of
black and 'mailed' basalt, somewhat resembling the old
Saracenic revetments of Hums, and of David's Tower
at Jerusalem.   It is evidently the bank formed by

LOHF BAGHAYLAH : THE TULUL OF THE SAME NAME AND JEBEL ZIRS.

the lava torrent when beginning to cool, and thus
becoming able to resist, like a dyke, the pressure
and thrust of heated matter in its rear.   The height
varied from 30 to 50 feet without a break, and the

cast - iron prism projected into the yellow wady capes, bluffs, and headlands, separated by dwarf bays. The feature is familiar to those who have crossed the Leja, and it gives the volcanic patch the shape of a frying-pan without the handle. We did not, however, sight the Eastern Lohf of this north-western dependency of the Safá; and when we thought to see it, the elevation proved to be merely an independent fragment of eruption. Small ruins and look-out places of the liveliest coal-black crown the coping, and in places where the outline droops it is crossed by paths practicable to horsemen. As the attack must be made in front, a small party taking shelter behind any natural breastwork on the crest could easily defend itself against Arabs in force. Near a spot called El Hezábah (الحزابة) we ascended the summit, and found the shape a tolerably regular prism, disposed in sections at right angles like giant fortifications. Here the western side was lamp - black, and the eastern was white with the normal cryptogam; there the rule was reversed; in fact, we could only determine that the lichen least affects the sunny southern frontings.

After one hour and fifty minutes up the Saut, which often became a scatter of stones, apparently

swept down from the Lohf, we turned sharp to the
right, and crossed the lava ridge-lip where it had a
break.   Here it was subtended by several parallels,
which bore much the appearance of earthworks and
cavaliers.   Within the rim the surface of the naked
plateau was rough to the last degree: now the
basaltic barrows showed heads blown off, where the
gases had converted them to suffiones and fumaroles;
then they were domed, where the force of the explosion was insufficient to burst them.   Upon the slopes
here and there lay concentric circles of ropy lava,
as if poured out upon a level and then tilted up.
This shield-like formation is not uncommonly seen in
the contortions of the limestone strata; near 'Cana
of Galilee' there is a remarkable specimen.   The surface was everywhere striated with longitudinal gashes
and fissures; between the lava-passages were circles
and long streaks of stoneless yellow clay, now dry
as summer dust, but impassable during the rains,
except by working round the stone-scattered edges.
It was a grim and grisly scene of volcanic struggle
and devastation, mocking all the ruins ever made
by 'Tamerlane' el Wahsh;[7] a landscape spoiled and

---

[7] The civil name of this mighty devastator is the Amir Taymúr, a
corruption of Dimir, Lord Iron. The Persian Shiahs, who hated his

broken to pieces, blistered, wrinkled, broken-backed, and otherwise tormented; here ghastly white, there gloomiest black, and both glowing under the gay sunlight of a Syrian June. The altitude was 1300 feet, some 900 below that of Damascus city; but the light sweet breath of the morning from the north ceased when we left the Ghadír, and the shape as well as the components of the Wa'ar or Trachon admirably condensed the heat; the air danced and recked upwards, the abnormal evaporation affecting man and beast with intolerable thirst.

The only sign that human foot ever trod this inhospitable wild was here and there a goat-Maráh, with a Mintar (sentinel-place) perched on some commanding spot. Bedawin, however strong and however safely camped, never fail to keep, at all hours of the day and sometimes at night, as sharp a look-out as the most prudent of old 'salts;' and their little parties of scouts, reduced not unfrequently to

---

orthodoxy, nicknamed him Taymur-i-lang, *i.e.* limping Taymur, whence our Tamerlane. He is called El Wahsh (the wild beast) by the Damascans, because he rode his horse over the corpses of their ancestors, whilst his people played at Chaugán or hookey with the heads of the slain. The city caught a Tartar when the Amir Taymúr stabled his horse in it. In the Haurán he is still accused of filling up the wells, and of throwing quicksilver into the springs so as to prevent the water rising to the surface.

a solitary tribesman perched on a Tell-top, are the
first to see and to be seen by the strangers. Our
guide, and the two Bedawin, apparently knew nothing of the way, and the latter were confused by
the perpetual interpellations of the Druze Mashaikh
(Chiefs). The road was simply a goat-track over
the domes of cast-iron ovens in endless succession.
I remember it as truly a 'maniac ride.' We should
have taken the south-eastern line, where the land
is higher and flatter: we preferred winding from
east to south, when our course was north-east. No
less than five halts were required, after periods
varying from forty-five minutes to one hour and
five minutes, in order to await the camels, of which
one was badly cut by the sharp basaltic edges. At
the Rajm el Shalshal ('of dripping water'), where
we took refuge in a shady fissure, we again saw
traces of our friend on the dromedary. We were
reminded of the world of life by the usual swarms
of flies, gnats, and fleas, and in one place by a
quaint pair of rock lizards, possibly Baron et feme ;
one of a bright French blue, the other with azure
head and coat of lively green and red. Our Arabs
of course called them Hardún (chameleons), like the
Brazilians of the São Francisco River and their

'Cameleâo.' The queer beasts, bobbing their heads with the action of the black lizard, that mocks the Moslem at his prayers and prostrations, watched us curiously as we watched them.

We were presently surprised, at 4.20 P.M., by seeing the advanced party spring suddenly from their mares, and by hearing the welcome words, 'Umm Nírán.' Day was wearing on, and the attempts at pointing out the site had become vague in the extreme. A night march over such a country would have been worse than a moonlight tramp up to the crest of the Camarones Mountain, or of Santa Isabel, Fernando Po. The transit of the ugly monotonous Wa'ar had occupied four hours twenty-five minutes, and the day's journey a total of eight hours fifteen minutes. From Taymá we had spent seventeen hours, whose result was a distance of twenty-three and a half direct geographical miles.

We hastened to inspect a feature concerning which we had heard so many curious and contradictory tales. It lies at the north-western foot of a scarped, round-topped, and fang-shaped block, which the Arabs call, from its likeness to a grinder tooth, El Zirs (ضرس). Dr. Wetzstein was therefore misled in changing it to El Turs (the Target).

MOUTH OF THE CAVE AT UMM NIRAN.

This accomplished writer, who was a philologist rather than a topographer, did not, I have said, visit in person the Umm Nírán and the Tulúl el Safá; hence his description of the former and his map of the latter abound in inaccuracies, which contrast remarkably with the exact descriptions of what he really saw. The mysterious cave, occupying the eastern slope of a rounded bubble of basalt, opens to the S.S.East (133°) with a natural arch of trap, which at first appears broken into artificial voussoirs; and it is fronted by a circular

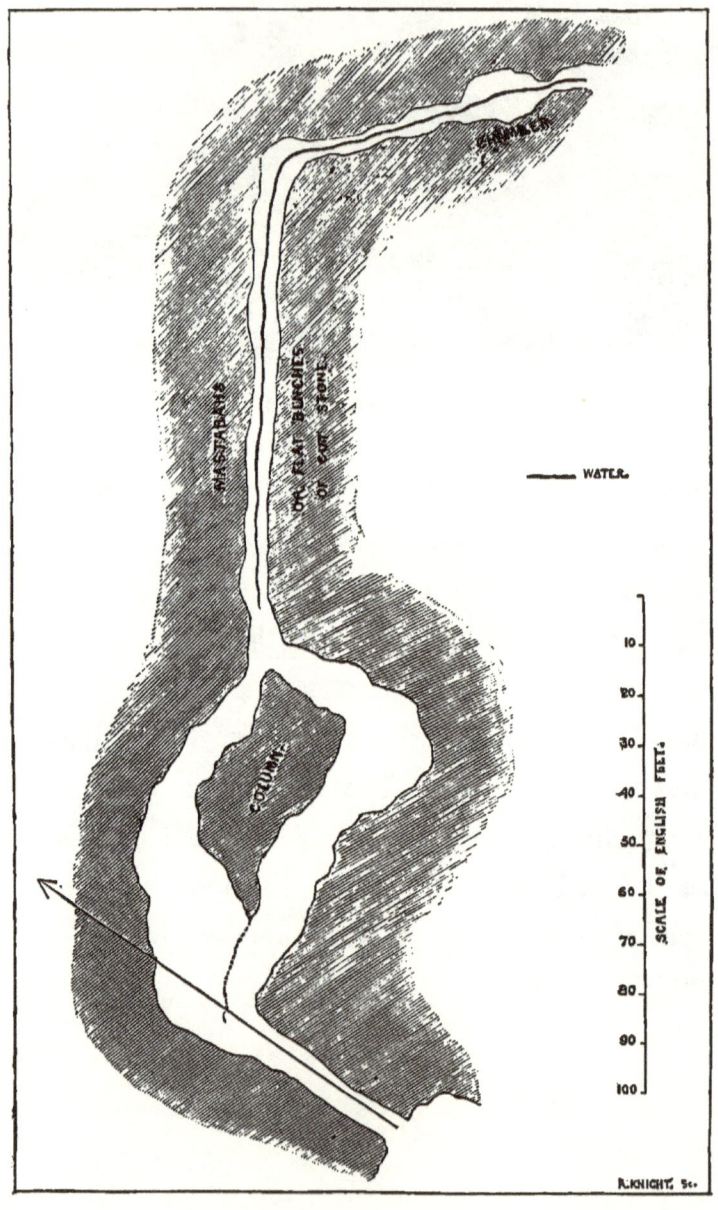

hollow of the usual yellow clay, to which rude steps
lead from the stony eastern edge. There is another
approach from the west, and both show that at times
the water is extensively used. All above the cave
is dry as the Land of Sind, and in the summer
sunshine the hand could not rest upon the heated
surface. After rain, however, there is evidently a
drainage from the fronting basin into the cave.

The preceding plan (p. 223) by Mr. C. F. Tyrwhitt
Drake will explain the form of Umm Nírán better
than any words of mine. The floor, coated with shallow dry mud, is of ropy and other basalt; therefore
the entrance, low as it is, can never have been more
than a few inches higher. The slope is easy and
regular; but we found no sign of the inside 'trep-
pen' alluded to by Dr. Wetzstein (p. 38). The roof
displays a longitudinal ribbing, as if the breadth
had, near the entrance, been almost doubled by the
handiwork of man. A sensible widening with a loz-
enge-shaped pier, the rock being left to act column,
succeeds the narrow adit through which a man
must creep; and boulders are heaped up along the
right side, apparently to show the way. Passing
this bulge, and entering a second tunnel, we came,
after a total distance of some 200 feet, to the wa-

ter; a ditch-like channel, averaging four feet in breadth, with mud-clothed Mastabahs, or flat benches of cut rock on either side, varying from two to six feet wide. The line then bent from N.N.East at an angle of 50° to the right (north-east). Here, by plunging his head below the water, and by raising it beyond where the roof-spine descended, my companion found an oval-shaped chamber, still traversed by the water, which gleamed fitfully in the candle-light. He could not, however, reach the end; a little beyond this point the rock ceiling and the water definitively met. The supply was perfectly sweet, depressing the immersed thermometer from 74° in the air to 71°-72°. The atmosphere was close and dank; and whilst the roof was an arid fiery waste of the blackest lava, the basalt ceiling of the cave sweated and dripped: apparently simple evaporation could not have been the only cause. The water, which varied in depth from a few inches to mid-thigh, is said by the Bedawin to be warmer in the morning; but that may be explained by the air being colder to the sense. The taped length of the tank was 140 feet, making a total of 340 feet; but the extent may be greater. According to the Arabs, it is supplied by springs as well as by rain,

and the hottest season fails to dry it. The altitude
by aneroid proved to be 2745 feet, or 446 feet above
our lowest level. A water-scorpion was the only
living thing found in the cave.

This curious tunnelled reservoir is evidently
natural; but it has been enlarged and disposed by
man. There is no local legend concerning the origin
of a work so far beyond the powers of the Bedawin
past and present; we could only conjecture that it
was made by some of the olden kings of the Damascene, who, finding a fountain and a rain-cistern
so inconveniently placed as to be almost useless,
enlarged the approach for the benefit of their flocks
and herds intrusted to Arab care-takers. The Bedawin knew naught of cut blocks, written stones,
or of ruins in the neighbourhood; and we could
see only the rudest of dry walls, used to shelter the shepherd from wind and rain. As regards
the Shitáyá clansman mentioned by Dr. Wetzstein
(p. 38), who went in with black locks, and who
after the third day came out with white hair, such
a visitor in such a place would be easily frightened out of his wits, and, losing his light, he would
grope and wander round and round the pier, in
mortal dread of the Jánn (genii) and other crea-

tures of his fancy. We carefully searched the bays and enlargements in the two branches around the pier, and we found no trace of human bones. Of course the Mother of Fires, which should be called the Father of Waters, situated and constructed as it is, would naturally be a theme for the grossest exaggeration. One of our Druze lads declared that he had taken an hour to reach the water; we timed the approach, which was on all-fours, and found it occupy three minutes.

Our straggling and losing way upon the march was the more regretable, as it prevented our inspecting the mountain El Zirs, whose bluff northern face, distant about three miles, suggested the necessity of a long détour. The 'Grinder-tooth' is the northernmost apex of the Tulúl el Raghaylah (رغيله), which Dr. Wetzstein's map, adopting the apocope of the Fellahin, erroneously calls El Ġele (Anglicè Ghaylah).[8] The Raghaylah range has three well-

---

[8] They will sometimes also, like the Bedawin, broaden the word to Ghāilah, as if written غايله. Raghl, the root of Raghaylah, means sucking (as a lamb sucks the ewe), grain fresh-formed in the ear, or fulness of grain in an ear of corn. Raghlat is also sucking, or a small animal (*e.g.* lamb or kid). Ghayl and Ghilat have also the signification of sucking; but the former more generally denotes thickly-tangled trees: hence Umm Ghaylán (literally Mother of Thickets), Egyptian thorn, *Acacia Nilotica.*

marked summits, without including the Hlewá (حلیوا)
—an un-Arabic term, which some pronounce Hle-
wiyyá (حلیویّا)—and other cones to the east, or the
detached volcanic cone El Mafradah (the Solitary),
which lies upon the southern decline. The minor
altitudes of all these Tulúl are technically known
as El Istirát, or the Outliers: thus the Bedawin say
Istirát Umm Izn, Istirát el Dakwah, and so forth.

We are now at the southern limit of the northern
Tulúl el Safá, a projection from the Safá proper,
the eastern Trachon (τράχων, or rough range) of
the classics, which apparently has been so puzzling
to modern translators. Strabo (book xvi. chap. 2,
par. 20, Hamilton and Falconer's translation; London, Bohn, 1857) says: 'Above [read beyond] Damascus are the two hills called Trachones [read
the two so-called Trachons, namely the twin Wa'ars
of the Leja and the Safá]; then towards the parts
(*i.e.* south and south-east) of Damascus occupied
by Arabians and Ituræans promiscuously are mountains of difficult access, in which are caves extending to a great depth. One of these caves (Umm
Nírán?) is capable of containing 4000 thieves.'
Pliny (vol. i. chap. 16, Bostock and Riley; Bohn,
1855) reckons Trachonitis amongst the Tetrarchies.

The 'revolt of the Trachonitis' is the subject of Josephus's essay (book xvi. chap. 9, *Antiquities of the Jews*); but though familiar with the sea and the shores of Tiberias, he evidently, knew nothing of the northern regions. Ptolemy (chap. xv. table 4) mentions among Syrian mountains the Alsadamus, whose centre would be in E. long. 71° and N. lat. 33°; and the *Bathaneæ provinciæ* (Bataniyyah, Bashan), *a cujus orientali parte est Saccæa* (Shakkah). *Et hujus sub Alsadamum montem sunt Trachonitæ Arabes.* Popular works (*e.g.* Smith's *Classical Dictionary*, sub voce) of course repeat that 'Trachonitis was for the most part a sandy desert, intersected by two ranges of rocky mountains called Trachones;' a grand 'elimination' from the self-conscious depths of the author. Similarly in the *Concise Dictionary of the Bible*, Trachonitis is represented 'to have included the whole of the modern province (!) called El Lejâh, with a section of the plain (?) southward, and also a part of the western (add eastern) declivities of Jebel (Durúz) Haurân. This may explain Strabo's two Trachones.' One fortnight's excursion will, it is hoped, introduce correct topography to future educational writers. The fact is, that the Safá or eastern Trachon, together with the western—

that is to say, the Leja proper—would be included in the Tetrarchy of Trachonitis, which thus extended from Auranitis, or the Haurán[9] Valley, to the Ruhbah Valley and the Hammád or Desert of the Euphrates.[10]

The shape of the Tulúl el Safá region is pyriform, like the Leja. The lone El Mafradah forms the stalk; the bluff end to the north is the Tell Shámát, together with its dependencies abutting upon the limestone range of the Anti-Libanus, at whose base runs the desert road to Karyatayn and Palmyra; whilst the boundary to the north-west is represented by a dark outpouring of lava known as the Arz el Jaháshiyyah (of Asses' Colts?), and looking like the dry bed of a torrent, brown and rust-stained upon the yellow surface of the limestone. We did

---

[9] Haurán is popularly derived from Hor (חור), a hole, a cave, therefore cognate with troglodyte or Horite—Firlbog, Terrigena, Cavigena —which is not satisfactory. The word occurs once only in Scripture; Ezekiel (xlvii. 16) speaks of ‘Hazar Hatticon, which is by the coast of Hauran.’ Haur in Arabic means only a poplar, and the region is as a rule utterly destitute of trees. The Hawárinah or actual tenants of the Haurán have a very bad name, and as far as my experience enables me to judge they merit it: Hayyarú Rasúl Ullah salasah marrát (‘They bewildered the Prophet of Allah three times’), is the punning explana- tion of the Arabs.

[10] Burckhardt had heard that this Hammád is sandy.

not lay down the eastern limit; but the villagers of Dhumayr pointed out certain unnamed cones ('Istirát') depending upon the Umm Rakíbah: this frontier may perhaps be extended to Jebel Says (the Ses of Dr. Wetzstein's map), bordering upon the Hammád region. The western Lohf projects a few yards beyond the second or middle Dayr, and the last heights in this direction are the outliers of Jebel Dakwah.

After bathing in the Mother of Fires, and a comfortable sleep upon the lap of Mother Hertha, we set out, in a cool west wind, at 5 A.M. on June 4th. Striking north, with a *tantinet* of westing, we made for the great red cinder-heap known as Umm el Ma'azah (Mother of the She-goat). The ground suggested that the eastern Lohf was not distant: it was mostly stony, and we passed on the right a crater whose surroundings when viewed from lower levels, the surface over which we were travelling, appeared like giant earthworks. The course was very devious, and frequently a stiff descent compelled us to dismount: at the base of the wall we found a dry well and a stone trough. After one hour and thirty-five minutes, in which we covered perhaps four and a half direct geographical

miles, we halted for observations at the southern
slope of the Umm el Ma'azah, and we then fell into
the trodden way which winds round the west of
this volcano. It leads from the Ghútah section of
the Damascus plain, about Harrán el Awamíd in
fourteen hours—twelve upon a good dromedary—
to the Ruhbah Valley. No Arabs, however, had
passed since the spring rains, as the camel-chips all
well washed showed, and our escort did not for
five minutes cease singing their war-song.

As we wound round the western side of the
great cinder-heap we found its crater in its lap, as
if it extended far out upon the plain two fat red
thighs, the Jarcath (ירכה literally thighs, hips,
loins) of the Hebrews, applied to the Libanus and
Mount Ephraim, the East African Tumbo la Mlímá
(Belly of the Mount). After twenty minutes of slow
march we ordered the camel-men to make straight
for the Bir Kasam, whilst we ascended a remarkable
feature, the Tell 'Akir (by the Bedawin pronounced
El 'Ajir).[11] Usually known as the Shaykh el Tulúl,

[11] By changing the Káf (ك) into Jím (ج). So they say Jiblah for
Kiblah, and Jaryatayn for Karyatayn. In the Hejaz the words would
become Giblah and Garyatayn. The eastern Bedawin, however, like ·
the Syrian, prefer Jawásim to Kawásim (the name of the noted pirates
of the Persian Gulf). There are several 'Akir villages in Syria and

this 'Headman of the Hillocks' rises some seven statute miles north, with a suspicion of westing from the Umm el Ma'azah. We then rode up in one hour and twenty minutes to the foot of the cone, which springs from a high plane with large outliers trending to the south, with a little easting. Seven minutes were spent in stiff climbing up the ridgy surface of exceptionally light and thoroughly burnt scoriæ, dark below, and above light red and yellow, containing sulphur. The angle of the north-western slope was 19° 30′; that of the north-eastern 22°; the southern range up which we walked showed 22° 30′; and the stoniest part above the lateral folds reached 24°. The altitude proved to be 3328 feet.

We had expected to stand upon the lip of a large crater; we found only a tall horseshoe open to the north and the north-west, without any sign of a bowl. Accordingly we ascended the eastern or highest point for a better view of the peculiar scene before us. Seen from this elevation, the volcanic Tells and craters, modern, tertiary and

Palestine; and one of them in the Philistian Plain represents the Ekron or Accaron of old. The word means a high sandhill, or (large tracts of) unfertile sands.

pleiocene, which before seemed scattered in wild confusion, fell into regular lines, with trifling interjections, towards north-south, slightly deviating to east-west. The parallels are distinctly three. The middle range is represented on the north by Umm Izn (Mother of an Ear), so called because the table-top, bearing 246°, has a projection at one end, a kind of 'cock-nose' breaking the straight line of features : the word is classical; we read in Joshua (xix. 34) of Aznoth Tabor, the ears or projections of Tabor. About the centre of the line stands the Monarch of the Mounts, Tell el 'Akir, and to the south project the Zirs and the Raghaylah blocks. The map will give the best idea of the meridional lines which flanked us on the east and west. The ground at the foot of El 'Akir was of silt upon a limestone floor, and its high level explained how from afar a yellow sheet appears shelving up to the very bases of the pyramids: it here represents the Arz Tanánír (Land of Gathering Water),[12] the system

[12] The Hebrew Tanur in our version is translated furnace; but it mostly applies to a baking-oven. The latter in modern Arabic would be Furn, opposed to Tannúr (plural Tannúrín and Tanánir), a smelting-place. In Jerusalem the Furn is still called Tabúnat. Tannúr also means the surface of the earth, or any place where water gushes out, or gathers in a depression.

of shallow and heated basins between the Hijánah village and the Dayrs or monasteries. The volcanoes rise from this sterile investment in naked heaps, black and white, red and yellow; they are conical, table-topped, or saddle-backed, whilst inky dots show the smaller fumaroles, and sable bars and lines denote the connecting bars and ridges of basalt. The section from Umm Izn to Jebel Dakwah, where the basalt preponderates over other formations, explains the low and widespread dark dome called at the Hijánah village El Mutallá. The effect of these upheavals displays itself in the tilting-up of the northern range of limestone hills about Dhumayr, where the strata have been raised almost to a perpendicular, and the intervening waves of calcareous ground are deeply fissured. We could not at the time explain why all the Tells, especially those to the north-west, projected immensely long black tails to the east.

In twenty minutes we walked down the whole height of El 'Akir, and remounting, we proceeded to cross the silty plain on the W.S.West, which was cut and broken by many shallow Wadys. A little southwards of our course was a detached block, a long ridge, red above and dark below, which seemed to be crowned by a castellated ruin ; this, however, proved to be a mass of rock. The gash of El 'Akir presently showed big and ruddy. After forty minutes we passed an extinct crater in the western range; it is known as El Halayyawát, probably a corrupted diminutive of El Hlewa, before mentioned ; forty-five minutes then placed us at the foot of the small black cone El Huwayfir, remarkable for the disproportionate bigness of its bowl; hence probably its name, derived from El Hufr, the digging.

The last of this day's march was wearying and monotonous. The only new feature was a fine white sand, composed mainly of triturated fresh-water and land shells (*Neritinæ* and *Helices*), the latter belonging chiefly to two species. They are produced in considerable quantities by the limestone region generally, and especially by the Fanges or swamps, when these basins bear water : after the death of the mollusk, they are swept up inland by the strong and regular west wind, which rushes from the Anti-Libanus to the Desert. It may here be mentioned, that during nearly two years in Damascus I never saw a drop of water upon the chalky-white surface of the so-called 'lakes.' Mr. Porter (chap. ix. *Five Years in Damascus*) assures his readers that he has established two points of some importance: the first being, that the Barada continues to flow into the lake during the whole summer; whilst the second is, that the waters of the lake do not dry up during the hot season. Between December 1869 and June 1871 I repeatedly followed the course of the Damascus river; and I also had 'ocular demonstration' that, firstly, the stream does not reach its basin (Bahrat el 'Utaybah);[13] secondly, that the said basin, like the three southern features which look so neatly and prettily blue upon the maps, showed nothing of the element, except in pits and wells. I shall not easily forget the disappointment of my first visit, when eyes accustomed to lake scenery in the four quarters of the globe fell upon an ugly expanse of dried and

---

[13] A small collection of shells made in Syria and Palestine was presented to the British Museum, where Messrs. Gwyn Jeffreys, F.R.S., and Edgar Smith kindly named the species as follows:

FRESH-WATER—Unio Niloticus, Férussac; Unio dignatus, Lea; Corbicula fluminalis, Müller; Neritina turris, Mousson; Neritina Numidica, Récluz; Melania tuberculata, Müll.; Melanopsis prærosa, Linné; Melanopsis cariosa, L.

LAND—Helix candidissima, Draparnaud; Helix candidissima, var. prophetiva, Bourguignat; Helix lactea, Müll.; Helix spiriplana, Olivier; Helix figulina, Jan, and var. minor; Helix simulata, Fér.; Bulimus Alepi, Fér.; Bulimus Syriacus, Pfeiffer; Clausilia Boissieri, Charpentier.

The fossil shells were in such bad condition that Mr. Woodward could not give specific names. He found the genera to consist of: 1. Pecten; 2. Ostrea; 3. Turritella.

flaky mud, varied only by dwarf white rises where
the salt outcropped, and by lines of thickety rush,
denoting that the subsoil was a trifle muddier
than usual. Our statements, however, are easily
reconciled. Mr. Porter visited the swamp region
during years of average rain-fall; I during two
years whose winters were remarkable for drought:
for the winter of 1870-71, the pluviometer at Damascus gave only 3·32 inches.

I may be allowed a few words touching these
so-called lakes, which have of late been made the
subject of discussion.[14] Moreover, some maps show
two, others three, and mostly four waters. They are
laid down with tolerable accuracy, and are correctly
named, in the map of Dr. Wetzstein, which Van de
Velde has evidently transferred bodily to his own.
The Prussian traveller, however, calls the northernmost basin 'Atêbe, and Dr. Beke Atabch; whereas
I would write 'Utaybah, with the initial Ayn moved
by Dammah, the name of the village on the western
plain, and also that of the ruffian tribe of hill-
Bedawin who fired upon our caravan as we were ap-
proaching Meccah. The terms Bahrat el Sharkiyah
(Eastern Tank) and El Kibliyah (Southern Tank),

[14] *Athenæum*, Nov. 1870 (passim).

applied by mappers to the same basin, are totally unknown to the people, and are simply absurd, because one 'lake' does not lie east of the other. The basin also is not bisected by a band of higher ground, as shown by Mr. Porter, although a shallow natural trench, connecting the northern half of the kidney-formed depression with the lower, is distinctly to be traced. In rare places I found mud, though the people spoke of dangerous quagmires. The dry bed is here and there white with a saltine efflorescence, and all the sheep fed upon the grass would become *près salé* perforce, as in Northern France, where mutton is now unknown. The ground-waves not usually submerged are known by the tamarisk-scrub, and the deeper depressions are overgrown with tall reeds and rushes, which rear colonies of shells and shelter wild pig. Ducks and aquatic birds also are said to abound when the place is flooded.

The second 'lake' to the south, called from a village also on its west Bahrat el Hijánah, receives, when there is any to spare, the drainage of the 'Awaj River. I found it a chalky-white surface, with mushroom-shaped pillars horizontally ribbed and left in the harder material by the water, which has washed away the rest. This ground is in spring and autumn the favourite camping-place of the Wuld Ali; they find water in pits some five to six feet deep, generally sweet, but here and there brackish. When riding from El Hijánah to visit my friend Shaykh Salih Tayyár, I crossed a deep drain which connects the basin with that of 'Utaybah, and down which Mr. Macgregor probably paddled the 'young lady.' I cannot agree with that traveller, who suggests that the Abana (Barada?) and the 'Awaj (Pharpar?) do not flood or dry up together; both are fed by the same rains and by the same snows, whilst their springs are perennial.

The Bahrat Bálá, so called from a village now ruined,[15] and at times swamped by the surplus of the Bahrat Hijánah, evidently occupies the lowest gradient of the plain, which is bounded eastward by the westernmost Lohf, a rim of the volcanic floods poured out by the Tulúl el Safá. The surface is of the light bistre-coloured soil (*goldgelbe humus*), called farther west Arz Haurániyyah: friable in the extreme, and in places rotten, it becomes after rain ankle-deep mud, and in the dry season it is full of

---

[15] There is a prosperous place of the same name upon the Damascus Plain, near the well-known Tell Sálihíyyah.

treacherous sinks and holes, attributed by the people
to the sinking of water. These man-traps often
widen below, and in one of them I have seen a horse
fall to the saddle-flaps. Similar to this is the formation of the fourth water, the Matkh B'rák (Burák),
the 'Flooded Plain of the Cisterns.' It takes its name
from an almost deserted town at the stalk or northern
end of the pyriform Leja. Here Ibrahim Pasha of
Egypt established his commissariat, and upon this
point, where the stone breastwork still remains, he
fell back when the flower of his army was destroyed
by the Druzes. The Matkh B'rák, separated from the
Hijánah basin by a high wave of rugged basaltic ground
called Fas'hat Tell el Ra'as, admits after heavy rains
the waters of the Wady Liwá or Luwá, a fiumara defining the eastern limits of the Leja. This rough and
rocky conduit receives, a little north of B'rák town, the
tributary Wady Abu Khunayfis, and the latter drains
off the southern slopes of the basaltic block through
which the 'Awaj Valley passes, and whose culminat-
ing point is the Jebel el Máni'a (the Forbidding or
Difficult Mountain). Rising from the northern slope
of the Jebel el Ashkárá (Schkâra in Dr. Wetzstein),
and the eastern gradient of Tell el Huzaynah, the
Liwá conducts, under a complexity of names, the

surface-water of the Jebel Durúz Haurán; and it often becomes a violent torrent with a rapid descent and overfalls, carrying with it boulders of basalt, and here and there forming little holms. In the dry season the bed is lined with the pinkest and greenest oleanders, and with the blue-flowered Ghár. Mr. Porter derives the Wady Liwá from the neighbourhood of Nimrah town, where a deeply-cut river-valley runs up far beyond it; and he terminates it in the Hijánah 'lake;' finally, he omits the third and the fourth basins.

The Druzes, as usual, rode on, leaving us to follow with the camels, and every hour and a quarter of march obliged us to halt, wearying us by want of exertion. We saw only a small drab-coloured snake and a few Katás, where the ground was faintly green. Pterocles once saved my life, and I never shoot him or his kind.[16] At last, after three hours and thirty minutes of actual riding, we came upon the scorched yellow-white plain of the Kala'at and Bir Kasam (the Fort and Well of an Oath), concerning which I could find no trace of tradition. Features now familiar

[16] Surely this is the bird alluded to by Isaiah (xxxiv. 10) when he speaks of the ' Land of Edom being abandoned to kath'—of which the commentators have by turns made an onocrotalus, a pelican, a bustard, a stork, and a cormorant?

stood before us: the Hermon hogsback, El Kulayb of the Druzes; Abu 'l Atá, on the Palmyra road; Jebel el Máni'a, on the way to Moab;[17] and others familiar to me for the last year and a half. The shallow silty basin in front was backed by what seemed to be plantations round villages, and a little to the south was the Tell Kasam; a small black rock, conspicuous from afar, supporting a ruin, which some Arabs call the fourth Dayr, others the Kasr (Palace) Kasam. We reached the fort in thirty minutes; and thus ended our total of nine hours and forty-eight minutes, the work of that day.

[17] I hope that the geographical reader will not understand me to agree with the Rev. Mr. Porter (*passim*), who, instead of assigning Wady Mújib (Mojeb, the ancient Arnon), about the middle parallel of the so-called Dead Sea, as the northern limit of later Moab proper, unjustifiably prolongs the latter region northwards through Ammon, and El Barriyyah, the chalky lands north-east of Jebel Ajlun (Gilead), right into the Hauranic Valley. By thus confusing the Roman city of Bostra (Nova Trajana), or Bosra in Bashan, which he calls (p. 67, *Giant Cities of Bashan*) 'this city of Moab,' with the true 'Bozrah of Moab,' the southern settlement of the same name, better known as Bosrah the Lesser, he is able to apply to the rich and well-peopled lands of the Haurán, still the granary of Syria, all the hideous curses and denunciations pronounced by the Jewish prophets against their illegitimate cousins. Strange to say, he is followed in this course by Mr. Cyril Graham (*Journal of the Royal Geographical Society*, vol. xxviii. p. 230). The curious student will do well to consult the 'Carte pour l'intelligence des Campagnes de Mesa, Roi de Moab,' which concludes *La Stèle de Dhiban* (see Appendix I. Vol. II.).

The arrival at the well was not, as it usually is, a time of rejoicing, of smoking long pipes, of coffee-drinking, and of rest upon cushioned carpets. The Druzes, who had finished the journey, twelve and a half direct statute miles from the Halayyawát cone, a good hour and a half before us—the camel escort—had dispersed wildly in all directions looking for water, which they could not find. We inspected the fort, a square of modern construction, sadly broken down; and to the west we were shown a large 'Jurn' or sarcophagus-trough, which, according to our guides, once denoted the well. My companion and I, obedient to the maps, took the south-eastern direction, in which the Bir Kasam is laid down by Dr. Wetzstein and his copiers. He had, however, passed it by night, with fear and trembling of his escort; and his mistake caused us a couple of hours of thirst and general discomfort. In the high west wind, fast stiffening to a gale, which seemed to confound earth and sky, and which filled the air with acrid and pungent dust, like a storm in Sind or the Panjáb, we could descry no trace of the water-pit, although I had taken a 'blind sight' to it in December 1869. On the south were two rubbish-filled pits, both evidently unused for years, and north of the fort lay

a third in the same condition. At last a wanderer
of the party, happening to go farther afield, was
lucky enough, when we began asking each other
what on earth could be done, to hit upon the well,
bearing 10° from the Kala'at, and 39° 30′ from
the Tell Kasam. The lip, well-worn and deeply-
grooved in the hard basaltic stone, shows how long
it has been used by the Bedawin. It is sunk some
twenty feet deep in the live rock, and it is flanked
by two shallow pans or vats, for the convenience of
watering cattle. The salt and silty plain around
had made its yield particularly unsavoury, and it is
never sweet except when copiously drawn. Our eyes
were peppered with pungent dust, and we felt in the
flesh what spoils the water.

The Druzes kept us waiting as long as possible,
each, according to custom, fighting to water his
mare first; and here, upon the very Darb el Gha-
zawát (the Road of Razzias from time immemorial),
they seemed unwilling to leave the well. A Bedawi
never commits the imprudence of lingering near
water, especially about sunset; so, leading the way
to a shallow bulge in a Wady south of the fort, we
made preparations for the night. As evening fell,
we found that a 'palaver' was to be held. Every

attempt was of course made to find out what our intentions were, and all equally failed. Presently we told our friends that we were not going direct either to Damascus or to the Dhumayr village ; and this item of news determined their action. All but one disappeared during the night; and when morning dawned, we felt a sense of relief in having seen the last of men and mares. The society of the Fellahin is not more wearying, and our horses had become utterly demoralised.

The next day (Monday, June 5) saw the last of our excursion into the desert. We set out from the well at 5.30 A.M., leaving the third Dayr or monastery to the north; whilst far beyond it, and a little westward, appeared the break in the limestone ridge which allows passage to the Ruhaybah rivulet of Dhumayr.[18] This was to be our resting-place; but luckily for ourselves, we bent to the north-east, intending to inspect the Dakwah

[18] Erroneously called in maps and plans the 'Mukabrit,' or Sulphur Water. This name is applicable only to the produce of the western influent, which flows, or rather which used to flow, for a few yards a little to the north-west of the gate or gap debouching upon the Damascus Plain. These waters would answer all the purposes of the Tiberias thermal springs; and formerly there was a Hammam for the accommodation of invalids. The cupidity of the peasants, however, has ruined all present prospect of reëstablishing it.

Mountain—the cone which from Damascus appears the best defined and the most picturesque.

Travelling slowly, in unusually hot and still weather, over an exceptionally rough country—a sea of basalt, a mass of lava, which, in the moment of its most violent commotion, appeared suddenly to have cooled—we reached, after three hours and forty-five minutes, the base of El Dakwah,[19] and we found the ascent a stiffer affair than usual. The height was 3370 feet above sea-level, and 580 feet above the plateau from which it rises. The slope must again be compared with a well-stuffed and legless arm-chair; or, to describe it less prosaically, it is

'Hook'd and crook'd like the horn'd moon.'

The 'Dakwah' is a kind of shell, with a hollow opening to the north-west. The inside of this crater of eruption is ribbed with semicircular rocks, whilst the outside is ridged with long shunts and shoots. My fellow-traveller ascended from the interior hollow; I tried the western rim, which had two slopes, the lower occupying eight minutes, and the upper ten minutes. The surface is the usual red and yellow

---

[19] The word is probably derived from Dakk, or Dukk, a hillock or low hill.

scoriacious matter, resting upon what seems to be hardened mud. At the highest point we found masses of rock, in whose shade grew lichens and small-leaved plants. The beetles were all elytra and exuviæ; but the big and little flies appeared lively enough. We cast scrutinising glances about the lowlands, which were a complete network of foot-paths; and we were easily consoled at not seeing a living thing. This had been the rule, since we left Taymá, with, but one exception, those ominous dromedary tracks. The shepherds evidently frequent the Dakwah in the days of grass; and, returning to Damascus, we were told that a Mangalah (Mankalah), a pitted stone used for a popular Egyptian and Syrian game, is found upon the very summit. We were afterwards shown from Dhumayr a cone to some distance north-eastward of the Dakwah, and called Milh el Kuranful (Salt of Cloves?). Upon this the stranger may pick up cloves; but if he does, he dies. It is said that snow falls upon the 'Hillock volcano;' but in this matter I am disposed to be incredulous.

The summit of the Dakwah explained to us the secret of the long dark brushes which the western-most of the three lines of cones project far to the east. The zebra-like stripes of black and white are the effect of the regularly blowing west wind, which disposes the shell-dust in thin sheets over the western slopes of the cones, whilst the latter shelter the basaltic ground to their lee or east. Thus on the Jebel Dakwah we found the line of wind to run about 60°; the leeward plain was a sooty stripe of naked lava about one mile broad: north of this lay a snowy band averaging about half that width; and farther north was a second black ribbon about one-third of a mile in breadth, kept clear and clean by the 'Three Brothers.' As will be seen in the map, this triple formation adjoins the Dakwah, whereas Dr. Wetzstein places it on a parallel instead of a meridional line, and distant some twelve direct geographical miles to the north. He also gives them the curiously corrupted name 'Tulesawa' for Salás Akhwán (the Three Brothers), which only the most ignorant of peasants would pronounce 'Tulays a'wwá.'

At eleven A.M., leaving the foot of Jebel Dakwah, we made for Dhumayr, to the north-west. The white shell-sand seemed to gather mostly around this western group of hills, and presently we passed out of it. The limestone flooring of the plain again exposed itself; it was more deeply fissured than usual by volcanic action, possibly by earthquakes.

This line led to an irregular north-western Lohf, composed of long narrow dykes and barrows, blow-holes and circlets, the drums of domes which had burst into space: all was of the blackest basalt. Gradually the igneous formation fined off, and we found ourselves riding over the Arz Tannúrín (the Land of Furnaces), and the Zuhúr el Surr (Ground-waves of the Billán-thorn), the rolling ground which outskirts the rich plain of Dhumayr. We passed the well-known features, Hayt Rambay (Rambay's Wall), which defends the entrance to cultivated land, and which runs straight up hill and down dale; and the Sadd Rambay (Rambay's Dyke), vestiges of a dam which, formerly spanning the narrow neck between the basalts on the south and the limestone outliers of the Anti-Libanus, pent up the eastern waters, and converted a widening expanse of meadow into a tank. Its large blocks of white limestone have been used to make two diminutive drains; according to the villagers, they were mill-races. A gallop over the plain placed us (4.50 P.M.) at the Maskabahs[20] of Dhumayr, where we were well received by the good Rashid el Bostají. We had covered twenty indirect

---

[20] Strips of arable or ploughed ground, fifty to sixty piks (cubits) long × five, separated by rough baulks.

miles from Jebel Dakwah, and a day's total of thirty.

Our arrival was in the very nick of time. The Druze traitor sent from Shakkah by Kabalán el Kala'ání, at the instigation of the Governor-general of Syria, set out on Friday, June 2d, and reached the Ruhbah Valley on the evening of the next day. The Sunday was employed in mustering the Bedawin: the Razzia missed us on Monday at the Umm Nírán, at the Bir Kasam, and upon the direct Lake-road to Dhumayr; they were, in fact, a few hours too late. On Tuesday they plundered, although some 600 Turkish soldiers were in camp within half an hour's ride, three neighbouring villages — Suwaydah, Abbádah, and Harrán el Awáníd;[21] the first mentioned belonging to M. Hanna Azar, dragoman to her Majesty's Consulate, Damascus. They also threatened the life of this valuable official; and the inspectors sent by the Governor-general pronounced the damage done to his property to have been the work of wild pigs! Such was the justice to be obtained by English-protected subjects at Damascus, and this

---

[21] It must not be confounded with Harrán in the Leja, famous for its bilingual inscription, Greek and Nabathæan. The first traveller who passes there is strongly advised to get a ' squeeze' of the stone.

was the state to which England in Syria has been allowed to fall.

We rode into Damascus before noon on Wednesday, June 7th, escaping by peculiar good fortune a plundering party numbering 80 to 100 horsemen and some 200 Radifs (dromedary-riders), two to each saddle. I duly appreciated the compliment—can any unintentional flattery be more sincere?—of sending 300 men to dispose of three. Our zigzag path had saved us from the *royaume des taupes*, for these men were not sent to plunder; besides, *honneur oblige*. The felon act, however, failed; and our fifteen days of wandering ended without accident.

APPENDIX TO VOLUME I.

I.

OBSERVATIONS TAKEN WITH ANEROID AND THERMOMETER (FAHR.) ON THE ROUTES TO THE LIBANUS, THE HAURAN MOUNTAIN, THE TULUL EL SAFA, AND THE ANTI-LIBANUS, BY R. F. BURTON AND CHARLES F. TYRWHITT-DRAKE.

THE aneroids used by me were two pocket instruments.

No. 1 (Spencer, Browning, and Co., patentees, London) was presented to me by the Royal Geographical Society in 1861.

No. 2 (L. Casella, London, 1182, compensated) was bought before I left England in 1869.

After each journey these pocket instruments were tested by comparison with a larger instrument (name and number unknown), which was kept at home; and eventually with mercury-filled glass tubes, also supplied by M. Casella.

The heights taken in October 1871 by Mr. C. F. Tyrwhitt-Drake are by aneroid, the latter corrected by comparison with tubes filled with mercury. Needless to say that we both agree with Captain Warren, that in Syria and Palestine aneroids, however useful for laying down moderate differences of elevation in neighbouring places, as in the process of drawing the contour lines of a country, are worse than useless for absolute determinations of height. The instrument has many disturbing influences. Owing to eccentricities of make, to not being regulated for extreme heat, and perhaps to rapid transition from one elevation to another, the index error changes to any extent ; and the readings show a greater variation than is due to the diurnal range, or to other alteration in the atmospheric pressure. Indeed, in these sub-tropical climates, even mercurial barometers do not keep relatively well together, because one is more sluggish in its movements than the other.

My friend Captain George, R.N., remarks :

' These aneroid observations have been reduced to the *level of the sea*, at which the reading of the barometer is assumed to be 29·92 in. The corresponding temperature at the sea-level was obtained from K. Johnston's Physical Atlas, sheet 18, in which the extremes of temperature are given, *i. e.* January 50°, and July 78° ; the intermediate months obtained by interpolation.'

Observations taken on the Route to the Libanus and upon the Cedar Block.

Place.	Date.	Aneroid.	Barom. tube.	Therm. local.	Sea-level.	Altitude.
						Feet.
1. Ba'albak[1]	Mean of obs. at different times	26·11	26·20	70°	78	3,847·5
2. Source of Litáni	July 26, 1870	26·39	·	69°	78	3,595·
3. 'Uyún Urghush, Eyes of Argus (Valley)	July 28, 1870	23·34	·	78°	78	7,147·5
4. Cedar Col	July 29, 1870	2·20	·	53°	78	8,351·
5. Summit of Zahr el Kazib	October 1871	20·87	20·98	·	61	10,018·
6. Jebel Muskiyyah (Cedar Block)	July 29, 1870	20·98	·	75°	78	10,131·
7. Jebel Makmal	Do.	20·98	·	63°	78	9,998·
8. Jebel Timárin[2]	Do.	20·68	·	75°	78	10,533·
9. Cedars of Lebanon[3]	July 30, 1870	23·16	·	78°	78	7,368·
10. Jebel Sannín[4]	August 3, 1870	21·84	·	67°	74	8,895·

Nos. 9 and 10 can hardly be depended upon, as the instrument was somewhat out of order.

[1] Captain Warren assigns to Ba'albak an altitude of 3450 feet; M. Gérard de Rialle 1170 metres.

[2] Van de Velde (Memoir to accompany the Map of the Holy Land) makes the highest point of the Lebanon Pass on the road from Ba'albak to the Cedars (v. Schubert) 7624 feet.

[3] Van de Velde gives the Cedars (Scott) 6315 ft.; (Russeger) 6400 ft.; (v. Schubert) 6364 ft.; (v. Wildenbruch) 5898 ft.

[4] Van de Velde gives Jebel Sannin (Scott) 8554 ft.; (Marshal Marmont, in *Voyage du Duc de Raguse*, &c., ii. 225) 8283 ft.; (estimated by Russeger) 7250 ft.

Observations taken on the Hauran Mountain (Jebel Durúz Hauran) and the Tulúl el Safá.

[N.B. The pocket instrument showed at Damascus 27·55; and the standard 27·555, after returning from this journey.

Place.	Date.	Aneroid.	Therm. (F.) local.	Sea-level.	Altitude.
					Feet.
11. Summit of Jebel Shaylhan	May 26, 1871	26·26	81°	69	3738
12. Summit of Jebel Kulayb	May 29, 1871	24·42	75°	69	5785
13. Taymá Village	June 2, 1871	25·64	69°	74	4399
14. El Naká	Do.	26·26	85°	74	3781
15. The Ghadir el Ka'al	June 3, 1871	26·69	78°	74	3980
16. On the Lohf	Do.	28·59	70°	74	1299
17. At the Cave Umm Nirán[5]	Do.	27·22	86°	74	2745
18. Top of Tell el 'Akir	June 4, 1871	26·64	74°	74	3328
19. Bir Kasam (a little above the Damascus swamps)	June 5, 1871	27·94	57°	74	1930
20. Top of the Jebel Dakwah	Do.	26·62	81°	71	3373
21. Dhumayr Village	Mean of several observations	27·78	72°	74	2124

[5] N.B. Inside the cave the aneroid showed 27·38; the thermometer 74 degrees; and the difference between the hygrometer was 11 degrees (dry).

Observations on the Anti-Libanus.

N.B. After returning from this journey, the pocket instrument showed at Damascus 27·28, and the standard 27·480.

Place.	Date.	Aneroid.	Therm. (Fahr.) local.	Sea-level.	Altitude.
					Feet.
22. Top of El Akhyár⁶	July 25, 1871 . .	22·78 + 0·20	65°	78	7736
23. Birkat el Mudawwarah . .	July 31, 1871 . .	23·53	65° (in winter 54°)	78	6827
24. Top of Abú 'l Hin . .	Do. . .	22·37	75°	78	8330
25. Ayn el Durrah	August 1, 1871 .	23·66	55°	76	6589
26. Western Cliff-ridge of Anti-Libanus .	Do. . .	22·99	62°	76	7441
27. Assal el Ward Village . . .	Do. . .	24·66	76°	76	5553
28. On Nabí Bárúh Block (50 to 60 ft. below cairn)	August 2, 1871 .	22·72	71°	76	7841
29. Top of Tala'at Músá . . .	Do. . .	22·06	75°	76	8721
30. Mu'arrat el Bashkurdi Village .	Do. . .	24·41	72°	76	5688
31. Top of Col Wady el Mál . .	August 3, 1871 .	23·20	79°	76	7321
32. Well of Kurrays	Do. . .	23·16	74°	76	7324
33. Top of Halímat el Kabú . .	Do. . .	22·40	73°	76	8257
34. Wells of Wady Katuín . .	August 4, 1871 .	23·20	70°	76	7245
35. Well of Wady Jubáb . . .	Do. . .	22·90	65°	76	7573

⁶ Van de Velde gives 'highest top of Anti-Lebanon near 'Ain Hawar' (Porter, about) 7000 ft.; also 'Zebedany' (Russeger) 4280 ft.: (Schubert) 3760 ft.; (Allen) 4135 ft. (the best); B'ludán or Belúdán (Porter, in *Rob. Later B. R.* 487, and in *Ritter,* xvii. 1318 ft.), 4842 ft.; (in his *Five Years,* &c., p. 280), 4529 ft.

*Aneroid Observations by Charles F. Tyrwhitt-Drake en route
from Telfita, near Damascus, to Hamah.*

N.B. These are calculated without allowing for local temperature or
temperature at sea-level.

Place.	Aneroid reading.	English feet.
Telfita	25·110	4845
Ka'ábet Kalkas	24·230	5625
El Watiy	24·480	5375
Ain el Durrah	23·600	6255
Ba'albak	26·110 }	3772 mean
„ (barometer)	26·200 }	
B'teddar	26·190	3665
Watershed above Yamunah . .	25·340	4515
Aináta (vil.)	24·830	5025
Cedar *Col*.	22·200	7665
Base of Dhahr el Kodhib . .	21·120	8435
Dhahr el Kodhib	20·870 }	9003 mean
„ (barometer) . .	20·980 }	
J. Tizmarún	20·680	9175
Pass to north of preceding . . .	21·000	8855
Sahlet el Jubab	24·050	5705
Merj Ahín	24·230	5625
Fenaydir	24·050	5705
Bayno	28·120	1735
Akkar	26·500	3355
El Abéyyát	28·050	1805
Antakít	27·750	2105
El Bukáya	28·800	1055
Plateau to east of former . . .	28·150	1705
Hums (mean of four observations)	28·125	1730
Mijmar el Sohun	28·560	1295
Shemmamit	28·160	1695
Tell above Arúneh	28·260	1595
Múrik (vil.)	28·650	1305
Mo'arrat el No'aman	28·150	1705
Abú Tín	28·700	1155
Hill above Abú Tabbeh	28·430	1425
Safíreh	28·750	1105

Aneroid Observations en route from Telfita to Hamah
(continued).

Place.	Aneroid reading.	English feet.
Howwayyith	28·180	1675
Aleppo	28·660	1195
Serákib	28·700	1155
Tarutin el Tujjar	28·620	1235
Jirjinnaz	28·420	1435
El Farajeh	28·800	1055
Temányeh	28·720	1135
Hamah (mean)	28·940	995

Aneroid corrected thus :
    Mean 23 days' standard barometer . . . 29·842
        ,,   aneroid ,,   . . . 29·697

              ,,   too low . . . . ·145

Aneroid Observations by Charles F. Tyrwhitt-Drake en route from Kara to Sadad and back.

N.B. These are also calculated without allowing for local temperature or for temperature at sea-level.

Place.	Aneroid reading.	English feet.
Peaks above B'ludan :		
1st (Northern)	22·520	7335
2d (Southern)	22·380	7475
Watershed near Khan Liban, north of Jebel Abú Ata	26·320	3535
Kutayfeh	26·620	3235
Watershed south of Kastal . . .	25·060	4940
Kara	25·340	4660
Sadad	26·640	3215
Yabrud	25·080	4775
Watershed near Buk-ha	24·390	5465
Máalúlah	25·480	4375
Watershed at head of Menin Valley	25·350	4505

II.

PROVERBIA COMMUNIA SYRIACA.

'The genius, spirit, and wit of a nation are discovered in its proverbs.'—BACON.

A writer remarks, 'If men at the lowest as well as the highest stage of civilization enunciate the same truths, the fact goes to prove that these truths are unimportant.' I can hardly assent to the conclusion, even were the premiss correct, whereas it is not. Those familiar with proverbial literature have remarked that some aphorisms are common in matter, and a few even in actual manner and form, to almost all nations and languages. The Syrian, for instance, will say, 'The egg of to-day, not the hen of to-morrow;' and 'A live dog is better than a dead lion.' On the other hand, the points of difference are far more important. Setting aside the sayings which 'bear the stamp of their birthplaces, and which wear the colouring and the imagery of their native climes,' we find that there are proverbs peculiar to every race—proper to it, as are its syntax and its idiom; that each people speaks out the truth or the half truth which is in it, and, consequently, that for the most part neither the idea nor the wording bear comparison. Moreover, were it a fact that all enunciate the same truth, it by no means proves the latter to be unimportant, except to the few. The student of the nineteenth century will not, for higher thought, consult proverbs or proverbial philosophy, or other saws and instances; but he will treat not a few of them as chapters of anthropological and ethnological history; showing how truth arose in the silent education of the world; how the experience of every-day life gradually took shape and status; how the appreciation of experience became concrete in the

pithy aphorism, till at last the 'wisdom of many' gained life
by the 'wit of one.' In it he sees the process of a pencil of
light stealing into the child-like savage brain, slowly but
surely dispersing the fatal glooms of ignorance and preju-
dice, of falsehood and barbarism; assuming various degrees
of illumination, and at last becoming the perfect day of
wisdom and judgment, of truth and civilization. No wonder,
as Count Lucann observes, that proverbs have ever been so
popular with the human race.

As regards these Proverbia Communia. The labours of
Pocock, Erpenius, Freytag,[1] and others, have introduced to
Europe the repertories of classical Amsal (الامثال), in which
the Arabs delighted from the days of the Khalifah Ali to
those of El Maydani. My object is not so high. Returning
to Western Asia, and resuming the studies which had been
interrupted by long service in Africa and South America,
I at once recommenced them at the commencement—the
alloquialisms of a people new to me. Presently I remembered Burckhardt's *Amsal el Masr* (Arabic and English,
1830), which aimed at illustrating manners and customs
from proverbial sayings current at Cairo, and it appeared to
me that the same might be done for Syria.

The modern dialect of Syria retains distinct traces of the
old Aramœan, and, as may be expected in a land where men
live much at home, every great city—Damascus, for instance
—preserves peculiar words and phrases. And without living
interpretation it is impossible to master sayings of purely
local use and unfamiliar allusion, further mystified by proverbial sententiousness and conciseness. They must, however, be learnt, and even committed to memory, before a
stranger can feel himself at home with the people. Here

---

[1] His 'Amsal el Arab,' in four vols. octavo, is an excerpt from the vast collection of El Maydani.

proverbs have not passed from the learned to the vulgar tongues; they are in universal circulation, amongst all degrees, from the ignorant to the man of highest cultivation; and the apposite use of aphorisms is, like wit and eloquence, a manner of power. Some of the sayings are mostly confined to women, and the nursery; not a few of them have some popular tale whose point they resume. Many are quoted only in part, the rest being suppressed for some obvious reason. So we, for instance, might say '*qui facit per alium.*' As will be seen, the peculiar vagueness inherent in Arabic speech allows them an immense range of application, and permits them to be used in a variety of senses, which require from us a certain amount of study. Nor is the labour of studying them for their own sake in vain. It is highly interesting to observe the modern succedaneum for the old aphoristic philosophy of Syria, which in some form or other has overspread the civilized world.

Of all the races known to me, the Syrians and certain West African tribes are those who delight most in proverbs. The Spanish type, immortalized in Sancho Pança, comes next; the Portuguese loses much of the characteristic; and the Brazilian, his descendant, has wholly lost it. When visiting Yoruba I was so much struck by the speeches and harangues—mere conglomerates of quotations—that I persuaded Messrs. Tinsley to publish, in 1865, a collection of 2859 proverbs, popular amongst seven Negroid and Negro nations. The volume, which bore the title of "Wit and Wisdom from West Africa," was not so successful as the *Adagia* of Erasmus, and of course brought out the remark that the 'sparkles of wit were few and faint, and the wisdom of the mildest order.' This was to be expected. But my object was to make the people describe themselves, to put them, as it were, in the witness-box upon their racial trial.

Pace the critics who differed from me, I cannot but think that the idea of the compilation was good. At any rate, it obtained the approval of one whose opinion in such a matter is worth a thousand cavils of men, who, ignorant of the subject, must borrow from the book itself the arms with which they would assail it. I need hardly mention the name of Mr. William Stirling, now Sir William Stirling Maxwell, of Keir.

1. الذى زوجها معها بتدير القمر باصبعها

'She who hath her husband with her, shall turn the moon with her finger.'

2. جيبوا بنات ولا تقعدوا بطّالات

'Bring girls, and sit not to no purpose.'—It is better (for a woman) to bear girls (if she cannot have boys), and not to remain childless.

3. بنيّه على بنيّه ولا حائل سنيّه

'Girl upon girl, and not retaining (barren) for a year.'— Meaning the same as No. 2.

4. ستّى من غير وحام مريضه

'My lady without (the) queasiness (of pregnancy) is unwell.'—Said of a woman who affects to be an invalid; to be delicate, to be interesting.

5. الحمل والحبل والركوب على جمل لايختفوا

'Love and pregnancy, and riding upon a camel, cannot be hid.'—Similar to the Persian 'Musk and murder cannot be concealed.'

6. كل شى تشتغل السمره لا يكفيها خطوط و حمره

'However much the brown woman works, it will not pay for her eye-paint and rouge.'—Applied to men and women who spend more than they make. So the Turkish proverb, *Fantasia chok, parah yok*

7. دور الدورة ولو دارت وخد بنت البيت ولو بارت

'Go the round way, though (it be) long, and marry the daughter of a house (*i.e.* good family), though she be stale (or has lain fallow, from بور).'

8. تتكنّى القرعه بشعر بنت خالتها

'The scald-headed woman prides herself on the hair of her (maternal) aunt's daughter.'—Said about a small or a bad man who boasts the greatness or the goodness of his relatives.

9. الحمار يتكنى بان الحصان خاله

'The ass prides himself upon the horse being his (maternal) uncle.'—Meaning the same as No. 8.

10. مثل اليهود على اخف الصنايع

'Like the Jew who (ever) chooses the meanest work.— Said of one who neglects important for trivial matters.

11. مثل فقرا اليهود لا دنيا ولا اخرة

'Like Jew beggars, who enjoy neither this world nor the next.'—Said of a man who fails in life. So they also say *Misl el Fawákhirah* (plur. of *Fakhúri*, a jar-maker) *wa la dunyá wa la ákhirah.* The jar-maker is proverbially a rascal, and his calling is a poor one. The first three words are generally found sufficient; and to make it more offensive to the Jews, Moslems say, *Misl el yahúd.*

12. تفشفشي يا خاله كل الدعاوى بطاله

Be wroth, O aunt! (here means a stepmother) for all thy curses are in vain.'—Said to any one who curses or uses bad language. *Fishfish* فشفش means literally 'vapid wine.'

13. الف دعوى ما شقت قميص

'A thousand curses never tore a shirt.'—So our adage, 'Hard words break no bones.'

لا الفاره طاهره ولا دعاها مستجاب .14

'The mouse is not pure, nor is her prayer answered (by heaven).'—Said to a bad man who curses.

طب الجره علی فمها تطلع البنت مثل امها .15

'Turn the jar mouth downwards: the daughter will turn out like the mother.'—The first half is merely for the purpose of rhyme. *Li ummihá* is also said, instead of *Misl ummihá.*

یا بنت من ملاکی مزتک و بیت حماکی .16

'Girl, who raised thee (so high)? Thine honour (*i.e.* husband) and the house of thy mother-in-law.' (*Bayt Hamá,* the husband's family; Hamu, حمو father-in-law; and Hamá, حما mother-in-law.)

رتعه شنعه ولا لحم بتال .17

'(Let a man wear) foul rags, but not show (a naked) skin.' —Said, for instance, to woman. Meaning that though poor she may be honest.

یا بنت لا تفرحی بثوب عرسک یا ما وراه من الشقا .18

'Girl! don't exult in thy wedding dress. Ah! how much trouble is behind it.'—Said to a man enjoying himself without thought of the future.

لا تروح بین القبور ولا تشم رایحة المنتنه .19

'Go not amongst the tombs; nor smell evil odours.'—Said to one, for instance, who wishes to meddle in troubles which do not concern him.

لا تقول للمغنی غنی ولا للمصلی صلی .20

'Say not to the singer, sing, nor to those praying, pray.' —Meaning, it is useless to ask a man to do what he is compelled to do; he will only make excuses, and perhaps refuse.

بدل ان تتقول الدجاجه كش اغربها واكسر رجليها .21

'Instead of saying to the hen Kish (pst! be off), strike her and break her leg.'—Spoken by one asking a favour from another; and when the latter, who can grant it, makes excuses and puts him off.

رافق الديك وشوف وين يوديك .22

'Befriend the cock, and see where he bears you.' Evil communications corrupt good manners. *(shúf* for *shâf:* others say بوم the owl.)

كل عنزه معلقه بكرعوبها .23

'Every goat is stuck to her circle.'—Said after giving good advice to a man who will not take it.

كل الدروب توصل للطا حون .24

(Or, *Kull ud durúb ala 't 'táhun.*) 'All the roads lead to the mill.'—Spoken to a man who tries roundabout ways, when he can go straight to the point.

مافى طلعه حتى قَبالها نزله .25

'There is no rising up without a falling down in front of it.'—Meaning, that any man will have his turn of good and bad fortune.

ما يجى الترياق من العراق حتى يكون ملسوع الهوام فارق .26

'The tiryak (Mithridate) will not come from Irak (where it is made) till the man bitten by the snakes is released (by death).'—Said by a man whose important business is deferred. Others say, *Malsu' el hawá, i.e.* the victim of love.

على قد بساطك مد رجليك .27

'According to the size of your carpet stretch your legs.'— The same as our 'Cut your coat according to your cloth.'

28. لِسانه مثل مقص السكاف لا يقص الا النجاسه

'Like a cobbler's scissors, which cut nothing but the impure (leather).'—Spoken of a foul-mouthed man.   Often the
first half of this proverb is found enough.

29. كل الكلاب احسن من حيمور

'Every dog is better than Haymúr (proper name of dog,
generally pronounced Hammúr).'—The speaker is supposed
to declare his dog worse than all others.   Said by a man
who complains of his wife, children, friends, and so forth.

30. مثل الكلاب شبعه او جوعه

'Like dogs, full or empty (it is all the same).'—Benevo-
lently said of a poor man, or of one who wants everything.

31. النذر للدّير و الوَخَم على سمعان

'Gifts to the convent and filth (polite people prefer البلوا
El balwá, toil and trouble) for Samaan (proper name of the
convent servant).'—Said of a servant or a slave working for
his master.

32. كل الديوك تصيح والصيت الى ابو قونبره

'All the cocks crow, but honour is given to the crested
cock (*Abu kumburah*, a bird with feathered tuft, and therefore more remarkable).'—Spoken of a man who carries off
honours or profit from those more deserving.

33. كل شى عند العرب صابون

'Everything is soap to the Arab.'—Meaning, all is fish
that comes to his net.

34. حتّا ابن منّا الذى عاش الف و مأة سنه و ما تهنّا

'Hanná, son of Manná, who lived a thousand one hundred
years, and never enjoyed himself.'—Said to one complaining
of a little misery.   The Spanish *Ommiad Khalifat el Nasr*.
'the heir of prosperity,' was more easily contented ; he owned
to two happy days in a reign of fifty years and seven months.

اذا امحلت حوران تساعِد هجانه .35

'When the Hauran (plain) fails, Hijanah (the swampy region east of Damascus) supplies (provision).'—Popularly said in praise of Hijanah.

الطيز طيزى والارض للسلطان .36

'My rump is my rump, and the land is the Sultán's.'—Spoken by a man, for instance, when another would turn him out of his place or property.

شُرّابةخرج لابتعدّل ولا يتميّل .37

'The tassel of a saddle-bag, which cannot straighten nor incline (the saddle).'—Applied to a ne'er-do-weel, a useless fellow, a man of no consequence.

رعيف برغيف ولا يبات جارك جيعان .38

'A loaf for a loaf (*i.e.* lend him a loaf), and let not thy neighbour remain hungry (for he will return thy loan).'—Meaning, assist thy brother man, and he will assist thee.

خبزكم اكبر من خبزنا عيرونا برثيف .39

'If your bread be greater than our bread, shame us with a loaf!'—Said to one from whom a favour is wanted, and who boasts that he can do it.

جارك القريب ولا اخوك البعيد .40

'Your neighbour who is near, and not your brother who is far.'—Meaning, your neighbour who does you good is better than a brother who does not. Also, a live dog is better than a dead lion.

العين ما ترتفع فوق الحاجب .41

'The eye cannot rise above the eyebrow.'—Said by an inferior to a superior, who would do him more honour than he deserves.

العين ما تقاوم مخرز .42

'The eye does not oppose a collyrium needle.'—Meaning,
you are too cunning of fence for me to fight you.

البومه لو كان فيها خير ما فاتها الصياد .43

'If there were any good in the owl, the hunter would not
pass her by (but would have shot her).' Spoken thus, a
man would buy an article ; he hears that it has been seen
and not bought by another whose judgment he values, and
then he applies the proverb. Also, it means that the value-
lessness of a person or thing is his or its safety.

يمصريّة كرفس ما بهينك يا نفس .44

'One para (*misriyah*) worth of watercress (is enough), and
I won't dishonour you, O myself!'—Better be contented
with humble fare (etc.) than support an obligation.

شهر الذى ما منه فايده لا تعد ايامه .45

'Of the month which does not profit you, count not the
days.'—Meaning, take no useless trouble about what will not
do you good.

يا ويل الذى ما له اضافر و يا ويل الذى ما له ظهير .46

'Woe to him who has no nails, and woe to him who has
(no one to) back (him).'—The man who has no nails cannot
enjoy King James's greatest pleasure, and the friendless man
cannot prosper.

كل ديك على مزبلته صياح .47

'Every cock crows loudly on his own dunghill.'

الحجر بمحله قنطار .48

'The stone in its place is a *kantár* (hundredweight).'—
The same as No. 47. Also they say, *Haswah saghirah tasnud
khábiyah kantáriyah*. 'The little pebble supports (upright)
the jar that holds a *kantár* (hundredweight).'

الذى يُخفف راسه يتعب رجليه .49

'He whose head is light soon tires his feet.'—Meaning, that the foot is always running about; or said of a man who does a thing without reflection, his bolt is soon shot.

الحكى من فضه و السكون من ذهب .50

'Speech is of silver, silence is of gold.'—An old proverb in Syria; a comparatively new saying amongst us.

فرس الاصيله لا يعيبيا جلالها .51

'A thorough-bred mare is not disgraced by her (bad) saddle.' They also say عدتها *iddat-há*, 'her packsaddle.' The *Jilál* is the flat pad, the *Sarj* is after the Frankish fashion.—Spoken, for instance, of a rich man in a bad hat.

مصفايه ما بيعيقيا ثقب .52

'The cullender is not hindered by a hole (more or less).'—Applied, for instance, to a man who habitually lies.

كل شى على بابه يشابه اصحا به .53

'Every thing in its place resembles its race.'—There is a similar saying, *Kullu aná yunzhah* (ينضح) *má fíh.* 'Every pot pours out its (own contents).' Good trees bear good fruits.

قال التا جرلابنه شوف الذبون واعطى على شكله .54

'Quoth the merchant to his son, look at the habitual buyer (the pratique), and deal to him accordingly.'—Meaning, treat every man as he deserves.

وقعت الفاره من الثقف قالت ليا استقطه الله .55

جوبتيا انت ابعدى عنى وانا بالف خير من الله

The mouse fell from the ceiling, and the cat cried "Allah." The mouse replied (generally *kálat liha el fárah*), "Go far from me, and I am with a thousand blessings from Allah."' Allah, is ejaculated when a man stumbles or falls. Said to a man who is getting into the hands of those who will harm him.

وقعت البقره وكثرت السلاخـين. 56

'When the cow falls, the knackers flock (to her).'—Meaning, when a man gets into trouble his enemies collect to injure him.

مستهزِى الرجال برأس لفت يقتل. 57

'He who despises men will be killed (for the sake of) a turnip.'—Meaning, that if a man oppose one stronger than himself he will be lost by the least *faux pas.*

لو ما جراده ما وقـع عصفر. 58

'Had there not been a locust, the bird would not have fallen.'—This alludes to a long story about a bird following a locust into a house, and being trapped. The king was anxious to take a young woman called Jerádah (the locust) from her old husband named Usfur (the bird); and the latter managed to escape by using the proverb. It is applied to a person who ventures too much. Also it means, 'If I had not bribed him, I should not have won my cause.'

يا ما اكثر اصحابى عند ما كان كرمى دبس ويا ما اقل اصحابى. 59
عند ما صار كرمى يبس

'Oh! how many were my friends when my vines produced syrup; and oh! how few were my friends when that same vine dried up.'—Familiar to all, *Donec eris felix multos numerabis amicos.*

مثل الدجاج دايما يهدس بالغرابله. 60

'Like the fowls which always think of the broken (or spoilt, corn, poultry food).'—Said to a man always talking shop, about money, or women, for instance.

ما دامك على دل حصيره لا هى طويله ولا هى قصيره. 61.

'As long as you lie on this mat, it will become neither longer nor shorter.'—Meaning, whilst you are so lazy and inactive, you will do no good, you will not prosper.

ايش المر للذي امرّ منه. 62.

'What is the bitter to one (who has tasted) the more bitter?'—Said when misfortunes or sorrows come one after the other.

لا عين تقشع ولا قلب يوجع. 63.

'Let not the eye discover what pains the heart.'—Meaning, wink at small annoyances. Also, the heart does not grieve at what the eye does not see.

مثل الدجاجه ما تملك على بيضها. 64.

'Like the hen who is not mistress of her own eggs.'—Said to a man of property who is not master in his own house.

كل قمحه مسوّسه لبا كيّال اعما. 65.

'Every worm-eaten (corn-)grain has a blind (others say one-eyed) measurer.'—Reproving a servant, for instance, who buys a bad article. Also, *Toute Fadette a son Fadet.*

الكذب ملح الرجال وعيب على من يصدق. 66.

'Lying is the salt (goodness) of men, and shameful (only) to one who believes.'—Said to a great liar, whose lies are, like salt, required for all kinds of food. It is also used in a literal sense, even as Bacon declared that the mixture of a lie doth ever add pleasure—only a little less usually than the Syrian adage. The first half is often said without the second, and then it becomes a curious index of material thought.

لا تلوم الغايب حتى يحضر. 67.

'Blame not the absent (who is doing your work) till he shall appear.'—Similar to our *De mortuis,* etc. *Les absents ont toujours tort.*

مثل المرابعين يفرح بفتح العدال .68

'Like the *Murábain* (hired labourers) who rejoice at the
opening of the grain-bags (which benefit the master).'—
Spoken to or about a man who works for another's advantage.

الحق الكذّاب لباب الدار .69

'Follow the liar to the house-door (*i.e.* to the end of his
lies).'—Said of a 'promising' man, push him as far as
possible.

الذى يلاعب القط يحتمل خراميشه .70

'He who plays with the cat must suffer her claws.'—
Addressed to one, for instance, who is insulted after speaking to a rude fellow, who has touched pitch, and has been
defiled.

من كثرة بناته صار الكلب صهره .71

'From the number of his daughters, even the dog (in the
streets) has become his son-in-law.'—The man with many
(plain) daughters must make presents to every one in order
to get them off his hands.

مثل حمار الزبّال يمشى عايق و محمّل وخم .72

'Like the dustman's donkey, who paces swaggering, and
yet carries only dirt.'—Spoken of or to a pretentious fellow.
Also they call him *Himar muhammal Asfär,* 'ass laden with
books.'

من يعتاز الكلب يقوله صباح الخير يا خالى .73

'He who wants the dog says to him, " Good morning, O
my uncle," (or, *Sabahak el khayr haji kalb,* " Good morning,
Mister Dog ").'—So the people of Trinidad wittily say,

> Dëir chein, cé chein ;
> Devant chein
> Cé, ' Missier Chein.'

74. اليد الذى ما تقدر تعضها بوسها و ادعى عليها بالكسر

'The hand which you cannot bite, kiss it, and pray that it may be broken.'—Same meaning as No. 73. They also say, 'He kisses the hands and he laughs at the beards.'

75. جهنم و بين البوابيج

'Hell and amongst the slippers!'—Meaning, for instance, that when you condescend to visit your enemy you expect to be civilly treated, and yet you are not—adding insult to injury. Also, don't let people say that I am in hell and also disgraced; I am lost in both worlds.

76. ما بقى احدا حتى قرص حتى دبان الفرس

'Every one has stung him, even the horse-fly.'—Said about a man who suffers from every one.

77. تلّم الاعوج من ثورالكبير

'The crooked furrow is (the work) of the big bull.'—Meaning that the fault is from the great man. A saying often used about the rulers, who, of course, should set the best example.

78. ما عُمره مقسّم دخل الجِنه

'Never in all his life shall the divider (arbitrator) go to heaven.'—Because the arbitrator in these lands is always a rascal; he gets the best portion—the oyster, not the shells.

79. فراق البدو بعبا ولا بسوق العبى كله

'Get rid of the *Badawi* (wild man) with a cloak, and not with the whole cloak-market.'—Meaning, sacrifice a little to save much.

80. اذكر الذيب وهيّ القصيب

'Speak of the wolf, and make ready the club.'—So our adage, 'Talk of the Devil,' etc.

81. ابن الحلال عند ذكره يبان

'The honest man appears when he is spoken of.'—Said as No. 80. Also about a man who does good.

82. لا تستكثر اولادك على عزرائل ولا مالك على الظلّام

'Do not boast of thy many children before 'Azrail (the angel of death), or of thy wealth before the tyrants.'—The first half of this phrase is the more used.

83. لا تقول فول حتى يصير بالمكيول

'Do not say "beans" before they are in the measure.'—So our proverb about counting chickens; the vision of Mirza, etc.

84. حساب العقله ما بيجى على حساب البيدر

'The estimate of the field (whose crop is still in grass) does not agree with the estimate of the thrashing-floor.'— Same signification as No. 83.

85. يا حواجبه يا عينيه على المغتسل بائن

'O his (fine) eyebrows! O his (fine) eyes! they show upon the *mughtasal* (place where the Moslem dead are washed).'— This is especially a woman's proverb, meaning, it is useless to praise a thing which is before your eyes. They generally say, *Ya hawájibhu, ya 'uyunhu*, etc.

86. شد الخيط ومطه الذى عليه شى بيحطه

'Tighten the thread and draw it close; whoso has a share let him put it down (contribute it).'—Said, for instance, to a shareholder, one of a picnic, etc., who grumbles.

87. عشرة حلبيه تحنك وشرب مويه

'A friendly party of Aleppines laugh, jaw, and drink water.'—Our 'tea and turn out.' *Tahannak* from *hanak*, a jawbone; in low language, as we say, to jaw, to chaff.

ديك النحيم من البيضه يصيح .88

'The clever cock crows from the egg.'—Alluding to a sharp boy: also meaning that the boy is the father of the man.

كل الجمال بتِعاركْ ما عدا جملنا باركْ .89

'All the camels are fighting together, except our camel, which is kneeling.'—Said by a man to himself when others are working round him, and he does nothing. *Jamal-kum* is used if applied to another. It also means all are employed except myself.

مثل الحمام حنيه بلا رضاعه .90

'Like the pigeon, fond (of her young) without suckling (them).'—Spoken of a man who is civil, but who will not spend his money.

انظر يا حمار حتى يطلع الربيع .91

'Wait (for grass), O donkey, until spring comes.'—Said to a man who works without getting his wage. *Unzur* is for *intazir*.

هل اقرع عمرى ما جمرت .92

'This scald-head all my life I never cured (cleaned).'— The *akra'* is always supposed to be a quarrelsome man. The saying would mean, I never met with such a tiger; I never interfere in this matter, and so forth. *Tajmir* is especially applied to burnishing gold and silver.

مثل شحمة قرد ما بيسلى ولا بيذوب .93

'Like the monkey's fat, which does not soften (*bi-yasli*) and does not melt (*bi-yadúb*).'—Said of an impracticable or avaricious man. سلو *sulu* means becoming semi-liquefied

احترت فيك يا اقرع كيف اداويك .94

'I marvel at thee, O scald-head! how I shall cure thee?'—
Said when a man will not consent to anything. Like No. 93.

الكحل احسن من العما .95

'Kohl (collyrium) is better than blindness.'—Meaning,
better to have a little than to lose all; because the use of
kohl for a month may save the eye. The better form is *el
ramad,* (ophthalmia) is better, etc.

كل ما شفت اعمى طبه   ما انت اخبر من ربه .96

'When thou seest the blind man beat him down; (for)
thou art not greater than his God.'—Punish the bad man,
because he cannot do good. The Creator made the blind
man blind. Also said of an ungrateful man. They tell a
tale of the Prophet Jonah, who prayed the Lord to heal a
blind boy, whereupon the latter began to stone him; the
prophet quoted the proverb as above.

كنيسة القريبه ما بتشفى .97

The church which is near does not cure.'—Said of a
man, for instance, who buys (or consults a doctor, etc.) from
afar, when he can buy as well near. Also of near relations,
one's cousins, for instance. Opposed to the Scotch idea of
blood being thicker than water.

حس الطبل يودّى الى بعيد .98

'The noise of the kettledrum goes far.'—Report flies
abroad: the end often omitted is *wa juwwáthu fárigh,* 'and
she is empty inside.' That would be said of a windy
boaster, etc.

صوت الطبل غطّا الذايّات .99

The sound of the (big) drum drowns the flute.'—Said of
a great man when a greater appears. Also in the form *Ajá*
(has come) *el Tabl,* etc.

جمل مطرح الجمل يبرك .100

'The camel kneels on the place of the camel.'—Spoken, for example, when dismissing a servant; another can soon be found. 'There are as good fishes in the sea,' etc.

كنت اصلّى حتى يحصلى لمّا حصلى بطلت اصلى .101

'I used to pray till I obtained (what I prayed for); but, when I obtained it, I left off praying.'—Meaning, for instance, women fawn and flatter till they get what they want.

المعروف مع غير اهله ضايع .102

'Kindness is wasted on the undeserving (the ungrateful).'

خذ الاصيل ولو انه على الحصير .103

'Take the noble, though (sleeping) upon a mat.'—Meaning, in marriage (or in hiring servants, and so forth) prefer blood to money.

الجمل لو شاف حردبته لوقع فك رقبته .104

'If the camel had seen his hunchback, he would have fallen and broken his neck.'—Corresponds with Burns's lines about the 'Giftie.'

قالوا للعميان على الزيت قالوا هذا الهم لا يعنينا .105

'They said to the blind (men), "Oil is dear!" They replied, "This is a sorrow which does not touch us!"'—The blind not wanting lamps. The saying is applied to those who spread reports that do not concern the hearer.

من جرّب المجرّب كان عقله مخرّب .106

'Whoso tries the tried his intellect is belied.'—Meaning that he is a fool.

حط قردك على قرده .107

'Put thy monkey upon his monkey.'—Meaning, if a man will not hear you, din it always into his ears; or try who is the better man. A favourite proverb with the Jews.

لا تدعى لصاحبك بالسعاده تعدمه .108

'Pray not for the prosperity of thy friend, lest thou destroy him.'—Meaning, that when prosperous he will forget you. Said to a friend who has waxed rich.

اذا انعاق مرسالك استبشر فيه .109

'If thy messenger delay, hold it (a sign of) good news.'—As we say, 'No news good news.'

لا تكثر الزياره على الملوك اذا كانوا اهلك يكرهوك .110

Visit not often the kings (*i.e.* the great), for even if related to you they will hate you.'—Said to a tuft-hunter; also an excuse popularly made to one who reproaches you with not visiting him often enough.

كن بعيد وانتظار الذى تريد .111

'Remain afar and await what you want.'—Equivalent to 'Await the opportunity.' Almost same signification as 110.

كثر الشد يرخى .112

'Too much tying loosens.'—Meaning that man loses by pushing too fast.

ان كان ماشى على هل درب خيط بغير مُسلّه .113

If he (the muleteer, etc.) be walking upon this road, let him sew with another pack-needle.'—Said, for instance, of one who asks an impossible favour, deeming it easy, 'Let him take some other thought;' this pack-needle can do no good.

البير الفارغ لا يملاه الندا .114

'Dew fills not upon an empty well.'—Said to a person who lives beyond his income.

هذه المِصفاة لا يملا طروف .115

'This filter will not fill the (water-) skins.'—Same as 114.

116. من يدق الباب يسمع الجواب

'Whoso knocks at the door hears the reply.'—Similar to our 'Knock, and it shall be opened to you.'

117. لا ظرف انخزق ولا زيت اندلق

'No skin has burst, and no oil has been lost (*lit.* poured out).'—Used when a man wishes, for instance, to decline a contract.

118. اذا دقيت على باب و ما فتحوا لك فتش على عرضك وروح

'If thou knock at a door which is not opened to thee, consult thine honour and go.'—Said when a favour is asked of one who makes excuses.

119. لا فاطمه بالعلم ولا حسن بالكُتّاب

'Is not Fatimah (my daughter) at her task? Is not Hasan (my son) at his school?'—Meaning 'What matter to me?' *Kuttáb* in low language means a school.

120. لا من الذين آمنوا ولا من الذين كفروا

'He is not of those who believe, or of those who disbelieve.' —Said of a man who does not care for anything. (Quoted from the Koran.)

121. مثل حمار المطران عاقل شيطان

'Like the archbishop's ass, a clever devil.'—Applied to a slippery fellow. They also say, *Misl himár el kháhhán,* 'Like the ass of the (Jewish) Scribe.'

122. اذا ضربت اوجع واذا اطعمت اشبع

'When you hit, hurt (*i.e.* let him feel it): when you feed, fill.'—Our *Age quod agis.*

123. يا شى يُصلح يا تركه اصلح

'Either the thing is good, or to leave it (undone) is good.'—Same signification as 122.

أُسرق على عدوك جيعان ولا تمر عليه عريان .124

'Pass by thy foe hungry; but pass him not naked (so that he can see you).'—Meaning that if you ask a favour of an enemy, do not let him see that you want it.

العما ولا هذه الدوله .125

'Blindness, and not (rather than) this government.'—Said when an enemy gets into power. They tell a tale that the bear, the fox, and the monkey were in conversation, and the former expressed a desire to be *Wali* (Governor-General) of Syria. 'What will you do for me?' said the fox. 'I will make you my *Kihaya* (secretary),' was the reply. 'Strike me blind,' cried the monkey, 'before I see such a government!'

نحس تعرفه ولا سعد تتعرف به .126

'An unlucky man whom thou knowest, and not (rather than) a lucky man whom thou dost not know.'—Meaning, if you dismiss a servant, or drop a friend, you will probably take one worse. For *Sa'ad* some say *Jayyid* (noble). They also say, *A'l Usman marhúmin bi yeji wahid anhas min el sani,* 'The sons of Usman (the Ottomans) are pitied, (because) he who comes is worse than the other (preceding him).'

من غير دف بيرقص .127

Without the timbrel he dances.'—Said of an excitable, passionate, fidgety man.

قالوا للاعمى ايش بتريد قال جوز عيون .128

They said to the blind man, 'What dost thou desire?' He replied, 'A pair of eyes!'—Said when you offer a thing which you know is wanted.

الذى ما هو من ظهرك كلما جنّ افرحله .129

'He who is not of thy loins, however mad he be, be glad.'
—Because his madness does not concern you. A rascal
proverb, and great contrast to the *Homo sum,* etc.

حبيبى مليح وا جاه هبة ريح .130

'My lover is handsome, and a breath of wind came to
him (and made him love me the more).'—Meaning, he was
glad (or grieved), and now he is the more gladdened (or
grieved). To whom much is given, more shall be given us, etc.

حبيب بحبّه ولو كان عبد اسود .131

'I love my friend, though he be a black slave.'—Said
when a man blames you for liking what is not worthy.

مثل معلم الاولاد حاضر الدقن وعايب العقل .132

'Like the teacher of boys, whose beard is there, but whose
wits are nowhere.'—Said to an absent man, one *cupo concen-
trato,* etc. There are the usual multitude of stories against
schoolmasters. It is enough to quote part of this proverb,
e.g. Házir el dakan.

عزيمة الحمار العرس يا للحطب يا لالمويه .133

'The invitation of the ass to a wedding is to (carry) wood
or water.'—Said, for instance, of a man who has no right to
be in a distinguished assembly; of one who works without
pay, etc.

بلادى ولو جارت علّى عدية واهلى ولو شحو اعلّى كرامة .134

'(It is) my country (home), although comfort has fallen
out with me: (it is) my family, although they fail to befriend
me.'—Used, for instance, when advising an exile to go home.

لو ما كان الوطن قتّال كانت بلاد السوّ خراب ‎.135

'If (one's) birth-place were not deadly, the poor lands (of the world) would be deserts, (as no one would go abroad).'— Almost the same as No. 134.

الذى ما بده يجوّز بنته يغلى نقدها ‎.136

'He who wisheth not to marry his daughter asks much (ready) money.'—*Nakd* is the same as *Mahr*, the pre-nuptial settlement made upon the *Moslemah*. Said of one who, not wishing to sell, asks a ridiculous price. In Syria, men do not refuse to part with an article to a superior, but demand something unconscionable, as £100 for a dog.

بيحكى من كل وادى عصا ‎.137

'He talks a stick from every valley.'—Said of one who talks much nonsense. A favourite proverb with the peasantry; not used in the city, but of course intelligible.

كما ستى كما سيّدى ‎.138

'Like my mistress, like my master.'—Supposed to be said in the language of a black slave girl. Applied to a man who cannot get satisfaction from or content any one. It would also mean, 'There is no good (to be got) from my mistress or my master.' Amongst Syrian Moslems the grandchildren address their grandparents *Sidi* and *Sitti*. The Christians for *Sidi* would say *Jaddi*.

ما بيحكك بدنك الا ضفرك ‎.139

'No nail can scratch (thy body) but thine own.'—Advising a man to do his own business, and not to ask the aid of others.

البصّه ما بتحرق الا مطرحها .140

'The (live) coal burns only its place.'—Meaning the heart knoweth its own bitterness, etc. Said to those who administer useless pity.

الذى تخدمه طيعه والذى ترهنه بيعه .141

'Obey the man thou servest, and sell the thing thou pledgest.'—Because it is useless to keep it. The proverb means, finish off your business—*Age quod agis.*

بيت الذى ربانى ما بينسأنى .142

'The house which brought me up will not give me up (forget me).'—Although you will not assist me, others will.

كل شى تربيه ينفعك الا بنى آدم يقلعك .143

'Every thing (which) thou plantest will profit thee, save the son of man, who will uproot thee.'—Ingratitude is apparently the rule in Syria.

جبناك يا اقرع توانسنا كشفت قرعتك وخوفتنا .144

'We brought thee, O scald-head! to be company with us; thou didst uncover thy scald-head and frighten us.'—Said of a friend whom you summon to your aid, and yet he goes against you.

من تزوج من غير ملته يموت بغير علته .145

'Whoso marries out of his faith, he dies a living death (*lit.* he dies of a disease besides his own disease).'—The signification is evident. The proverb is also said to one who meddles with what does not concern him.

من آمنك لا تخونه ولو كنت خوان .146

'One who trusts thee, deceive not, though thou be a deceiver.'

ان ضاعت الامانه اعمل مخزنك جُبك .147

'If trust be broken make thy pocket thy store.'—Spoken to a man when you lose confidence in him.

يقتل القتيل و يطلع فى جنازته .148

'He kills the killed (man) and goes to his funeral.'—Applied to a man who tricks you and pretends sympathy or friendship.

هلى بِدّه نِح ما يقول اح .149

'He who wants nah (goodies), says not Ah.'—Meaning, who wants to be a rich or great man must not show funk or doubt.

In Syria, and especially in Damascus, there is a child's language, which may perhaps number a hundred words, and which has found its way into literature. Witness the following rather pathetic 'Rubai' of the Shaykh Abd el Ghani el Nablusi :

طعميتك النم و نمنم وَنِح النح

وسقيتك انبو والبستك حرير الدح

وتطلب التس منى ما اقدر اقل لك بح

اليوم يا منيتى انا البعبع و غيرى الدح

'I fed thee with the nam (goodies) and the nam-nam and the nah-nah (goody-goodies) ;

And I gave thee drink (unbu), and I clothed thee in silk the dah (nice) ;

And when thou askest a tip (tiss) I could not say thee bah (there is none) ;

But to-day, O my beloved ! I am the bugbear (bu'bu'), and another man is the nice (dah).'

In the proverb *nah* is a child's word for sweetmeats. *Ah* is the exclamation when eating something too hot, or when wanting to be led to the closet; in the latter sense *kikh* and *kukh* are used by the nurse. *Daadah* means 'walking,' *du*, 'falling,' *'a-'a* (ﺋﺎﺋﻲ), 'going near something dirty.' The camel, the horse, the ass, all have their nursery names, and these are sometimes by no means easy to write.

150. خاص التجاره لا مكسب ولا خصاره

'The specialty of trade is not to gain and not to lose.'— Said to a man when disappointed of a great profit.

151. مثل الذى اسلم الظهر ومات العصر عيسى تبرّ منه ومحمد ما عرف فيه

'As one who Islamized at noon, and died (before prayers) in the afternoon; Jesus got rid of him, and Mohammed has not learned him.'—Between two stools you fall to the ground.

152. كلشى عند العطار الا حبنى شصب ما فيش

'Everything is (to be found) in the druggist's shop, but "love-me-by-force" is not there.'—Applied to one who would force his friendship upon another.

153. لا نحلتك ولا تعقصنى

'(Give me) not thy bee, and do not sting me.'—Said to a treacherous man who pretends to be friendly or who talks 'honey-mouf.'

154. الذى يموت يوصيك باولاده

'He who dies bequeaths to thee his children.'—Quoted of a person who has not done the good you expected him to do. Some end the proverb—*yamútu min al jua*, 'they (the children) die of hunger.'

155.   لبس العيرة ما بيدفّى

'The borrowed cloak never warms.'—Spoken by a man to whom a favour is done ungraciously.

156.   شغل الذى ما بيطلع من القلب عناينه صعب

'The thing which comes not from the heart; its assistance is hard.'—Almost the same as No. 155.

157.   دق الماء وهى ماء

'Beat the water, and (still) it is water.'—Meaning a pig-headed man who agrees to nothing.

158.   الذى ما تتعب به الإيادى ما بتحزن عليه القلوب

'What the hand has not toiled for, the heart does not moil for.'—We say, 'Soon won, soon lost.'

159.   كبر البيدر ولا شماتة الاعدا

'The greatness of the thrashing-floor, and not the exulta-tion of thine enemies.'—Meaning, he works hard in order to disappoint those who would revel in his misfortunes.

160.   المجنون ما له الّا اهله

The madman has none (to care for him) but his own (people).'—Said to a man who is friendly, and from whom you want a favour. Also meaning, 'No one will have patience with your ill-haps but a relative.' A similar say-ing is, *Má li yahinn al 'al úd illa kishruh,* 'No one sym-pathizes with the lute except its wood' (its shell). Applied to the wife taking the part of her husband, etc.

161.   تعلّم من العشق كلمة اوحشتنا

'He has learned from love (only) the word *Auhashtaná.*' ('You have made me sad by your absence,' 'it is long since I saw you.')—He learns only that, and he pretends to know much. Applied to a man who would be a sage, a doctor, a merchant, etc.

المولّى ما له صاحب .162

'The departed (from this world) has no friend.'—Spoken of a man always changing his friends during life.

يوم الله يعين الله .163

'On God's day, God helps.'—Said, for instance, to a person who predicts your failure.

ارض الواطيه تشرب ماها وما غيرها .164

'The lowland drinks its own water and the water of the other (upland).'—Meaning, he keeps friendly with all.

الذى يا خذ امى يصير عمى .165

'He who marries my mother becomes my (step-) father.'— We must be resigned to those who govern us. '*Amm* is the paternal uncle, the step-father, or the father-in-law.

ما يكفى الميّة موته بل عصمته بالقبر .166

'Death is not enough for the dead, he must be squeezed in his grave.'—Meaning, a man not only dies, his family must spend money on his funeral. Said also, when, for instance, a man has too much to do, and more business comes. A similar saying is *khurkah* (for *khirkah*) *fauk el khurdah*, a wad or rag upon the (charge of small) shot; and *Shankulah fauk el himl*, a package upon the load—the last straw that breaks the camel's back.

قلنا لك شوّيه ما قلنا لك احرقه .167

'We said to thee, "cook it," not burn it.'—*Pas de zèle.*

انفخت الطبل وتفرقت العشّاق .168

'The timbrel burst and the lovers were scattered.'— Quoted when offence is taken in company and all part displeased.

كل جديد له بهجه وكل عتيق له دفشه. 169.

'Everything new brings joy: everything old brings re-
pulse.'—The new broom expels the old.

احفظ عتيقك جديدك ما بيبقا اك. 170.

'Preserve thy old; (for) thy new will not last thee.'—
Opposed to the former. In Syria also these sayings are in
pairs.

قلبه من الحامض لاوى. 171.

'His stomach from (eating) sour things is crude.'—Said
when trouble (or business) comes upon trouble, etc.

كثير الغلبه راح لجهنم قال الحطب اخضر. 172.

'Much meddling went to hell (and) said, "The fuel is
green" (there).'—Of course it is useless to tell those there
what the state of the fuel is. *Ghalabah* is mostly applied to
excessive talking, *e.g.*, *Lá takassar el ghalabah !* in Persian,
Fuzuli ma-kun.

من ذكرني بعظمه كنت عنده عظيم. 173.

'He who remembers me with his bone, honours me with
his bone.'—Meaning, he shows that he remembers me. The
play of words is upon *'Azm* and *'Azim; induh kalb 'azim* is
said by the baser sort.

اطلب الخير لجارك تجده بدارك. 174.

'Seek the good of thy neighbour, and thou wilt find good
at home.'—Benefit yourself by benefiting others.

نفع لالضيف ولا لاسيف ولا لغدرات الزمان. 175.

'He is no good; neither to the guest, nor to the sword,
nor to the treachery of time.'—Said of a man utterly worthless.

نفع ما منه دخانه يعمى .176

'There is no profit from him, and his smoke blinds.'—
Spoken of one utterly worthless, and harmful withal.

ان كان طبّاخك جعنيص لا تبالى من القَرَف .177

'If Yaís be thy cook, take no thought of thy squeamish-
ness.'—Yaís was a notoriously unclean cook, who put too
much water in his *marak* ('kitchen' poured on rice, etc.).
The saying means expect no good from a bad workman.

كثرة الطباخين تحرق الطعام .178

'The number of cooks burn the food.'—'They spoil the
broth,' as we say. A similar proverb is, *Kisrat el ruasa
be yagharsik el markab*, 'Too many captains sink the ship.'

مفتاح البطن لقمه ومفتاح الشر كلمه .179

'The key to the belly is a bit (to eat, a mouthful), and the
key to quarrel is a (hot) word.'—Used when people are to be
dissuaded from quarrelling, or when persuading them to eat.

نارك ولا جنة غيرك .180

'Your (hell) fire, and not another man's heaven.'—Meaning, I prefer a poor gift from you to a rich one from another.

وعَلى الكبير يساع الصغير .81

'The big vase contains the small one.'—That is to say,
'Be patient, you are a greater (or wealthier) man than he is.'

لا بد يذوب الثلج ويبان الوحم .182

'The snow must certainly melt and show the filth' (also
خرأ). Spoken of a man who makes much fuss about business
of no importance.

مثل دجاج داريا بيترك القمحه وبياكل الخَّريه . 183.

'Like the hen of Dáraya (village) that leaves the wheat and eats the filth,' which explains itself.

التثايه عوجه 184.

'The cucumber is crooked.'—Meaning, you can't make the cucumber straight, or the liar a truthful man. So they say, *Zanab el kalb a'awaj wa lau hattuh alf sanat li 'l kálib,* 'The dog's tail is crooked though you put it in the mould for a thousand years.' Applied to bad government, etc.

ما شفت ولا قشعت ولا بعرف 185.

'I have not seen, and I have not perceived, and I don't know.'—It is said that this is the first sentence of the catechism taught to the Jewish child at Damascus.

كل فعل جائز و كل مطلوب حرام . 186.

'All (things) done are lawful; all (things) asked for are unlawful.'—Used when encouraging a man to act upon his own responsibility.

مثل خوري عين طينه 187.

'Like the priest of Ayn Tinah.' They relate that the parishioners having complained of their tyrannical parson to the Moslem authorities, found him sitting amongst and in high favour with the latter. A kind of Vicar of Bray. Said of one from whom you cannot escape.

III.

ON WRITING A ROLL OF THE LAW.

THE RULES PRESCRIBED BY MAIMONIDES AND OTHER HEBREW
AUTHORITIES.

I WAS led to investigate the rules established for the guidance of scribes in writing a roll of the Law by noticing the
remarkable differences to be found in manuscripts of various
dates, both as regards the arrangement of columns and the
spaces left between certain words or portions, as well as in
the forms of the letters and other minor points. I especially
observed these in some old rolls from Saná in Arabia, mostly
written upon red leather, in the possession of Mr. Shapira
of Jerusalem.

Feeling sure that much curious matter would be contained in Jewish writings—not only interesting in itself, as
coming from sources but very little known, and scarcely
available to any but Hebrew scholars, and showing in what
regard, nay even how infallible, the laws and traditions of
the scribes and elders are held, but also valuable in aiding
to settle the date of MSS.—I determined to devote some time
to the subject. In this I have received most valuable assistance from Mr. Shapira, a German-speaking Jew by birth,
thoroughly read in the Talmud and traditional lore of the
Hebrews, and now a member of the Protestant community
at Jerusalem. The gist of these notes is taken from Mai-

monides' מישנה תורה, Mishna-Torah—Deuteronomy, or Repetition of the Law—which is also known as יד.החזקה, or
Strong - hand; while the remarks and explanations are derived from various sources.

This Maimonides is frequently spoken of as Rambam,
from the initial letters of his name — *Rabbi Musha Ben
Maimon*. He lived in the twelfth century, and wrote about
the year 1170 A.D., as we know from finding that date mentioned in his treatise on the calendar. He resided chiefly at
Cairo, but visited Jerusalem in his capacity of physician to
Salah-el-din, commonly known as Saladin. In addition to
his knowledge of medicine, he was well versed in astronomy
and Jewish traditional lore, on which subject he is still the
chief authority of the Sephardim, or Spanish and Maghrabi
Jews. After his death, his writings were attacked by certain Rabbis, but never with much success; many of the Safat
school vigorously defended him, especially Yusuf Kara; a
most learned and bigoted teacher in that then famous centre
of Rabbinical learning, who flourished about the year 1540
A.D., and whose tomb is held at the present day in great
reverence by the Jewish colony of Safat, one of the four holy
cities of Palestine in Jewish estimation.

The first statement of Maimonides with regard to the
duty of writing the Law is found in ch. vii. sect. 1, where he
says, 'Every member of the house of Israel is commanded
to write a roll of the Law for himself, as it is written (Deut.
xxxi. 19), "Now therefore write ye this song for you."' This,
he goes on to say, must be done by every one for himself;
and not the song only, but the whole of the Law in which the
song is contained, it being forbidden to write separate portions of Scripture by themselves.

In the Talmud, tract Sanhedrim, p. 21, according to the .

teaching of Rabeh, it is necessary for every male Jew to write a roll of the Law. This argument is founded upon the plural 'ye' in the above-quoted passage, and the Rabbis take it to mean every one of the house of Israel, although there is no such injunction given in the Bible. 'Ye' clearly means Moses and Joshua, who (ver. 14) were ordered by the Lord to present themselves in the tabernacle of the congregation. And again (ver. 22), it is said, 'Moses therefore wrote this song the same day, and taught it to the children of Israel.' Thus we see that the Talmudical rule is based upon a misinterpretation of Scripture, and supplemented by a purely Rabbinical command (Talmud, tract Gittin, p. 60), where the teaching of Abai and Rabeh forbid the writing of detached portions of the Law. No reason is given for this order, but it was issued seemingly to prevent men from transcribing some favourite portion more frequently than another, which would lead the unlearned to believe that these sections were more worthy of reverence and honour than others, and thus the integrity of the Scriptures would be impaired. Hence the command to write the whole Law or none. Our author goes on to state, that even if a man inherits a roll of the Law from his ancestors, he is nevertheless in duty bound to write a new one for himself; and that it is reckoned to every one who writes a roll of the Law with his own hand as though he had received it in person from Mount Sinai. This is fully enunciated in the Talmud, tract Menachoth, p. 33. Again, should the man be unable to write himself, he is bound to commission another to write a roll for him; and if he then corrects but one letter of the roll so written, it will be the same as though he had written the whole of the Law. This easy method of writing a roll is given in the teaching of Rabb Sheshath (Talmud, tract Menachoth,

p. 30). It is even now a common custom among the Jews, when a roll of the Law is written for the use of the synagogue, to omit a few words at the end. The roll is then completed by several members of the congregation, each writing a single letter; and thus each one is able to declare that, as the roll of the Law would have been unlawful should that one letter have been wanting, he, by writing it, has made the roll correct and lawful, and thus it is reckoned to him as though he had written the whole Law with his own hand, and fulfilled the supposed command of God.

The passage (Deut. xvii. 18, 19), 'And it shall be, when he (the king) sitteth upon the throne of his kingdom, that he shall write him a copy of this Law in a book, out of that which is before the priests the Levites; and it shall be that he shall read therein all the days of his life,' &c. is taken to mean that a king must write for himself a roll of the Law, in addition to the one he possessed before coming to the throne; and this book is to be corrected from the roll of Ezra through the great Sanhedrim. The roll he held before he became king is to be deposited in his treasury; but the second, written by him or by his order, must always remain with his person. When he goes to battle, it must go with him; so when he sits upon the judgment-seat. At his meals it must be placed before him. Should, however, the king not be in possession of a roll of the Law at the time of his coming to the throne, he is bound to write two rolls on the day of his accession; one to be deposited in his treasury, and the other to be always near his person, except in the night-time, or when he is going to sleep, even if it be in the day-time, when he is at the bath, or in unclean places. Maimonides, however, does not state so much as the Talmud, tract Sanhedrim, p. 22, where the king is ordered to make the roll like a charm, and bind it to his arm, or let it hang from his shoulder by a strap, in support of which fashion Ps. xiv. 8 is quoted, 'I have set the Lord always before me, because he is at my right hand.'

The Hebrew word *mishna* in the above passage of Deut. is translated 'copy' in the Authorised Version; but according to the Talmud, tract Sanhedrim, p. 21, it is interpreted by Rabbi Elieser son of Simeon, on the authority of Rabbi Elieser of Modahi (who lived about A.D. 80), 'a repetition.' Hence the command for the two rolls of the Law.

The Karaïte Jews, as well as many of the Rabbinical grammarians, call the book of Deuteronomy Mishna-Torah— Repetition of the Law—and they consequently believe that the king is bound to write for himself, and always carry about his person, the book of Deuteronomy, which contains most of the moral law, as well as many precepts which he, in his regal position, is specially bound to observe.

The custom still prevails among the Jews living in Arabia, that a chief Rabbi, on coming into office, should write out for himself, and always wear, the book of Deuteronomy. I am not aware that this usage holds amongst any other community of Jews than those of Arabia proper, who thus invest their chief Rabbi, partially at all events, with regal honours.

In ch. vii. sect. 4, Maimonides states that a roll of the Law which is not written upon marked lines is unlawful, as is the case if it be written partly upon Gevil (גויל, parchment), and partly upon Kalaph (קלף, vellum). The letters must be regular, correct, and well formed. The scribe is to leave as much space between the words as is required for a small letter, and between the letters a space of a hair's breadth; between the lines the space is to be equal to the breadth of a written line.

In the Jerusalem Talmud, tract Megila, ch. i. it is said that three oral commands were given to Moses on Mount Sinai: viz. 1. that all rolls were to be written upon skins, not upon cloth, papyrus, or any other material; 2. that they were to be written with *deyow* ink; 3. that they were to be written upon marked lines.

With reference to the first of these injunctions, we find that the roll must be written upon the skins of clean animals, that is to say, those lawful for food. It is unlawful to write upon the skins of unclean animals, or of fishes, even though they be clean. The skins must be tanned by an adult male Jew, who is responsible and a true believer, not by a Gentile or slave, nor by a Jew that is insane or not arrived at manhood, nor by a Jewess. The tanner must tan the skin with the full purpose that it be used to write the Law upon; in fact, on putting it into the pit, he must repeat this formula: 'I do tan this skin on purpose that a roll of the Law be written upon it.' The process of curing the skin must be gone through in the following order: first, to shave off the hair; secondly, to soak it in salt water; thirdly, to lay it for a time in meal-paste; fourthly, to tan it with gall-nuts; and lastly, to clean it. The skin so prepared is called Gevil (parchment), and was orally bidden to Moses, who at the same time was enjoined to write only on the outer or hairy side of the skin, the side towards the body being unlawful.

Two other preparations of the skin were used, by splitting it into two thicknesses, the outer part being called Kalaph (vellum), and the inner Ducsustus (דוכסוסטוס). The law of tanning these is the same as that for Gevil. It is said to have been orally commanded to Moses to write the four portions of the arm and head phylacteries upon the inner side of Kalaph, and the door-post phylactery upon the outer side of

Ducsustus. Thus a scribe is enjoined to write a roll of the Law upon Gevil, arm and head phylacteries upon Kalaph, and door-post phylacteries upon Ducsustus.

Should it happen that a roll, by ignorance, had been written upon Kalaph, and there were no other at hand to read from, it would still be lawful to make use of that in such a case, provided that the whole of it were written upon one preparation. Should part, however, be on Gevil, and part on Kalaph, the roll must in any case be unlawful.

As regards the ink, *deyow*, דיו (for the word see Jer. xxxvi. 18), we find in the Talmud, tract Shabath, p. 133, the recipe for making it, viz. to take soot deposited by the smoke of burning oil, resin, wax, and suchlike things, knead it up thoroughly with gum and honey, make it into small cakes, and dry it; then pound it very fine, and mix it with infusion of gall-nuts or some acid. This is an ink which does not leave an indelible mark; for if the ink dyes or stains, or gold letters be used, then the roll becomes unlawful.

The marked lines must be made (Talmud, tract Sophrim) with a hard piece of wood or iron, or some other substance which does not leave behind it any coloured mark. If more than three—or, as some say, four—words be not written upon marked lines, then the roll is unlawful. The writer too, in transcribing, must always have a correct copy before him; and it is forbidden, even to the most learned scribe, to write one single letter without copying it from the text that lies in front of him.

Maimonides continues, that the length of the line should be such as to contain thirty letters, or three times the length of the word למשפחותיכם ('to your generations'). This word is only twice used in the Bible, viz. Exod. xii. 21 and Num. xxxiii. 54; and in both these places the vau is omitted after the cheth, thus making it a word of nine letters instead of ten. It is curious that so careful a writer should have made this mistake; and that it should have been quoted and copied, without comment or correction, by his very numerous followers, is still more remarkable. In the Talmud the word is given, but no number of letters assigned to it; thus the correct number of letters in a line would be twenty-seven. This breadth is ordered for the column in order that the MS. may not have the appearance of an Agiroth, or epistle. This word אגרת is only used in those portions of Scripture which were written after the Exile, as Ezra, Nehemiah, Esther, and 2 Chronicles; and it seems that letters were written on narrow strips of skin or parchment; the word itself, in Hebrew, means a gathering together, a collection, and is used in old Karaïte writings for a lexicon.

The scribe is farther specially enjoined not to make any words or letters smaller than the rest, and not to cramp his writing in order to make space for the necessary divisions. If at the end of a line he meets with a word of five letters, he is to be careful to write three letters in that line, and two in the next, not *vice versâ*. If there is not room to write the three letters, he is to leave a blank space, and begin another line. If a word of two letters come at the end of a line, he is not to write it beyond the edge of the column—though this is allowed in the case of two final letters of a long word —but begin a new line with it. Half a long word, as of ten letters, may be written at the end of a line, and the other half beyond the column; but should there not be room for the half, the space must be left blank, and the whole word put at the beginning of the new line.

Most of the Rabbis, however, disagree with Maimonides about this last rule, and prove from the Talmud that of words

of five letters and upwards it is allowable to write at most
two letters, while of words of two, three, or four letters it is
permitted to write one only beyond the edge of the column.
Most authorities, too, forbid the leaving of a blank space at
the end of a line, because it has too much the appearance
of a division; and to obviate this they allowed the letters
ם ת ל ה א to be spread out thus, רׄ אׄ, so as to fill up or cover
the required space.

In ch. viii. sect. 7, our author says that the scribe is
bound to leave four blank lines between each of the five books
of Moses, neither more nor less; the following book is to be
commenced at the beginning of the fifth line. Care must be
taken to end the book of Deuteronomy in the middle of the
last line of the column; should the scribe calculate that the
writing will not reach to the end of the column, then he must
gradually reduce the length of his lines, so that the last word
but three may reach to the end of the penultimate line of
the column; the first half of the last line must then contain the three final words, לעיני כל ישראל ('in the sight of all
Israel').

These rules are taken from the Talmud, tract Baba-Bathra,
p. 13; tract Menachoth, p. 30; tract Sophrim, ch. ii.; and
from the Jerusalem Talmud, tract Megila, ch. i., where it is
also added, that the books of the Pentateuch must end and
begin at the middle of a column; while the books of the
Prophets are to end at the bottom and begin at the top of a
column. This is so arranged that a man, if he wished it,
might cut out any one of the books of the Prophets for his
own convenience, but would be obliged to keep the five books
of Moses together, it being unlawful to separate them.

Some rolls in the possession of Mr. Shapira, which were
brought from Arabia, have all the books conterminous with

the columns. These may possibly have been written before the end of the third century A.D., when this rule was promulgated.

In sect. 8 of the same chapter the writer is admonished to be very careful about those letters which have to be made large or small, about the words which have to be pointed, and those which have to be written differently from the others; the winding *p*'s and crooked letters are to be written in conformity with the traditions handed down from the scribes of old till the present day. The Tagim תגים too (dots or crowns) must be scrupulously attended to; some letters must have no dots at all, some three, and some seven. Every crown must have the form of a י, but as fine as a hair.

There is one complete alphabet of letters larger than the others, and one of smaller letters, in the whole of the Old Testament. These are not only pointed out by the Masoretic school, but mentioned in the Talmud, especially in tract Sophrim. Thus we see that they are as early as the end of the second or beginning of the third century A.D.

The words in the Pentateuch were required to have a point over some of their letters, as we see from tract Sophrim and other passages in the Talmud. In tract Aboth of Rabbi Nathan we find that Rabbi Elieser, son of Simeon, gave reasons for some of these. For example, he asks, ' Why is the word וישקהו (" and he kissed him"), Gen. xxxiii. 4, pointed ?' It is to show that this was the only time that Esau gave Jacob a true kiss, all the others being false. This punctuation, consequently, has nothing in common with the grammatical points for helping the reader, which are of much later date, and are not mentioned in the Talmud. No points are prescribed to mark the ends of verses, chapters, &c. Some say that the division of the books into verses dates from the

eighth century A.D.; this I shall disprove from passages in
the Talmud. In tract Sophrim, ch. iii., the following is
contained in the seventh doctrine: 'A roll of the Law which
has a division of verses, or has points at the beginning of a
verse, is unlawful to read from. If the points have afterwards been scratched out or mixed up with the letters, the
roll nevertheless remains unlawful.' (The tract Sophrim was
written in the third century A.D.)

In certain of the old rolls before mentioned there is a
single point at the beginning of the verses, and three ∴ at
the beginning of portions. Some of these points have been
scratched out, but some have been overlooked. These rolls
have other points under the letters, in places one, and in
others as many as four, in a verse. It seems impossible to
assign any reason for these eccentricities, as it is difficult to
imagine that a scribe, a learned man, should be ignorant of,
or inattentive to, the doctrine of the Mishna, unless we say
that the rolls were written before the promulgation of the
above-mentioned rules or the publication of the Mishna.

With reference to the Tagim (from Syriac *tag*, a crown),
see Talmud, tract Menachoth, p. 30, where Rabeh (who lived
A.D. 300, and is not to be confused with Raba, who lived
thirty-five years later) says that seven letters must have three
crowns[1] each, viz. ש ע ט נ ז ג צ. Thus we see that the dots upon
these seven letters are not only a tradition of the scribes, but
a doctrine of the Talmud. There are other letters which,
by tradition of the scribes, supported by anecdotes scattered
through the Talmud, ought to have one crown apiece, viz.
ב ד ה ח י ק.

---

[1] The single crown would be represented by our acute accent; the
triple by an acute and a grave, forming an acute angle and bisected by a
perpendicular. See note at end of this Appendix for these illustrations.

The rules for crowns on certain letters in the portions of Scripture used for arm, head, and door-post phylacteries, need not here be enlarged upon. It is an established rule, however, that all the crowns should be above the letters. A curious case of the non-observance of this regulation is to be seen in a MS. now in the hands of Mr. Alt of Frankfort-on-Maine. The letters have not only crowns and flourishes above but also below.

Maimonides states (ch. vii. sect. 9), with regard to the above-mentioned rules, that it was a virtue to follow them exactly; but should it happen that the scribe omitted some of the crowns, or made the lines too near together or too far apart, too long or too short, still, if none of the letters touch another, if no single letter has been omitted or inserted out of place, if all the letters are properly shaped, &c., then the roll is lawful in case of need.

It seems from the Talmud, and the demonstration of many later Rabbis, that our author referred only to the crowns on the letters which are ordained by tradition of the scribes. The seven which are so clearly mentioned in the Talmud must be crowned, and the roll in which they are not so written becomes unlawful, as though some of its letters were misshapen and improperly written.

In tract Menachoth, Rabbi Yehuda said, in the name of Rab (who lived A.D. 210), that every letter must stand distinct and separate, or else the roll is unlawful. The form of all the letters of the alphabet is nowhere mentioned collectively in the Talmud as a doctrine; but from scattered sayings, debates, teachings, and questions in the Babylon and Jerusalem Talmuds, we can pick out the form of nearly every letter. From these authorities it seems that the letter ת, as it now stands in printed books, was formerly written otherwise. It is forbidden too to make any separation between the members of the letters; so the Yod of the Aleph must touch the body; and the three Yods of the Shin must be joined to the basal line. There are, however, two letters whose parts must be separated, viz. ה and ק: it is unlawful, according to the Talmud, to write them otherwise; and if they are so written, it is not enough to scratch out the necessary space, but the whole letter must be re-written : see tract Menachoth, p. 29, and tract Shabath, p. 104, for the reason of these rules. Here we find that if there was any doubt as to whether a letter was correctly written or not, it was to be shown to a moderately-intelligent boy. If he could read it without difficulty, then it was lawful, and *vice versâ.* In some of the MSS. before mentioned, we find nearly all the left feet of the letter Koph obliterated; a few have been overlooked, and these touch the main body. From this we may be led to imagine that these rolls were written before the promulgation of this rule, which is, however, very old. In the latter passage of the Talmud, we find that Rabanan told Rabbi Joshua son of Levi (who flourished about 250 A.D.), that among other things taught on a certain day in the synagogue was this : The letter Koph ק represents the word קדוש, the Holy One; and the letter Resh ר the word רשע, the sinner. 'Why does the Koph turn away its face from the Resh ?—it being written thus קר. It means that the Holy One has no pleasure in looking on the sinner. Why does the crown of the Koph incline to the Resh ? To show that the Holy One holds out the crown to the sinner if he repent. Why is the space left between the foot and main body of the Koph ? To tell the sinner that the door of the holy place is open to him if he repent.'

There are many rules observed in writing, which, though

not mentioned in the Talmud, have been handed down by tradition of the scribes. For instance: Maimonides directs (ch. vii. sect. 10) that every column of a roll should have not more than sixty nor less than forty lines. In tract Sophrim, ch. ii. doct. 6, the number of lines is to be forty-two or sixty, seventy-two or ninety-eight; and the reason for these numbers is there given. The blank space between the portions, which I enter into fully in another place, is to be of sufficient length to write nine letters in it, or thrice the word אשר. In the column which contains the Song of Moses after crossing the Red Sea, there are to be five lines preceding the Song itself, the first line to begin with the word הבאים, ' that came;' the second with ביבשה, ' upon dry land;' the third with יהוה, ' the Lord;' the fourth with מת, ' dead;' and the fifth with במצרים, ' the Egyptians' (Ex. xiv. 28-31). After the Song there must also be five lines to begin with the words ותקה, ' and she took;' אחריה, ' after her;' סום, ' the horse;' ויצאו, ' they went out;' and ויבאו, ' they come,' respectively (Ex. xv. 20-23). At the top of the column which contains the Song of Moses before his death there are to be six lines, to commence respectively with the words, ואעידה, ' to record' (or rather, ' to witness'); אחרי, ' after;' הדרך, ' the way;' באחרית, ' in the latter;' להכעיסו, ' to provoke him to anger;' and קהל, ' congregation' (Deut. xxxi. 28-30).

After this Song there must be five lines in the column, having these initial words: 1st, ויבא, ' and he came;' 2d, לדבר, ' of speaking;' 3d, אשר, ' which;' 4th, הזאת, ' this;' and 5th, אשר, ' which' (Deut. xxxii. 44-47).

The exact form in which the two Songs themselves are to be written will be described in another place.

In ch. vii. sect. 10, Maimonides states that the above-mentioned rules are given in order that the writer may prepare to conform to them; and it will be considered a virtuous action on his part if he does so. Should the scribe even depart from these rules, the roll does not become unlawful, unless he has written those words defective (חסר, *versio defectiva*) which ought to be written full (מלא, *versio plena*), or *vice versâ;* or has written the Keri קרי, 'reading,' instead of the Katib כתיב, 'written' version; or has made open instead of closed divisions, or *vice versâ;* or has written the prose portions of Scripture in the form of a song. In any of these cases the roll becomes unlawful, and must not be regarded with the reverence due to a roll of the Law, but only as a book suited for the teaching of children.

A full list of the defective words here spoken of is nowhere given in the Talmud, this wearisome task being left to the so-called Masoretic school; but there are many notices of them scattered throughout the book. The difference between the reading and written texts is frequently adverted to by the Talmud, and reasons given for it. As an example, we may take the words 'ishkabena' and 'ishgalena' (Deut. xxviii. 30), which have almost the same meaning, the former being the Keri, and the latter the Katib text; or again (Deut. xxviii. 27), 'ubatchorim' and 'ubapolim.'

The roll may be used for teaching children to read from, if the inaccuracies consist only in the open or closed divisions, or in the manner of writing the poetical and prose portions. If, however, the spelling of words or shape of the letters be incorrect, then it is unlawful even to keep the roll in a house; it must be buried.

A man is forbidden—see Talmud, tract Ketuboth, p. 19, where Rabb Aini quotes Job xi. 14 in support of his doctrine—to keep in his house, or even in his possession, an incorrect roll of the Law for more than thirty days; but he must either correct or bury it. Later on there will be occasion to speak more fully of this custom of burying rolls of the Law. A roll may be corrected even though it has three inaccuracies in every column; but if there are four mistakes in half or more of the number of columns, even though there be no other faults at all, then the roll may not be corrected, and must consequently be buried. If, however, the majority of the columns be correct, and in the minority there be one that has less than four errors, then it is lawful to correct such a roll. See the teaching of Rab (who lived about the end of the second and beginning of the third centuries, A.D.) in tract Menachoth, p. 29.

These rules only refer to the case of words which have been written as defective (חסר) when they ought to have been full (מלא), as these must be corrected by writing the omitted letters over the word. In the case of full words being written instead of defective, any number may be corrected, as it is only necessary to scratch out the superfluous letters (Maim. ch. vii. sect. 13). This is also mentioned in the Talmud, tract Menachoth, p. 29, where Agra, the father-in-law of Rabbi Aba (flourished in the third century), having superfluous letters in his roll, asked Rabbi Aba what he should do with them, and received this reply: 'Where it is forbidden to make corrections applies only to the case of wanting, not of superfluous letters.' This, however, hardly tallies with the rule (Maim. vii. 4) before mentioned, which prescribes a hair's breadth as the space to be left between the letters.

It is allowable to write the five books of Moses separately, one by one; but in this form they are not holy as a roll of the Law. It is not, however, lawful to write portions or selections of Scripture, even for the purpose of teaching children from them; but a man may commence a roll, and .

use it as a book of instruction, if he has the intention of finishing it within a reasonable time. The only condition under which a person may write a portion of Scripture is, that he put no more than three words in each line (see Talmud, tract Juma, p. 37).

It is permitted to join the Prophets and the Scriptures to the Pentateuch in one roll; but the scribe must leave four blank lines between each book of Moses, and three between each book of the Prophets, whether the Greater or the Lesser. This rule was given as early as A.D. 120 by Rabbi Mair, in Talmud, tract Baba-Bathra, p. 13.

The order of the Prophets is: 1, Joshua; 2, Judges; 3, Samuel; 4, Kings; 5, Jeremiah; 6, Ezekiel; 7, Isaiah; and then the twelve minor Prophets. The Scriptures stand thus: 1, Ruth; 2, Psalms; 3, Job; 4, Proverbs; 5, Ecclesiastes; 6, Song of Solomon; 7, Lamentations; 8, Daniel; 9, Esther; 10, Chronicles. The blank lines for the purpose of dividing the books has already been noticed, ch. vii. sect. 7.

It is explained in the Talmud, tract Baba-Bathra, p. 14, that although Hosea prophesied before Isaiah, his writings are put after the greater Prophets, for fear of their being lost by reason of their smallness; and although Isaiah's prophecy is earlier than that of either Jeremiah or Ezekiel, the former of these two is made to follow Kings, because that book ends with the Captivity of Judah, and the whole contents of Jeremiah relate to this time of bondage. Ezekiel then follows, as he prophesied during the Captivity; and his book, which ends with words of comfort, is suitably followed by Isaiah. Notwithstanding that Job lived in the time of Moses, his book is put in the third place, it being judged unadvisable to begin the Scriptures with a book of suffering.

In the list just given, Maimonides has left out the book

of Ezra, seemingly by mistake, as it is clearly mentioned in the Talmud—Nehemiah there being included in it—which says that Moses wrote the whole of the Pentateuch, except the last eight verses of Deuteronomy (here we see incidentally that the division into verses was recognised as early as the beginning of the third century); that Joshua wrote his book, except the verses relating to his death; that Samuel wrote the books called after him, and also the books of Judges and Ruth; the verses, however, relating to his death were written by Gad and Nathan the prophets. David and ten prophets were the joint authors of the Psalms. Jeremiah wrote his book of prophecy, Lamentations, and the books of Kings. Hezekiah and his disciples are said to have written the book of Proverbs, the Song of Solomon, Ecclesiastes, and the prophecy of Isaiah, who, according to the Talmud, tract Jebamoth, had not time to complete his work, being slain in the prime of life by king Manasseh, who sawed him in two as he was hiding in a hollow cedar-tree. Ezra wrote the book of Chronicles, and part of the book called by his name, which was finished by Nehemiah. The members of the Great Synod wrote the books of Ezekiel, Daniel, and Esther, as well as the twelve Minor Prophets.

The whole of the Scriptures must be written upon marked lines, which I have already described, even though they be upon paper, which seems to be allowed for the use of schools, though it is distinctly contrary to the command stated to have been given by God to Moses on Mount Sinai (see Talmud, tract Megila, ch. i.). The doctrine of marked lines is at least as old as the second century A.D.; for we find in the Talmud, tract Megila, p. 18, and tract Menachoth, p. 82, Rabbi Jeremiah, quoting Rabbi Jehudah (the author of the Mishna), says that phylacteries need not be written on marked .

lines, &c. Some of the rolls from Arabia, which I have before mentioned as frequently differing from Talmudical regu-
lations, are not written upon marked lines.

As regards the peculiar sanctity attached to a roll of the
Law, it seems that if the Scriptures and the Prophets were
joined to the five books of Moses, then the roll was only to
be regarded with the reverence due to one book of Moses.
The reason given for this curious decision is, that too much
is equally a fault with too little. The promulgator of it seems
to have feared that the holiness of the Pentateuch would be
diluted by contact with the other books of the Bible, or its
odour of sanctity absorbed by some chemical process.

Chapter viii. of Maimonides commences with the rules
for open and closed, or broad and narrow, partitions (petucha,
פתוחה, and stima, סתימה). The open partition is of two
forms: 1st, if the scribe ends one section in the middle of
a line, and there is still space in that line to write nine letters, then he must begin the next section at the beginning
of the following line. 2d, if there is no blank space at the
end of the line, or not sufficient to write nine letters in it,
then a whole line must be left blank, and the succeeding
section must begin with the third line.

The introduction of the open and closed partitions seems
to be earlier than the time of the Mishna; for we find in
the Talmud, tract Menachoth, pp. 31, 32, mention of Rabb
having written the door-post phylacteries with closed partitions, as in the Pentateuch. The texts used for these phylacteries are Deut. vi. 4-9 and xi. 13-21. A saying of Rabbi
Simeon is also quoted, to the effect that he once saw Rabbi
Mair writing a door-post phylactery upon a piece of Ducsustus
like a board (*i. e.* long and narrow), and leaving blank borders
at top and bottom, and open partitions. Rabbi Simeon asked

the reason of this, and was answered, that though they were closed partitions in the roll of the Law, yet the two texts are not near one another in the Pentateuch, and have consequently no right to closed partitions. .

We see here that the doctrine of closed and open divisions is as early as the time of Rabbi Mair (flourished A.D. 120), though they are not mentioned in the Mishna, which generally left rules of this kind to the Masoretic teachers. In the Talmud, tract Sophrim, ch. i. doct. 14, and in the Jerusalem Talmud, tract Megila, ch. i., rules are laid down about them. Many of the later Rabbis disagree strongly with Maimonides, and most modern rolls are written in conformity with his first rule.   There is great difference of opinion too about the size of the blank to be left; Maimonides maintains that it must be sufficient for nine large letters, as in the word אשר; while other Rabbis hold that space for nine yods is enough.

We now come to the closed partitions, which are of three forms : 1st, if the scribe ends a section in the middle of a line, he must leave room for nine letters, and then write one word of the following portion at the end of the line.   2d, if there is not space for the above rule to be carried out, then the latter part of the line is to be left blank, and the next section to be begun in the middle of the second line.   3d, when a section is conterminous with a line, sufficient space must be left blank in the next line, and the next section made to begin in the middle of the line.

Some of the Rabbis allow a smaller space for the closed than for the open partitions ; but most rolls, even the oldest, are written in conformity with the rules given by Maimonides, who lays great stress upon their being rigidly adhered to ; for he says that a roll which is incorrectly written with regard to the defective or superfluous letters may be easily corrected, as already shown; but if the blank spaces are not left in their proper places; if an open be put for a closed partition, or the contrary; or if a blank space be put where it ought not to be, or be omitted; or if the form of a poetical portion be changed, then the roll becomes unlawful, and can only be remedied by cutting away the whole of the incorrect portions, and substituting properly-written ones in their places.

Maimonides then goes on to tell us (ch. viii. sect. 4) that, owing to the great confusion in all the treatises on these partitions, he has judged it expedient to give a full list of all the passages in the Pentateuch which require open or closed divisions. Of the former there are 290, of the latter 379. (The chapters and verses in this list are taken from the printed Hebrew Bible, not from the Authorised Version.) The roll which Maimonides used as his standard was one for many years in the possession of, and corrected by, Rabbi Ben Asher, who lived about the beginning of the tenth century. It contained, he says, all the twenty-four books of the Bible, and was considered so trustworthy, that it was taken from Jerusalem to Egypt, in order that all the MSS. there might be corrected by it. The twenty-four books are counted thus by the Jews: 1-5, the Pentateuch; 6, Joshua; 7, Judges; 8, Samuel; 9, Kings; 10, Jeremiah; 11, Ezekiel; 12, Isaiah; 13, the twelve Minor Prophets; 14, Ruth; 15, Psalms; 16, Job; 17, Proverbs; 18, Ecclesiastes; 19, Song of Solomon; 20, Lamentations; 21, Daniel; 22, Ezra and Nehemiah; 23, Esther; 24, Chronicles.

In Genesis

The open partitions are :		The closed are :	
Chap.	Verses.	Chap.	Verses.
I.	6, 9, 14, 20, 24.	III.	16, 17.
II.	1, 4.	IV.	1.
III.	22.	V.	1, 6, 9, 12, 15, 18, 21, 25,
VI.	5, 9.		28, 32.
IX.	18.	VI.	13.
X.	1.	VIII.	15.
XI.	1, 10.	IX.	8.
XII.	1, 10.	X.	15, 21.
XIV.	1.	XI.	12, 14, 16, 18, 20, 22, 24,
XVIII.	1.		26.
XXI.	22.	XV.	1.
XXII.	1, 20.	XVI.	1.
XXIII.	1.	XVII.	1, 15.
XXV.	1, 12, 19.	XX.	1.
XXVI.	1.	XXI.	1.
XXXII.	4.	XXIV.	1.
XXXV.	1, 9, and in middle of v.	XXVI.	34.
	22.	XXVII.	1.
XXXVI.	1, 31.	XXVIII.	10.
XXXVII.	1.	XXXIII.	18.
XXXVIII.	1.	XXXIV.	1.
XL.	1.	XXXVI.	20.
XLI.	1.	XXXIX.	1.
XLVIII.	1.	XLIV.	18.
XLIX.	1, 5, 8, 13, 14, 27.	XLVI.	8, 28.
		XLIX.	16, 19, 20, 21, 22.

In Exodus

The open partitions are :		The closed are :	
Chap.	Verses.	Chap.	Verses.
I.	8.	III.	1.
II.	1, 23.	VI.	2, 14, 29.
IV.	18, 27.	VII.	14, 19.
VI.	10, 13.	VIII.	1, 12, 16.
VII.	1, 8, 26.	IX.	13.
IX.	1, 8, 22.	X.	12.

In Exodus (*continued*)

The open partitions are:		The closed are:	
Chap.	Verses.	Chap.	Verses.
X.	1.	XI.	4, 9.
XI.	1.	XII.	29, 51.
XII.	21, 37, 43.	XIII.	17.
XIII.	1, 11.	XV.	22, 27.
XIV.	1, 15, 26.	XVI.	4, 28.
XV.	1, 20.	XX.	1, 2, 7, 12, 14, 15, 16, 17, 22.
XVI.	11.		
XVII.	1, 8, 14.	XXI.	7, 12, 14, 15, 16, 17, 18, 20, 22, 26, 33, 35, 37.
XVIII.	1.		
XIX.	1.	XXII.	4, 5, 6, 9, 15, 17, 19, 27.
XX.	8, 18.	XXIII.	1, 4, 5, 6, 26.
XXI.	1, 28.	XXIV.	12.
XXII.	13, 24.	XXV.	10.
XXIII.	20.	XXVI.	1, 31.
XXIV.	1.	XXVII.	1, 9, 20.
XXV.	1, 23, 31	XXVIII.	1, 13, 15, 31, 36.
XXVI.	15.	XXIX.	1, 38.
XXVIII.	6.	XXX.	34.
XXX.	1, 11, 17, 22.	XXXI.	1, 18.
XXXI.	12.	XXXIII.	1.
XXXII.	7, 15.	XXXV.	1.
XXXIII.	12, 17.	XXXVI.	8, 20.
XXXIV.	1, 27.	XXXVIII.	1, 8, 21, 24.
XXXV.	4, 30.	XXXIX.	6, 27, 30, 32.
XXXVI.	14.	XL.	17, 20, 22, 24, 26, 28, 30, 33.
XXXVII.	1, 10, 17, 25.		
XXXIX.	2, 8, 22, 33.		
XL.	1, 34.		

In Leviticus

The open partitions are:		The closed are:	
Chap.	Verses.	Chap.	Verses.
I.	14.	I.	10.
III.	1, 6, 12.	II.	1, 4, 5, 7, 14.
IV.	1, 13, 22, 27, 32.	V.	11, 14.
V.	1, 17, 20.	VI.	7.

In Leviticus (*continued*)

The open partitions are:		The closed are:	
Chap.	Verses.	Chap.	Verses.
VI.	1, 12, 17.	IX.	1.
VII.	1, 11, 28.	XI.	29, 39.
VIII.	1.	XIII.	24, 38, 40, 47.
X.	8, 12.	XIV.	21.
XI.	1.	XV.	16, 25.
XII.	1.	XVIII.	6, 7, 8, 9, 10, 11, 12, 13,
XIII.	1, 9, 18, 29.		14, 15, 16, 17.
XIV.	1, 33.	XIX.	33.
XV.	1, 10.	XXI.	10, 16.
XVI.	1.	XXII.	26.
XVII.	1.	XXIII.	15, 26.
XVIII.	1.	XXIV.	10.
XIX.	1, 23.	XXV.	8, 25, 29, 35, 39, 47.
XX.	1.	XXVI.	27.
XXI.	1.	XXVII.	9.
XXII.	1, 17.		
XXIII.	1, 4, 9, 23, 33.		
XXIV.	1, 5, 13.		
XXV.	1.		
XXVI.	3, 14.		
XXVII.	1.		

In Numbers

The open partitions are:		The closed are:	
Chap.	Verses.	Chap.	Verses.
I.	22, 24, 26, 28, 30, 32, 34,	I.	20.
	36, 39, 40, 42, 44, 48.	II.	10, 17, 18, 25.
II.	1, 32.	III.	27, 40.
III.	1, 5, 11, 14, 45.	IV.	29, 38.
IV.	1, 17, 21.	VI.	24, 25, 26, 27.
V.	1, 5, 11.	VII.	1, 12.
VI.	1, 22.	VIII.	23.
VII.	18, 24, 30, 36, 42, 48, 54,	IX.	15.
	60, 66, 72, 78, 84.	X.	29, 35.
VIII.	1, 5.	XII.	4.
IX.	1, 9.	XV.	22, 27, 35.

In Numbers (*continued*)

The open partitions are :

Chap.	Verses.
x.	1, 11.
xi.	1, 16, 23.
xii.	1, 14.
xiii.	1.
xiv.	11, 26.
xv.	1, 17, 32, 37.
xvi.	1.
xvii.	6, 16, 25, 27.
xviii.	8, 25.
xix.	1.
xx.	1, 7, 22.
xxi.	4, 21.
xxv.	1, 10, 16, and in middle of ver. 19.
xxvi.	1 (in the middle of the verse), 52.
xxvii.	6, 12.
xxviii.	1, 9, 11.
xxix.	1.
xxx.	2.
xxxi.	1.
xxxii.	1, 20.
xxxiii.	1.
xxxiv.	1, 16.
xxxv.	1, 9.
xxxvi.	1.

The closed are :

Chap.	Verses.
xvi.	20, 23.
xvii.	1, 9.
xviii.	1, 21.
xx.	12, 14.
xxi.	1, 17.
xxii.	2.
xxvi.	12, 15, 19, 23, 26, 28, 35, 38, 42, 44, 48, 57.
xxvii.	1, 15.
xxviii.	16, 26.
xxix.	7, 12, 17, 20, 23, 26, 29, 32, 35.
xxxi.	13, 21, 25.
xxxii.	5, 16.
xxxiii.	40, 50.

In Deuteronomy

The open partitions are :

Chap.	Verses.
iv.	1, 25, 41.
v.	1.
vi.	4.
vii.	12.
viii.	1, 17.
ix.	1.

The closed are :

Chap.	Verses.
ii.	2, in middle of ver. 8, 17, 31.
iii.	23.
v.	6, 11, 12, 16, 17 (as well as three others within this and the following

In Deuteronomy (*continued*)

The open partitions are:

Chap.	Verses.
x.	1, 12.
xiii.	2.
xiv.	22.
xv.	19.
xvi.	1, 13.
xvii.	8.
xix.	11.
xxi.	1.
xxii.	6.
xxv.	17.
xxvi.	1.
xxvii.	1.
xxviii.	1, 15.
xxix.	1, 9.
xxxi.	1, 14.
xxxii.	1, 44, 48.
xxxiii.	1, 8.

The closed are:

Chap.	Verses.
	ver.), in the middle of ver. 19.
vi.	10, 16, 20.
vii.	1, 17.
xi.	10, 13, 22, 26, 29.
xii.	20, 29.
xiii.	7, 13.
xiv.	1, 3, 9, 11, 28.
xv.	1, 7, 12.
xvi.	9, 18, 21.
xvii.	1, 2, 14.
xviii.	1, 3, 6, 9.
xix.	1, 14, 15.
xx.	1, 10, 19.
xxi.	10, 15, 18, 22.
xxii.	1, 4, 5, 8, 10, 12, 13, 20, 22, 23, 25, 28.
xxiii.	1, 2, 3, 4, 8, 11, 16, 18, 20, 22, 25, 26.
xxiv.	1, 5, 7, 8, 10, 14, 16, 17, 19, 20.
xxv.	1, 5, 11, 13.
xxvi.	12, 16.
xxvii.	9, 11, 15, 16, 17, 18, 19, 21, 22, 23, 24, 25, 26.
xxviii.	69.
xxx.	1, 11, 15.
xxxi.	7.
xxxiii.	7, 12, 13, 18, 20, 22, 24.
xxxiv.	7.

As no reason is given for the form of these divisions, one would imagine that the open partitions would be used as a break in places where there is but little connection between sentences or relations; but this is not the case, for we find open partitions even in the middle of verses, and frequently between two sentences closely connected by sense, while closed partitions are often put between passages whose contents have no relation to each other.

The rules given for writing the Song of Moses before his death are very precise, but it is enough to say here that the whole Song be written in seventy lines, and that a blank space is to be left in the middle of each line.

The Song of Moses at the Red Sea (Ex. xv. 1-19) is to be written in thirty lines in this form:

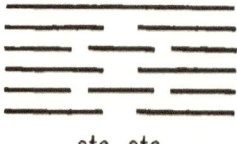

etc. etc.

The exact words with which each division is to begin will be found by reference to any printed Hebrew Bible.

In ch. ix. of our treatise we are told that the circumference of a roll should not exceed its breadth or height—in fact, they ought to coincide. If the roll be written upon Gevil, it should be twenty-four fingers or six hand-breadths' wide, and the same applies to Kalaph. The exact width, however, is not considered of very great importance, so that it equal the circumference. The blank margins ought to be three fingers broad at the top of the columns, four at the bottom, and two between the columns: so that a blank of one finger's breadth must be left at each side of a sheet of parchment, as well as a piece sufficient for the stitching. The doctrine of the size of the roll is as early as the second century; for we find it enunciated by Rabbi Jehuda, the author of the Mishna, in the Talmud, tract Baba-Bathra. The size of the margins is prescribed in tract Menachoth, p. 30, and in tract Sophrim.

Then follow rules for cutting the parchment to a convenient size for a roll, the number of lines and letters in a column, and various calculations and pieces of advice given by Maimonides to assist the scribe: these, as of no general interest and not being dependent upon any maxims of the Talmud, are best omitted. The finger-breadths before mentioned are stated to be equal to the width of seven ordinary barley-corns placed side by side, or to the length of two such grains. A hand's-breadth is four fingers, and a cubit six hands'-breadth: this is the standard of all measurements given in the Bible or the Talmud. The roll which Maimonides wrote for himself is recommended as a pattern: it was made from rams' skins, and contained 226 columns, each four fingers wide, except the three which contained the Songs, and these were each six fingers broad: there were fifty-one lines in each column. The whole length of the roll, including the margins, was thus 1366 fingers.

In ch. ix. sect. 12, a Beraita is quoted from the Talmud, tract Menachoth, p. 30, or tract Sophrim, ch. ii., to the effect that it is not permitted to write more than eight or less than three columns on one sheet. If the scribe has a piece of skin on which he could write nine columns, he is advised to cut it into two, and write four columns on one and five on the other. This rule does not apply to the final sheet of a roll, for on that he may write even a single verse.

This expression, ' a single verse,' is most difficult to understand; for in ch. vii. sect. 7, we have shown that the last three words of Deuteronomy must be written in the first half of the last line in the page or column, which (see tract Sophrim, ch. ii. doct. 6) must not have less than forty-two lines. To write nine words, containing thirty-five letters in all, over this space would not be easy. We cannot even get out of the difficulty by supposing that the verses were formerly larger than now; for in the Beraita of tract Baba-Bathra, p. 14, the number of verses in Deut. xxxiv. from the words, ' So Moses the servant of the Lord died,' to the end, is given as eight; this corresponds to our division. We can only imagine that the Beraita is not to be taken at the letter, but to mean that a small portion at the end of the Law may be written on a separate sheet.

When the roll is written, the sheets are to be sewn together with sinews, taking care to leave the stitches a little open at the top and bottom to prevent the sheets from tearing asunder; the whole is then to be sewn on to two sticks or rollers. The sinews must be taken from clean animals; the best and whitest are found in the legs. The rule for sewing with sinews is at least as early as the second century, as we see in Talmud, tract Makoth, p. 11, where, in a dispute between Rabbi Jehuda and Rabbi Mair, it was decided that cotton threads were unlawful for the purpose of sewing a roll together. Phylacteries, too, were to be sewed with sinews, on the authority of Hillel, who was chief Rabbi B.C. 30 (see Jerusalem Talmud, tract Erabun, last chapter; and also tract Sophrim, ch. i. doct. 1). The regulation for leaving the stitches open at the top and bottom of the sheets is found in tract Megila, but as it was not one of the oral commands given to Moses, the neglect of it does not make a roll unlawful. The custom of using two sticks to roll the manuscript upon is at least as early as the beginning of the Christian era, as we learn from the testimony of Rabbi Elieser the son of Rabbi Zadek, who says that he saw the scribes of Jerusalem making use of them, and who lived at this period (see the Beraita in tract Baba-Bathra, p. 14).

When a roll is torn, it must be sewn together, even if the

rent be only in the margin or between the words. If, however, the tear go through more than two lines in an old manuscript, or three in a new one, then it is necessary to put in a
new page. By a new roll is meant one on which the marks
of the acid or infusion of gall-nuts are still visible, otherwise
it is accounted old. All rents must be mended with sinews,
but great care must be taken not to injure the letters by sewing through them. On the authority of Rabb in tract Menachoth, p. 31, it is allowable to paste a strip of parchment
under a rent; but this doctrine seems not to have been generally recognised, or we should expect to find it in the Beraita.

In ch. x. sect. 1, we find a list of twenty causes for a roll
of the Law becoming unlawful, in which case we are told that
it is to be considered merely with the reverence due to one
book of the Pentateuch: it may be used for the instruction of
children (except in certain cases, as No. 10), but it is forbidden
to read from it in the synagogue.

The twenty causes are :

1. If it be written on the skin of an unclean animal.

2. If it be written on the skin of a clean animal which
has not been prepared according to the rules given in ch. vii.

3. If the skin has not been prepared in the name of God
and for the purpose of writing the Law upon it.

4. If it be written on the inner side of Gevil or the outer
of Kalaph.

5. If part be written on Gevil, and part on Kalaph.

6. If written upon Ducsustus.

7. If not written upon marked lines.

8. If there be no margin.

9. If it be written in any language other than Hebrew.

In the Talmud, tract Megila, pp. 8, 9, it is permitted to
write with Greek characters, and even in the Greek language,

because the seventy-two Elders translated the Law into Greek by order of king Ptolemy. Here, too, we find the reasons for the variation of the Greek translation from the original. In tract Sanhedrim we are told why Ezra changed the form of the letters from Hebrew (as the Samaritan character is called in the Talmud) to Ashirith, as the character in use at the present day is called.

10. If written by an Epicurean, or any other person who cannot lawfully be a scribe.

In tract Gittin we find that a roll of the Law written by an apostate, by a man who takes money from Jews on behalf of Gentiles, by a man who denounces a Jew to a Gentile, by a slave, a woman, or a boy, must be buried: one, however, written by an Epicurean must be burned.

11. If any of the names of God are carelessly written.

The names of God are as follow: יה, Lord; יהיה, Lord; אהיה, I am; שדי, Almighty; צבאות, Heavenly Host; אדני, Lord; אל, God; אליה, God; אלהי, God; אלהים, God.

Some of the names, as Adonai, Elohim, and Sebaoth, did not always apply to God Almighty. These are considered as profane in the Talmud, and most of the passages of the Bible in which they occur are found scattered here and there throughout the book. It will be sufficient if a few examples be given: 'For God doth know that in the day ye eat thereof . . . . . ye shall be as gods,' Gen. iii. 5. In this passage the first 'God' is holy and 'gods' is not, nor is the word 'God' in Gen. xx. 13: 'And God caused me to wander.' In Isaiah, ch. viii. 7, the word Immanuel is not considered holy, but in v. 10—where the Authorised Version translates it 'God with us'—it is holy.

The laws relating to the use of the names of God in vow-ing, swearing, or cursing, have no reference to our subject,

but those which have to do with writing the Law are as follow: 1. A scribe must say before writing a holy name of
God, 'I am ready to write the name of the Lord with mind
and understanding.' If he omit this formula even once, the
roll is made unlawful. 2. He must not write the name of
God with a freshly-dipped pen, for fear of making a blot, but
must fill his pen when he has at least one letter to write
before the holy name. 3. He is not allowed to put a single
letter of the holy name either out of, or between, the lines.
4. According to the Talmud, it is forbidden in Deut. xii. 3, 4,
to scratch out, destroy, or blot out even a single letter of a
holy name, in the words, 'Ye shall hew down the graven
images of their gods, and destroy the names of them out of
that place. Ye shall not do so unto the Lord your God.' If
a holy name be written incorrectly upon anything, whether
an earthen or stone vessel or a sheet of parchment, that thing
must be buried, and replaced by a correct one. 5. The scribe
is not allowed to think of anything else, or to speak, while he
writes the holy name, nor to give an answer even to the
greeting of the king (see Jerusalem Talmud, tract Brachoth,
ch. v.). Some of the cabalistic scribes went so far as to wash
their whole body in water before writing the holy name.

12. If a single letter be wanting.

13. If there be a single letter too many. As before shown,
however, these may, under certain conditions, be corrected.

14. When one letter touches another.

Most Rabbis also include under this head letters which
are written partly in the empty spaces of other letters, though
they do not absolutely touch.[2]

15. If a letter be illegible, or can be mistaken for another
letter on account of its being badly written, or worn by age,

[2] See terminal note.

or blotted. (This will of course refer also to omission of Tagim, &c.)

16. If space has been left in the middle of a word, so that it has the appearance of two, or if two words are so close as to seem like one.

This rule seems to contradict that mentioned in ch. vii. sect. 13, where it is permitted to scratch out superfluous letters, even if there be many in a page; but if a letter be thus scratched out from the middle of a word, then that word will seem like two, and the roll will become unlawful. In one of the old rolls from Arabia words are frequently written so close together that there is no more space between them than what is required to prevent the letters touching.

17. If the form of the partitions be changed.

18. If the form of the songs or poetical portions be not properly observed.

19. If the prose portions be written like the poetical.

20. If the roll be sewn together with sinews of an unclean animal (and, as has before been shown, with cotton or silk).

All the other rules mentioned in the foregoing chapters are to be carefully kept in mind whilst the roll is being written; but the neglect of them will not make the roll unlawful.

Our author, however, omits some points which would render the manuscript unlawful, viz. 1. If it be not written with *deyow*. 2. If written with blue, green, red, or any other dye; coloured inks being forbidden orally to Moses on Mount Sinai. 3. If written with gold or any other metallic matter. 4. If written on papyrus, linen, cotton, or other substance than skins. 5. If the scribe write with his left hand. The neglect of any of these rules makes a roll unlawful, so that it may not be read from in the synagogue even in time of need. It is curious to find them left out by Maimonides in his recapitulation, and none of the commentaries seem to have remarked this omission.

A kind of Fetish worship seems to have attached to a roll of the Law, and every stick or stone touched by it immediately acquired the odour of sanctity, and lost its market value. In ch. x. sect. 2 of Maimonides, we are told that a properly-written roll of the Law is most holy, and that the greatest honour and reverence must be paid to it.

A man is not allowed to sell it even if he be starving, although he possess many others, nor even may he sell an old one to buy a new one. In two cases a man is permitted to sell a roll, provided he have nothing else in his possession which would fetch any money: they are, first, to get means for studying the Law by help of the purchase-money; or secondly, to marry a wife (see Mishna, tract Megila, p. 27). It seems, however, from tract Baba-Bathra, ch. i. that it was allowable to sell a roll in a third case, viz. to ransom captive Jews with the money.

We are farther told that a roll of the Law which has become decayed or otherwise rendered unlawful must be placed in an earthen vessel, and buried near the grave of some learned man. This is called treasuring up a roll. The cover of a roll which has become worn out ought to be made into a winding-sheet for a 'virtuous deceased.' By this term is meant one who has left neither money nor relations behind him to pay the cost of his funeral. It is esteemed a virtuous act to help to bury such an one, or even to attend his burial.

A bag made to hold a roll of the Law—even if it had never actually been used, but only made for that purpose—or one in which a roll of the Law had been kept, as also the linen in which it was wound up, and the box and case in which it was kept, even though it were never put in without its cover;

and lastly, the stool made to lay it upon, and which had been used for that purpose (seemingly the stool was only holy when both made and used for laying a roll on it, see tract Megila, p. 27); all these partook of the sanctity of the roll. It is forbidden to cast them away till they be decayed or broken, and then they must be buried. The gold or silver pomegranates used to ornament a roll are not to be sold unless the money is to be used in purchasing a roll of the Law or the Pentateuch. The platform on which the Rabbi stood to read the Law, and the tablets on which the master wrote for the instruction of his scholars, are not to be reckoned sanctified.

The Pentateuch is to be considered the most holy part, then the Prophets, and next the Scriptures; and consequently it is forbidden to lay the Scriptures or Prophets upon a roll of the Law, nor the Scriptures upon the Prophets. In tract Eribon, p. 98, it is forbidden to throw from place to place not only any portions of the Bible, but even books containing divine doctrines and sermons. In tract Shabath, pp. 61, 62, it is ordained that charms containing portions of the Scriptures should be covered with pieces of parchment when the wearer enters latrinæ or other unclean places. A man is enjoined (tract Sanhedrim, p. 21) never to enter latrinæ, baths, or burial-grounds with a roll of the Law about his person, even though it be enclosed in its linen cover and case; he must not read from it till he is at a distance of four cubits from these unclean places; he is forbidden to touch a roll when undressed, and to sit on a couch or divan on which it has been laid (see tracts Megila, p. 32, and Moed-Ratan, p. 25).

In certain cases a roll must either be taken into another room, or placed in a box or vessel not intended to receive it, or must be bestowed in a chamber specially prepared for it and cut off from the rest of the room by a wooden partition ten hands'-breadth high (see tract Berachoth, p. 25).

A roll of the Law does not become unclean by an unclean person reading from it and touching it, provided that he has — as is required of every one — previously washed his hands.

If a roll of the Law is carried by any person from one place to another, all those whom he passes must stand up and remain on their feet till either the roll has reached its destination or the bearer be out of sight (tract Kedushin, p. 33).

In tract Berachoth, p. 18, it is declared to be a most virtuous action to prepare a separate place for the roll of the Law to be kept in, and to honour and glorify it exceedingly, as the words written upon the two tables of stone are contained in every roll. A man must never spit, undress himself, or stretch out his feet—it is still a sign of great disrespect in the East for an inferior to do this before his betters; rules of politeness require him to cover both hands and feet —before a roll, nor must he turn his back towards it unless it be at least ten hands'-breadth above the place where he is; he must not carry it on his head as if carrying a burden, but in his arms or bosom. If a man be on a journey, he must not lay the roll on the animal he rides and sit upon it, nor even beside it, but he must carry it in his bosom next his heart: in case of danger from robbers, he may lay it on the animal.

Elsewhere these precepts are enlarged, and we find: (1.) That when a man hands a roll to another, it must be given and received with the right hand, the reason being that God himself gave the Law on Sinai with his right hand: 'From his right hand went a fiery law for them,' Deut. xxxiii. 2. (2.) When a manuscript is being rolled up, the reader must not touch the writing, only the outside. (3.) The skins must not be folded under or back by the reader. (4.) The roll must not be laid upon the reader's knees, nor must he put his elbows on it. (5.) If a roll be placed on a stool, one end must never be allowed to hang down, but must be held in the hand. (6.) A roll must never be put under a bed; if upon it, only at the end towards the head.

A man before a roll of the Law must sit with humility, fear, and trembling, because it is a true witness to all mankind to bear witness against him; as it is written, 'That it may be therefore a witness against thee,' Deut. xxxi. 26. Therefore he must pay it all honour. A wise man of old wrote (see Mishna, tract Aboth, ch. iv., in the name of Rabbi Josi), 'Every one who despises the roll of the Law, his person shall be despised by the whole universe; and he who pays due honour to the roll, his person shall be honoured by the whole universe.'

From these scattered notes may be gathered with what scrupulous care the Jews were obliged to write a roll of the Law; and how, when their work was finished, they mistook the creature for the Creator, and turned their manuscript into a kind of demigod, honoured as is no saint by Catholic devotee, or unique sheet of papyrus by the most rabid bibliomaniac; and how, finally, to spite palæographists, they buried it as food for worms.

Note explaining certain peculiarities of Hebrew Bibliography.

1. Specimen of single crown : צ ק ח ז ח
2. Specimen of triple crown : ט נ ל ג ז צ. ש פ ע ד ק
3. Foot-crowns and head-crowns (M. Alt of Frankfort) : (Vaw) ו, (Yod) י, ל ח י ב ה א

4. Ancient form of letter ה ‏ﬡ

5. The Yod of the Aleph must touch the body thus א, not א ; and the three Yods of the Shin must be joined to the line ש, and not written thus ש. There are two letters whose parts must be separated, viz. ה and ק : it is unlawful, according to the Talmud, to write them thus ה ק.

6. Most Rabbis also include under this head letters which are written partly in the empty spaces of other letters, though they do not absolutely touch : thus ש or ש

IV.

NOTES ON THE HAMAH STONES, WITH REDUCED TRANSCRIPTS.

I VISITED Hamah between February 28th and March 5th of 1871; and my first care was to inspect the inscriptions, as Mr. Walter Besant, M.A., Secretary of the Palestine Exploration Fund, had asked me to do in his letter of Dec. 7, 1870.

The Stones were noticed as early as A.D. 1812. Burckhardt (*Travels in Syria*, p. 145) says of them: 'In the corner of a house in the Bazar is a stone with a number of small figures and signs, which appear to be a kind of hieroglyphical writing, though it does not resemble that of Egypt.' They remained in obscurity till 1870, when Mr. J. Augustus Johnson, of New York, Consul-general for the United States at Bayrut, and the Rev. S. Jessup, of the Syrian Mission, remarked them while looking through the Bazar of the old town. The former presently printed, in the 'First Statement of the Palestine Exploration Society' (No. I. July 1871, New York; published by the Committee), a reduction from a facsimile of No. 4 inscription—that noticed by Burckhardt, and still embedded in a wall near the bridge. The latter also 'endeavoured to purchase a blue (basaltic) stone[1] containing two lines of these strange characters; but failed to obtain it, because of the tradition connected with, and the

---

[1] The term may remind us of the 'blue stones' of Stonehenge, which differ from the others, and which were brought, it is supposed, either from Cornwall, or preferably from Ireland.

income derived from it. Deformed persons were willing to pay for the privilege of lying upon it, in the hope of a speedy cure, as it was believed to be efficacious in spinal diseases.' I heard nothing of this superstition.

A certain Syrian Rayyah, of the Greek orthodox faith, named Kostantín Khuri bin Daud, made sundry transcripts of the inscriptions, and a copy was deposited with Dr. Bliss, President of the (U.S.) Syrian Protestant College at Bayrut. Here they were inspected by Messrs. Tyrwhitt Drake and Palmer, the latter then acting under the (English) Palestine Exploration Fund, before their return to England in September 1870. Herr Petermann published some details concerning the inscriptions in the *Athenæum* (No. 2267) of April 8, 1871. In March 1871 I bought from Konstantín the originals of the copies possessed by Dr. Bliss; and I proposed sending them home to the Secretary of the Anthropological Institute, when Mr. Tyrwhitt Drake apprised me of his intended return to Syria with the object of photographing and ' squeezing' the Stones. He set out for Hamah on June 13; and on June 24, 1871, he brought back good ' squeezes,' and sun-pictures which were not wholly successful. I believe that his second visit gave better results; and he also found a similar inscription at Aleppo.

The local Dryasdust, Kostatín el Khuri, had not visited the country to the east of that venerable town, Emesa (Hums), and he had only heard of the interesting region on the north-east known as the 'Aláh (الْعلَى) or ' upland.' The extent may be roughly laid down as two days' riding west-east towards the Euphrates, and from Salamiyyah, the *avant-garde* of the Palmyrene, on the south, to six hours north of Mu'arrat el Nu'umán, on the Aleppo-Damascus road. Here, according to tradition, although our maps inscribe the region ' Great

Syrian Desert,' are some 360 villages—a favourite popular number—almost all, if not all, in ruins. I was able to visit only four of them : their stone-built floors and ceilings, with monolithic doors, shutters, and rafters of basalt, reminded me of the 'Land of Bashan,' that is to say, the Leja and the Hauran valley and mountain. Two ruins showed sundry large clean-cut and raised inscriptions, with crosses which suggested their origin. It is not a little curious that in this section of the country, lying east and west of the Orontes valley, many inscriptions are found in cameo, not incised, as is the general rule of Syria and Palestine ; thus perpetuating the style of the Hamah Stones.

It was at first my intention to employ Kostantín el Khuri in copying these monuments. He proved himself, however, so ignorant, leading me a long way to see a Hebrew inscription which proved to be Kufic; so greedy of gain, and so untruthful a *Græculus esuriens*, that I was compelled unwillingly to abandon the project. Although Mr. Tyrwhitt Drake has successfully accomplished his somewhat perilous task of exploring the 'Aláh, the country east of Hums still awaits a reconnaissance.

The ten sheets accompanying this article had been applied to the blackened or reddened faces of the four Stones, one of which has, it will be seen, a double inscription ; and the outlines were afterwards drawn with a reed pen. In a few cases the fancy of the copyist had been allowed to run wild : these vagaries have been corrected. The size of the facsimiles shows, *cela va sans dire*, that of the Stones.[2]

The material of all four is compact black basalt, polished as if by hard rubbing. The characters are in cameo raised from two to four lines, separated by horizontal framings also

---

[2] They have here been reduced to quarter size.

in relief: they are sharply and well cut. The first thing
which strikes the observer is, that they must date from the
metal age, and that they are the work of a civilised race. No
Bedawi would take the trouble to produce such results, nor,
indeed, has he any instruments which would answer the purpose. I proceed now to a short description of each Stone.

No. 1 (three lines) is in the north-western or Christian
quarter of Hamah, known as the Hárat el Dahhán (of
the Painter). The house (No. 28) belongs to one Sulayman
el Kallás (the Lime-burner), and it is tenanted by Khwájah
Jabbúr el Nasrani. The Stone stands, or rather lies, on its
side in the eastern wall facing the front impasse: it is close
to the left jamb of the doorway to one coming out of the
tenement, and the height of the lower margin is five feet
from the ground. Under the three lines is a plain surface;
and the general appearance of the Stone is shown by the
accompanying sketch.

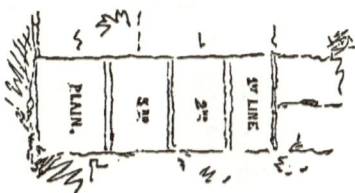

No. 2 (two lines) is lying in the lane called Darb Tak
el Tahun (Road of the Arch of the Mill), that runs south of
the same garden. It is a roughly-shaped block of basalt, with
more length than breadth or thickness, and presenting this
appearance:

No. 3 (three lines) is in the orchard or so-called 'garden' of Sayyid Umar bin Hajj Hasan, a little to the west of the ruined Bab el Jisr, the gate at the southern end of the third bridge which spans the Orontes, the whole number being four. This tablet is built up with common stones around it, close to the ground, in the northern face of the southern wall, whose upper part is of unbaked brick. It is remarkably well and sharply cut, with long raised lines separating as in No. 1 the three rows of writing.

No. 4 (total, nine lines) is at the north-west corner of a little shop belonging to Mohammed Ali Effendi, of the great Kilani house, the Emirs descended from that arch-mystic Abd el Kadir el Kilani. Its site is the dwarf Bazar, a few paces from the west end of the Jisr el Tayyarah, also called Jisr el Shaykh, the second of the four bridges beginning from the south. It is easily found : fronting it to the east is the Hauz or tank belonging to the small Jámi' (Mosque) el Nún, and it is within a few paces of the French Vice-consulate.

This Stone, unlike the others, shows two inscribed faces. To the north, where its breadth is least, appears inscription No. 4 (four lines), with the upper part plain, after this fashion :

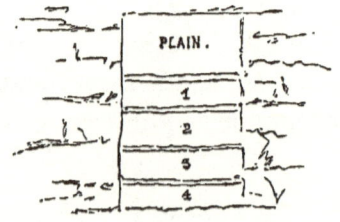

The other inscription (No. 5), in five lines, is upon the western side of the wall : it is considerably larger than the other; hence the transcriber has called it the 'long lines.' The five compartments are here again divided by well-raised horizontal ribs, and the lower row of characters is not so easily read as its neighbours: the upper line also does not cover more than half the breadth of the stone.

Besides obtaining photographs and facsimiles, it would, I believe, be highly advisable to secure the Stones; and Nos. 1 and 3 might be bought at a reasonable price. But this will require a Vizierial letter, intended to be obeyed, and not like the tons of waste-paper issued during the reign of the late 'Ali Pasha. A direct order will at once enable the Governor-general of Syria to take the Stones from their owners, paying just compensation, and to send them out of the country. When at Hamah, I began to treat with the proprietor of No. 1, the Christian Jabbúr, who, barbarously greedy like all his tribe, began by asking a hundred napoleons. And if the purchase of the Stones be judged advisable, the less said or written about them, on the spot at least, the better, as they may share the fate of Mesa's Stele.

I borrow the following notice of the Stones from Mr. Johnson's notes before alluded to:

'We should naturally expect to find in this vicinity some trace of the Assyrian and Egyptian conquerors who have ravaged the valley of the Orontes, and of their struggles with the Hittites on this ancient battle-field, and of Solomon, who built stone cities in Hamath (2 Chron. viii. 4), of which Palmyra was one. But we find nothing of the Palmyrene on these stones. The arrow-headed characters are suggestive of Assournasirpal. In the inscription on the monolith of Nimroud, preserved in the British Museum, in relating his exploits 915 B.C., he says: "In this time I took the environs of Mt. Lebanon. I went towards the great sea of Phœnicia.

... I received tributes from ... Tyre, Sidon, &c. ... They humbled themselves before me." And a little later, 879-8 B.C., Salmanazar V. says: "In my 21st campaign I crossed the Euphrates for the 21st time; I marched towards the cities of Hazael, of Damascus. I received the tributes of Tyre, Sidon, and Gebal."

'Until the interpretation of these mysterious characters shall be given, a wide field is open to conjecture. Alphabetic writing was in use 1500 B.C., but the germs of the alphabetic system were found in the hieroglyphic and hieratic writing of the Egyptians upwards of 2000 B.C. Some of the attempts at picture-writing on these Hamath stones suggest the Egyptian system, which consists of a certain number of figures to express letters or syllables, and a vast number of ideographic or symbolic forms to represent words. Other characters represent Phœnician letters and numerals not unlike the Phœnician writing on the foundation stones of the Temple at Jerusalem, recently deciphered by Dr. Deutsch of the British Museum.

'In framing their alphabet the Phœnicians adopted the same process previously employed in the Egyptian phonetic system, by taking the first letter of the name of the object chosen to represent each sound; as, A for aleph (a bull); B for beth (a house); G for ghimel (a camel): in the same manner as the Egyptians represented A by an eagle, *akhem;* M by an owl, *moulag,* &c.

'Some scholars have designated Babylonia as the true mother of the characters employed in very ancient times in Syria and Mesopotamia. And it appears that, besides the cuneiform writing found on Assyrian and Babylonian monuments, a cursive character was also employed identical with the Phœnician, and therefore possibly borrowed by the latter.   Kenrick, however, remarks on this theory, that the occurrence of these characters only proves the intercourse between the two people, and not that the cuneiform was the parent of the Phœnician.   We have in these inscriptions of Hamath a mélange of all three, and perhaps a connecting link between the earliest systems.   To suppose them to be bi-lingual or tri-lingual only increases the difficulty of interpretation in this case, for there is not enough of either to furnish a clue to the rest.

'The "Carpentras Stone" contains an analogous inscription ; it comes near to the Phœnician, and has been thought to present the most ancient specimen of the Aramean series. This and the Palmyrene writing form the links between the coin characters and the square characters, and are supposed to represent a language in a state of transition.   That the Hebrews borrowed the use of writing from Mesopotamia or Phœnicia has been universally admitted ; and according to Gesenius, the old form of their writing was derived from the Phœnician, and retained by the Samaritans after the Jews had adopted another character of Aramaic origin.

'Now may it not be that in these Hamath inscriptions we have fallen upon a transition period, when the Phœnicians, or their predecessors in the land, were using the elements of writing then in existence, and before the regular and simple Phœnician alphabet had been perfected ?

'The "Carpentras Stone" has been considered by Gesenius to have been executed by a Syrian of the Seleucidan period.   The "Rosetta Stone" dates back to 193 b.c.   The characters on these stones have much in common with those of Hamath.   Champollion's *Key to the Hieroglyphics* will be of aid perhaps in solving the present mystery.   But we shall be surprised if the inscriptions of Hamath do not prove to be older and of greater interest than any recent discovery of Egypto-Aramean or hieroglyphic characters.'

Dr. Eisenlohr, Professor of Egyptology, Heidelberg, in a letter asking permission to publish these inscriptions, writes: 'Though I believe we are at present not able to give a translation of them, I am still persuaded they will be of the highest interest for the scientific world, because they are a specimen of the first manner of writing of the people of that country.'[3]

My conviction is, that the Hamah inscriptions form a link between picture-writing and alphabetic characters: and I would suggest, that the most feasible way of deciphering them would be by comparing them with the 'Wusúm' (وسوم) of the several Bedawi families, tribes, and clans. These marks are still branded on the camels, and are often scrawled or scratched upon rocks and walls, as a notice to kinsmen that friends have passed that way. I need hardly say that the origin of 'Wasm' is at present unknown; it doubtless dates from the remotest antiquity, and it has probably preserved the primitive form of the local alphabets. For

---

[3] I cannot, however, believe, with Mr. Johnson, that the bas-reliefs on the monument called Kamu'a Hurmul (the column of the Hurmul village) can date from the same period. The people declare that it was built upon a basaltic mound to denote the source of the Asi or Orontes; we (that is, Messrs. Tyrwhitt Drake, Palmer, and I) thought it the tomb of some hunter; our reasons being that, 1. there are no inscriptions; 2. the rude alt-reliefs on the four sides represent weapons, and wild beasts wounded in the act of flight; and 3. the solid three-storied building is near the ancient Paradisus (παράδεισος, or hunting-park), identified by Dr. Robinson with the ruins at Jusyat el Kadimah. Mr. Porter's *Five Years in Damascus* represents the solid square structure as it stood some twenty years ago—now the southern side has fallen to ruins, and the pyramidal capping will soon follow.

instance, the Anezeh mark is the circle; and this we find,
to quote only two instances, representing the 'Ayn (eye,
fountain, 'eye of landscape') in the Asmunazar or Sidonian
epitaph, and in the Phœnician, or rather Canaanite, characters of the Moabite stone.

Again, the circle is shown on the sculptured stone of New
Grange, and in the ornament at Howth (figures 68 and 71,
Fergusson's *Rude-Stone Monuments*; London, Murray, 1872).
Captain Warren (p. 148, *Palestine Exploration Fund*, No.
IV. December 31, 1869) saw the signs ♀ △ upon the pointed
archway of Sabbah, the ancient Masada; he also saw the
former symbol upon the flanks of the Fellahín camels, and
he 'believed it to be a Bedouin mark for the district (?)
or tribe. In Spain there are marks peculiar to districts and
families, and the horses are all branded with them, just as
we mark our sheep; and the camels here appear also to be
branded according to their tribes or owners.' Other Eastern
travellers must have collected hundreds of these 'Wusúm;'
and were the want made known, we might soon produce a
volume of lithographs, which would not only supply a special
want, but also prevent future writers confusing, as lately done
by more than one, Bedawin brands with 'Nabathæan characters.' Messrs. Tyrwhitt Drake and Palmer neglected no
opportunity when mapping the Sinaitic Tih or Desert of the
Wanderings, and I have also been able to fill up sundry pages
of note-books.

'Hamah of the Asi,' or Orontes, the Hamath of Scripture
(חמת, *arx*, *munimentum*, e.g. Hamath-Soba, or Zobah),[4] was the

---

[4] We find the name again in Amathus of Cyprus and Laconia. It
must be remembered that the Talmuds, the Targums, and the ancient
Syriac version of the Old Testament all explain Hamath by Antioch—a
city which must have had a name before conquered by Alexander. The
northern 'entrance to Hamath' would be viâ Seleucia.

capital of a little kingdom at the period of the Exodus. Its
king, Toi, yielded allegiance to David (2 Sam. viii. 9); it was
called ' great' by Amos (vi. 2), and was, we have seen, ranked
by an Assyrian monarch with the most important of his conquests. Originally inhabited by the Canaanites (Gen. x. 18),
it is frequently mentioned as the northern border of the Land
of Promise, although it has as yet formed no part of the
' Holy Land.' Every guide-book will tell how, under the name
Epiphaneia, it became famous in the days of the Seleucidæ,
and how Seleucus Nicator, founder of Apamea (Kala'at el
Muzík), kept his stud of 500 elephants and 30,000 brood-
mares in the rich lands which the twin curses of Syria, the
Bedawin and Misrule, have converted into the Great Syrian
Desert; how subsequently it became, as it is now, a bishop-
ric; and how, under the Moslem rule, it produced (A.D. 1743)
the celebrated savant Abú 'l Fida (Abulfeda) prince of Hamah,
the worthiest scion of the Kilani house.

If Nablus occupies the most beautiful, Hamah certainly
owns the most picturesque of sites in modern Syria. It
has a cachet peculiarly its own, yet the general aspect of
the valley somewhat suggested Bath. And it has its own
sounds. Here the traveller hears for the first time the Na'úrahs,
those gigantic undershot box-wheels, one of them said to be
forty metres in diameter, which, creaking and groaning night
and day, continually raise the waters of the Orontes from their
deeply-encased bed to the level of the houses and the fields,
and which serve adventurous gamins as merry-go-rounds.
Each aqueduct and wheel, the latter built up of infinite piece-
work, and with axles playing upon the summits of masonry
triangles, has its own name—for instance, El Mohammediyyah, mentioned by Burckhardt in 1812; and each is the property of a (very) limited company.

The situation of Hamah is a gorge-like section of the Orontes (Asi) Valley, which, sweeping from the south-east, winds off to the north-west. The highest part of the city is on the south - east; here El Alaliyát ('Les Hauteurs') measure 140 feet above the stream. There are four other elevations: 1. the Castle - mound to the north; 2. the Báshúrá quarter, north-east; 3. Shaykh Ambar el Abd, above the left bank of the stream; and 4. Shaykh Mohammed el Haurani, a continuation of the older and much larger river-valley. The ancient city has no walls, and few gates; and the orchard separating the various cemeteries and the clumps of cottages into thin dwarf conical domes, make it a veritable oasis; the Bedawin, however, have long ago destroyed the once celebrated oliveta of the neighbourhood. Four bridges span the stream; which at this season (March) is coloured *blond de Paris*, that is to say, dirty yellow: three have parapets; all have rough and uneven floors, and mostly they rejoice in Saracenic arches of different sizes and shapes, here and there zebra'd with white and black stones (lime and basalt). The second from the south is the Jisr el Shaykh, or El Tayyárah, the 'flying,' possibly so called from the palace of Harun el Rashid at Baghdad. At the end, upon the right bank, rise the mansion and quarter of the Kilani Emirs; the tall walls stained with dirt and green mould poorly represent the 'very fine palace' of Pococke's day. The visitor will find much to admire at Hamah in the lofty and peculiarly graceful minarets, the perfection of lightness married to strength, which, numbering twenty-four, vie with the larger cupolas in adorning the sky-line. They usually consist of three sections: the finial; the balcony, with wooden awning against sun and rain, applied upon a smaller shaft; and the main body, a tower of larger dimensions. The most remarkable are the Mádnahs of Bab el Hayyah, of Khizr (El Maksúrah), and of the Suk el Shajarah : the model is that of the Jámi'a el Kabir, or Cathedral Mosque ; it consists of the following structures, and the dwarf buttresses, or rather bevels, that break the basal angles, refer it to the days of Sinán Pasha, when architectural taste had not wholly died out of El Islam :

An urn-like domed finial of solid (?) stone.
Cornice and pendentives.
Eight light pillars and ties.
Smaller octagonal shaft.
Flat-topped wooden awning.
Larger octagonal shaft.
Three archlets sunk in each face of shaft.
Rose-light between two horizontal bands of black stone.
Plain circular light between ditto.
Base of octagonal tower.

The traveller will do well to visit the splendid saloons of Muayyad Bey, son of the Sherif Pasha who fought the French in Egypt. The hideous dome contrasts strangely with the interior : such a mixture of Persian writing, painting, and gilding, with granite pillars, porphyry, marbles of all colours, and infinite variety of decoration, all gorgeous in the extreme, but tasteful, from the admirable proportions in which colours apparently discordant are made to blend, he will not see even at the capital. An architect might fill a small volume with the beautiful geometrical intricacies which everywhere meet the eye, and his study would add not a little to our northern ideas of ornamentation.[5]

[5] In consequence of a suggestion by Mr. D. F. Crace, I made careful inquiries at Damascus from the books of patterns, coloured and plain, which contain the models still used by house-decorators. It is believed

A local curio is also to be found at the Jámi'a el Hayyah, whose variegated dome rises conspicuously from the large cemetery in the Khan Shaykhun road at the southern extremity of the city. It derives its name, 'Mosque of the Snake,' from a block of the purest white marble, forming plain double capitals and bases, whilst the highly-polished shafts have been twisted into cables, writhing, as it were, in imitation of two huge boas locked in the closest embrace. I tried, but in vain, to buy this gem—it was 'church property.' A similar *tour de force*, but not so large nor so perfect, is found in the Mihrab, or praying niche, at the south-east angle of the Jámi'a el Aksa at Jerusalem, and I lately saw a sketch of it, by the Rev. J. Niel,[6] at the rooms of the Palestine Exploration Fund.

One of the most interesting parts of modern Hamah is the Castle-mound, whose green feet approach the left bank of the 'Rebel River.' Like that of Hums, it probably served for a Sun-temple; but it has suffered even more severely from time and man. The hillock is evidently natural; a core of chalky rock is suggested by the silex and the agates which bestrew the summit. Naked stone also appears in parts of the scarp and the counterscarp. To the east and south the material stands up in dwarf cliffs showing artificial strata of different colours, formed by charcoal, strews of pebbles, broken pottery, and other rubbish. The terrepleine was

that upwards of three hundred different arabesques are to be collected. Unfortunately we were obliged to leave Syria at the very beginning of my search.

[6] *Palestine Exploration Fund*, No. IV. p. 176. But why the reverend gentleman should call the pillars 'Solomonic twisted pattern,' I cannot guess. Did Solomon invent any masonic patterns or orders of architecture?

prepared for supporting the fane by layers of earth to which ruins have added; it is still tolerably regular, except where the people have dug into it for materials. The Saracens probably revetted the slopes with an armour of stone, which has almost entirely disappeared in building and rebuilding the venerable city. The length of the oval summit from north to south is 350 paces; the shorter diameter from east to west measures 250, and the height (by aneroid) is 90 perpendicular feet. The green sides of the rain-seamed mound have not yet assumed the natural angle: here and there they are *bombés;* and whilst the talus in many parts measures 60°, at the south-east it is almost vertical. The lower folds, as in the mound at Hums, fall into a fosse which in olden days could probably be swamped by means of conduits; now the broad expanse is cultivated, like the grounds around the temple of Ba'albak. The main entrance was at the eastern fort, and here the rocky counterscarp was cut to resemble the buttresses of a bridge: in the scarp appears a silo, shaped like a soda-water bottle. The path winds easily up to the left; on the southern side there is another track, but this is steeper and less used. I need hardly suggest here, as at Hums, the necessity of a few shafts and tunnels.

The Hamathites have gained for themselves a very bad name in the guide-books. 'They are haughty and fanatical, living in entire ignorance of the world beyond their own little sphere.' The fact is that they are somewhat unused to the visits of strangers, and the turban, especially the green turban, still expects the hat to make way. Fortunately for me my friend Abd el Hadi Pasha, an honest and honourable man, was occupying the Serai, and he assisted me through the little 'difficulties.' On the day after my arrival, a crowd assembled near the bridge to see me compare Kostantín's

facsimile with inscription No. 4, and two men who behaved
rudely, refusing to 'move on,' soon found themselves *au
violon.* The red-cloaked owner of No. 2 stone also charged
me with entering his garden, where women might, as is the
custom, have been walking about unveiled. I asked him if
it was the practice of his family to leave the gate wide open
on such occasions—an innuendo which brought the blood to
his pale face—and a reference to the Mutasarrif (Governor) ·
soon settled the question. Beyond this I met with no in-
civility from the people. It must, however, be confessed that
much of their good treatment was owing to my host, the excellent M. Fazli Bambino, Vice-consul de France for Hums
and Hamah, whose energy and *savoir faire* have given to the
European name an importance before unknown to it in these
regions, and who is distinctly not one of the 'time-servers
that write home their semi-annual reports, glossing over
everything unpleasant to the official ear, and carefully omit-
ting to mention the many opportunities they have missed of
doing their duty.' M. Bambino's nephew, Prosper Bey, soon
showed me all that was worth seeing at Ḥamah, and guided me
during a day's exciting ride over the outskirts of the 'Aláh.

The population of Hamah is laid down by Mr. Johnson,
probably from Murray, at 30,000 souls. They own to 38,000
or 40,000, and I believe the number to be nearer 45,000.
Of these, some 10,000 are 'Greeks,' that is to say Fellahs
belonging to the Greek Orthodox Church under their Matran
(Metropolitan) Jermanos. The Jacobites range from 200 to
300; there are two or three Syrian Roman Catholic families,
who 'sit under' their priest Khuri Mikhaíl. The French
colony, including dragomans and all protected subjects,
amounts to a total of thirty-nine souls, of whom two are
settled in the 'Mountain' (Jebel Kelbiyyah). The Christian ·

quarter in the south-western part of the city is the most filthy
and miserable of the twenty-four 'Hárát.' As a rule the
Nazarenes are poor; one man owns 200,000 francs, another
100,000 francs, and two others have 100,000 piastres. The
Jews have entirely disappeared, leaving only a cemetery,
which is also rapidly disappearing. The Moslems therefore
number at Hamah more than three-quarters of the population.[1] They boast of three great houses. The highest is the
Kiláni, above alluded to : at their funerals all the names of
their ancestry are recited, after the fashion of Dahome. The
chiefs of this family are the Mufti Shaykh Sujjádat el Kádiri
and Shaykh Mohammed el Azhari : from a visit to the tent
which some of the juniors had pitched on the hill of Zayn
el Abidin I judged that this *jeunesse dorée* had no absolute
dislike to a guitar or to a glass of strong, very strong, waters.
Second rank the Meccan Sherifs ; and third the house of
Mullah Khunkhwar of Kuniah (Iconium). I may end these
notes on Hamah by saying that my visit took place during
the Id el Kabir, or greater festival—a season when fanatical
Moslems are apt to become extra-fanatical.

NOTE ON THE HAMAH INSCRIPTIONS.

BY HYDE CLARKE.

THE Hamah inscriptions excite great interest; and as they
will soon be in the hands of scholars, I think it may be useful to publish the results of a cursory examination. This
I do, because while in some quarters it is believed these will
prove to be ancient and valuable inscriptions, yet in others
they are pronounced by men of high authority not to be inscriptions at all, but vagaries of ornamentation. It is like-

wise doubtful if, on the supposition that they are inscriptions, the characters are ideographs, syllabics, or letters.

My inspection has been, as stated, a cursory one of the copies in the hands of Captain R. F. Burton, and of the small portions printed by Mr. Wilson in the Journal of the American Palestine Fund. The results are consequently open to verification, but they are already sufficient to throw some light on the questions mooted. Thus it appears that the matter consists of recurrent symbols, and that it is presumably composed of characters. I estimated the number of characters at upwards of 500, but they may be found to be more, when the opportunity of careful analysis is obtained.

Of one of these types I found thirty-three examples, of one twenty-one, of two eighteen, and of others the proportions which would appear in an alphabet. Other reasons support this view.

Although there is a figure something like a man with a club and two hands, the bulk of the inscriptions are not ideographs or hieroglyphs, but characters. There appear to be double letters, and possibly ligatures and abbreviations; but so far as can be at present judged, the characters are rather alphabetic than syllabic, though some may be found to be so. The hands are found in Himyaritic.

On examining the most frequent characters, I am disposed to assign five as the vowel-aspirates of the old alphabets. Using the most convenient type-symbols for the characters which are not available, these would be represented thus:

÷	equal to	א, Λ, ᴠ,	*i. e.*	A vowel	Kh	aspirate.
I	,,	ת	,,	E ,,	H	,,
Θ	,,	ו	,,	Oo ,,	Y	,,
U	,,	ו, U, V, O	,,	U ,,	V, F, Ph.	,,
O	,,	ע, O	,,	O ,,	W, Hw	,,

Ꝩ is probably S.

∇ appears to be D.

Other common forms include I I, I I I I, ٦, I, Ⴌ, Σ, ⊥,]. These are sufficient to show elements of an alphabet; but many of them conform to the characters of the Himyaritic inscriptions, in which, as translated by Dr. M. Levy, I recognise as identical ע, ז, ב, ד, ר, שׁ, שׂ, ל, &c. The mode of writing is different in Hamah. The alphabet is in actual use in Abyssinia.

÷ thus gives us the type of א. This is not really connected with **A**, but is another type to be recognised in Aramaic, Italic, Palmyrene, and square Hebrew. ÷ is the analogue of א. If this be so, the א of the latter square alphabet has been borrowed from a source more ancient than A in the Phœnician and other alphabets. In Himyaritic I is a bar of division between words; and ÷ sometimes assumes the same character.

Θ appears as a new type, but is the analogue of the Phœnician, which has a corresponding form, as in Greek, ε. It is the most frequent letter, occurring thirty-three times. This letter may also be recognised in Phœnician, Aramaic, old Hellenic, Italic, and Palmyrene. It appears to possess a double form, one less frequent, in which a dot appears on each side of the bar.

U needs little comment; it occurs eighteen times. Its value is 100.

O occurs about ten times. Its value is perhaps 1000.

The Hamah inscriptions confirm my former opinion that the alphabet as named by the Hebrews is not in its right order, and that the names are not the original names having the significations usually attributed to them, but are representatives of the ancient names, adopted to avoid idolatrous references. All the alphabets of the Hamah class are chiefly founded on the intersections of two crosses, still used by Rabbis, &c. as a secret alphabet.

The words or phrases appear to be read from top to bottom, and may then possibly return, as in boustrophedon and in Himyaritic.

The remains, on comparison, suggest that there are at least two inscriptions differing in character.

The inscriptions are of such antiquity that if, on transliteration, they do not conform to a Semitic rendering, I would suggest they should be tried for Georgian, the nearest representative of the Caucaso-Tibetan languages spoken in the region before the Semitic.

———

Since these lines were in print, Mr. Hyde Clarke kindly addressed to me the following note upon the relations of the Hamah Inscriptions:

With regard to the Hamah inscriptions, it is the more difficult to say anything, since doubts are entertained by men of learning whether they are inscriptions at all. Such being the condition of public knowledge or ignorance, we are yet at the first steps of the investigation, when we have to make out our road and may go astray. Some of those who are best fitted are afraid to venture because they fear failure, much as they covet success. We must, however, make a beginning, even at the risk of going the wrong way and having to retrace our path. At all events, in any such attempt this good will be obtained, that we shall know where not to go in the future. In fact, while the very prudent are waiting the whole course of labour is stayed, and the task of research in this instance does require much, and very possibly protracted, exertion.

هذا رسم نسخ طبق الأصل لكتابة الموجودة بجانب جارة

NO 1.
INSCRIP
1ST LIN

وهنا رسم لخط الثاني من التاريخ

NO 1
INSCRIP
2ND LI

Nº 1.
INSCRIPTION.
1ST LINE.

هذا رسم لاحد علية القوم السابع الدوجه بجاد جاءة فلطان جعفر بي بي سلطان الكوس باعزالكط

Nº 1.
INSCRIPTION.
2ND LINE.

محن رسم لخط الثاني من النقايخ المصور وكذلك بجان الزمان بالقدسين بنيت سليمان الكلك باعذالغايف

SAYYID OMAR

نابع التاريخ الذى لى بستان اكبر

هذا سلم و الكذاب

Apparently the lines never had any character here

3RD OR LOWEST LINE OF
INSCRIPTION №2 BRIEF THE GARDEN OF SAYYID OMAR

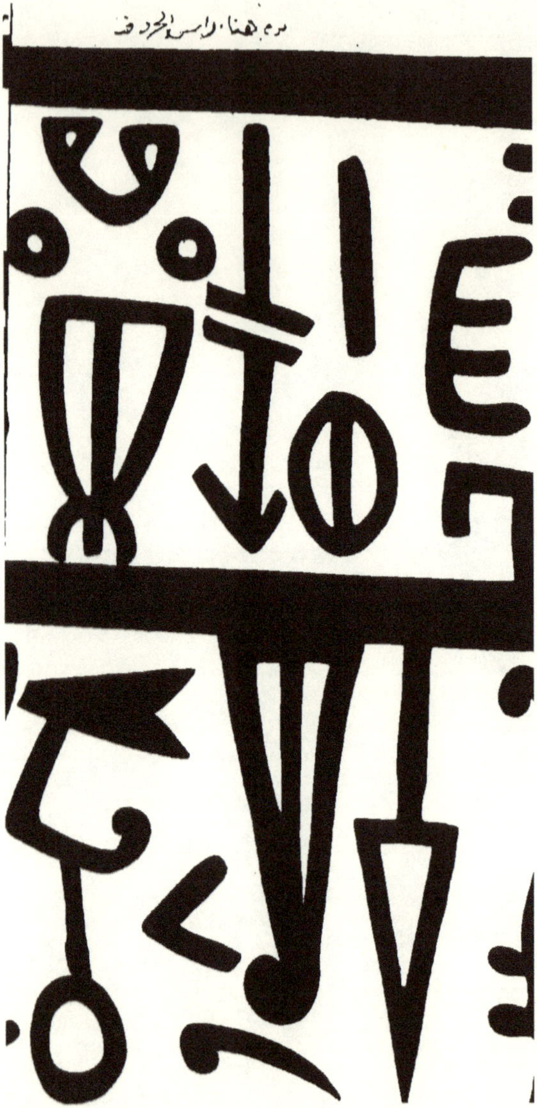

SHOP IN BAZAR.

Stone here
broken.

بما هاىو حير ىسع بنىه عرضا ارل سف ىه ونصب لكن ىكالة ىمقط بالجر محرف د سنفرد ووعاب

Stone here
broken

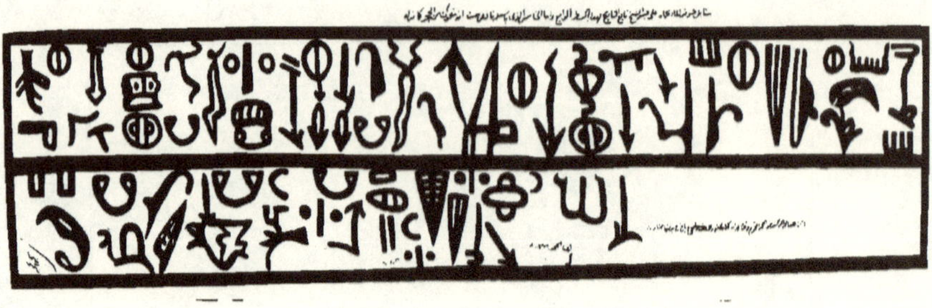

In making such an essay, no assurance of accuracy can be entertained, and it is quite possible that much of what is here written may, in the moment of its perusal, be superseded. In my own case my views have been modified from week to week, and one day's observations have tended to modify all the previous records. The toil is not, however, to be regarded as thrown away. It is as in a painting, where the first rough sketch in chalk is rubbed out, drawn over, and at last lost in the finished outline; but yet that fleeting embodiment of thought was the foundation of the perfect presentment upon which, touch by touch, from loose forms, sharp and accurate definition was reached, to become a lasting memorial.

In this case the very first question before us is, whether these drawings, reproduced by Captain Burton, are to be considered inscriptions or not; and the best answer will be to prove that they are. The appearance of them is uncouth and unpromising. They are not Egyptian hieroglyphs; they are not entire ideographs; and any semblance they show to Cadmean, or Phœnician, or such characters, is susceptible of other explanations. In No. 5 there are two unmistakable hands; there is a figure like a man or a monkey; and there appear to be darts, knives, bracelets, and other objects. The plates themselves do not afford exact representations; but they are much more useful for current reference and for study than the photographs or rubbings.

With the miscellaneous assemblage referred to we might associate some rude enumeration of tribes or of tribe-marks, such as are suspected to be inscribed on some Irish stones, and as are to be found painted by savage races. One mode to ascertain what may be the nature of these signs is by the simple statistical method of counting them.

The number of characters enumerated is about 300, but

there are others not as yet defined. These characters present
about 50 different types, but of these 17 have each only a
single representative. Of the remainder, the characters (sym-
bolised by common printing types) exhibit the following re-
sults: Φ 27, ÷ 26, ⊃ 24, Ð 21, V 15, | 11, || 11, Q 9,
ⵝ 7, ▽ 7, and so on. Thus we get indications of the dis-
tribution of the characters in the way in which an alphabet
is distributed into vowels and consonants: but some of these
may be stops or determinatives.

The next step is to search whether these signs are to be
found in other alphabets. There are few of them like the
Phœnician alphabet, but still there are familiar forms; as O,
Φ, |, C, ▽, and V (Λ reversed). Nevertheless they are
not to be classed as Phœnician. Another kind of alphabet
found in the northern region is the Himyaritic. In this case
the correspondence is greater, and a dozen forms can be compared with the Himyaritic.

The main seats of Himyaritic inscriptions are near Aden
and in Abyssinia, and the descendants of the alphabet are
the Ethiopic and the Amharic or Abyssinian.

It has long since been pointed out by Professor Newman
and M. Judas of Paris, that there are resemblances of this
Eastern African group with a Western African group, the
ancient Libyan of Carthage (not the Phœnician), and its modern descendants the Berber and Tamashek alphabets. It is
worthy of note, and indicative of our being in the path of
truth, that following the Himyaritic as we ought, we get a
number of identifications with the Libyan—a dozen.

We obtain out of the Hamah characters at least sixteen
identifications of form with Himyaritic and Libyan, leaving
no reasonable doubt that the Hamah characters are partly
related to one alphabet, in its origin allied to the others.

This is a clue we have obtained, but the whole Hamah alphabet is identical with neither; and as we cannot yet determine precisely the direction of the letters, we cannot tell the absolute value, this differing in some cases in both Himyaritic and Libyan. As to the Libyan alphabet, the value of its letters is as yet undecided, the latest views of M. Judas being opposed to those of his predecessors. What the Libyan language may be, is also an open question.

There is much resemblance between the Hamah and the Cypriote characters in the dart form, and this probably indicates a cuneiform alliance.

The characters on the bricks from Warka in Babylonia are allied to Hamah, and present another connection with cuneiform.

To increase difficulties, the Libyan and Cypriote are unknown tongues, though the Himyaritic is not. We have, however, a bilingual inscription, that of Thugga, now in the British Museum, Libyan and Phœnician; and some from Algeria, Libyan and Latin. We have therefore hope, and perhaps, as the Hamah so nearly resembles the Libyan, the Hamah will in time throw light on the Libyan.

Under all circumstances, we may consider we have materials for our investigation, and these we may proceed to apply. The hands have been referred to as a disturbing element. In No. 5, top line, we have a hand with the thumb and fingers displayed; and in the second line there is another, with the thumb but not the fingers displayed.

In the Himyaritic inscriptions published by the British Museum we have two examples of the hand with the thumb and fingers displayed. In one case there is a pair of hands, and in another about nine pairs of hands. These are above the inscription, but pointing downwards. These inscriptions are dedicated to Almakah (whom I regard as Moloch) and Ba'al.

In Phœnician and Carthaginian inscriptions the hand is common, accompanying the sun, moon, and stars.

In the worship of the Israelites the application of the two hands with the thumbs displayed is still a form of blessing, and undoubtedly of great antiquity.

The presumption is, that No. 5 Hamah inscription is dedicated to the fire-gods, possibly Moloch and Ba'al.

Then comes the question of the dedicator. No. 5 is unfortunately imperfect in an important part, but in the lowest line we find =. This is near ঙ . Let us resort to No. 1. In the third and second lines we find ঙ , and also =. The position of the former character shows us that No. 1 is reversed, as is No. 2. Proceeding to No. 3, we have the like characters.

These inscriptions are presumably at least four in number and beginning in the same way, and that is at the bottom, and reading from right to left. The Himyaritic and Libyan inscriptions read from right to left; one Himyaritic inscription winds to and fro. The Libyan Thugga inscription reads from right to left, beginning at the top, but then each line corresponds with the Phœnician. The Algerian bilingual Libyan inscriptions read from left to right and from bottom to top in columns; and this appears to be the case in Hamah, with the characteristic that the lines also begin at the bottom.

The Hamah inscriptions are divided by partitions or bands. This is to be found also in the Himyaritic.

A dedicatory inscription in the Himyaritic character, and so also in that of Thugga, begins with the genealogy of the dedicator. A *son of* B, *son of* C, *son of* D, &c. In Phœnician this *son of* reads ﺑﻦ. Not so in Libyan: what it reads is not known; but what was determined by Gesenius, and generally admitted, is that ן‎ב is represented by =.

= is consequently the genealogical sign, and such is apparently its application in Hamah, the groups ending with ঽ being names. In Warka, however, II corresponds with a cuneiform character.

With regard to ঽ, which ends the words, in my opinion it is equivalent to ꝣ in the Thugga inscription, but it is to be found in its own form in one Algerine inscription. Gesenius reads the Thugga character as ꝣ, but M. Judas does not. M. Judas has a wish to make it conform to the Berber genitive in N. In my view it is equivalent to S; and both in the Thugga and the Hamah inscriptions it may be the Caucasian genitive in S; a solution, according to my historical investigations, very probable.

On the subject of the Caucasian or Tibeto-Caucasian epoch in the Hamah region and surrounding countries, my papers in the *Palestine Exploration Fund Journal* and the *Athenæum* may be referred to. If the inscriptions prove to be Tibeto-Caucasian, they may or may not be comparatively ancient or modern; for on the evidence of words in the Book of Kings, I communicated to the *Athenæum* a solution of Mephi Bosheth, &c., as signifying the king's son in Georgian, and as implying the use of Caucaso-Tibetan terms in the time of King Saul as a court language adopted from the Canaanites.

The supposed ideographs are possibly determinatives or official symbols. The character like a celt is found as a technical mark on enamelled tiles all over Babylonia, and others are to be so recognised.

The first word in No. 2 and No. 3 is evidently the same, being chiefly composed of the same letters, a ▽, followed by

▽ traversed by |. This is possibly Tomb, conforming to such inscriptions in Himyaritic and Phœnician. The same words occur at the end in the last line of No. 5. The beginning of No. 5 is missing. It is, however, a remarkable circumstance that these characters occur on the most ancient Warka bricks, and have a cuneiform parallel, of which translations have been given.

On examining the inscriptions, No. 1 is seen to be chiefly composed of single characters; and so, apparently, is No. 2; but there must be some double letters. No. 3 is of the same class, but with occasional ligatures of characters bound together. No. 4 is very different from these, as it contains double letters and ligatures. It is to be noted, the characters are coarser and less well-proportioned. No. 5 has many ligatures or monograms.

In Himyaritic we have one example of the monogram in the published British Museum inscriptions, and there are others in the gems from Babylonia treated by Dr. Birch and Dr. M. Levy as Himyaritic, but which I am inclined to regard as possibly Hamah. The monogram or ligature is therefore to be accepted as a true type. These monograms are to be decomposed and read from bottom to top. A sufficient example is found in the word supposed to be Tomb. In Nos. 2 and 3 this is composed of single characters, but in No. 5 they are tied together.

As to double letters, they are found in the Tamashek alphabet, presumably a survival from Libyan.

Himyaritic, Libyan, and Phœnician inscriptions possess stops dividing the words. The words in Hamah appear to be so divided, apparently by O and C. Whether ÷ is a letter or a stop is not yet clear, for it has both values in other alphabets. It appears to be the same as ∗, and in the cuneiform it is a determinative for 'God.' If a letter, it is A, and the same as ℵ. In two cases, and possibly three, it accompanies the supposed word for Tomb.

The beginnings of the Hamah inscriptions when divided into words and written out in straight lines present a great conformity with the Thugga inscription, though not an identity.

Putting forward an opinion based on my observation, the Hamah alphabet appears to me to be of the same origin as the Himyaritic and the Libyan, and possibly the Cypriote, Lycian, and Warka, but intermediate between the two groups, and more nearly related to the latter or cuneiform type.

The original type of the Himyaritic and the Libyan, and also of the Phœnician, the Cypriote, the Etruscan, the Celt-iberian, and the square Hebrew alphabets, is a series of angular forms preserved in a cabalistic or magic alphabet still in use as a secret alphabet, and the observation of which may assist in giving the key to the Libyan and Hamah alphabets. The nearest approximation to this type is found in the Himyaritic and square Hebrew class.

As to the age of the inscriptions, they can hardly be lower than the latest date assigned to the Himyaritic, namely 100 of the common era, but they may be as old as the oldest Himyaritic are supposed to be, 600 before the common era; and there is a great possibility of their being of the age of the Moabite Stone, or even earlier—of the age of King Saul. The Warka characters were in use 1500 years before the common era. The palæographic indications already given show that the Hamah characters partake of the elements of the ancient alphabets and inscriptions; but the ligatures rather suggest an earlier date than the simplicity of the

Phœnicians, the Himyaritic, or the Libyan. The real value of the Phœnician alphabet must have consisted in its reduction of the number of characters, in its abolition of ideographs and determinatives, and in the simplification of writing. Thus ligatures, monograms, and boustrophedon inscriptions had to give way to Phœnician simplicity; and the probability is, that the Himyaritic and Libyan were made to conform to this influence, as the Etruscan and Hellenic inscriptions did. It is interesting to observe that Tamashek still uses double characters and winding lines for inscriptions. Oriental monograms begin from the bottom, as is exemplified in the Sultan's Toghra, and from right to left. These are examples of survival.

Whatever may prove to be the positive date of the Hamah inscriptions, they probably give us the records of a very ancient alphabet, and they are certain when deciphered to add to our stores of knowledge for the epoch preceding the Phœnician and Semitic. When the Phœnicians came to Carthage they found an earlier civilisation; they found the Libyan writing there, and did not import it. Presumably this latter style of writing is also earlier in the East, and that we must strive to ascertain. The cuneiform undoubtedly was.

HYDE CLARKE.

END OF VOL. I.

PRINTED BY ROBSON AND SONS, ST. PANCRAS ROAD, N.W.

www.ingramcontent.com/pod-product-compliance
Lightning Source LLC
Chambersburg PA
CBHW030825110726
47900CB00006B/1754